SHOOTING STAR
THE BEVO FRANCIS STORY

YLE KEIDERLING • FOREWORD BY GEORGE STEINBRENNER

SHOOTING STAR
THE BEVO FRANCIS STORY

THE INCREDIBLE TALE OF COLLEGE BASKETBALL'S GREATEST SCORER

www.sportclassicbooks.com

Published in the United States of America by Sport Media Publishing Inc., Wilmington, Delaware, and simultaneously in Canada.

For information about permission to reproduce selections from this book, please write to:
Permissions
Sport Media Publishing, Inc.,
21 Carlaw Ave.,
Toronto, Ontario, Canada, M4M 2R6
www.sportclassicbooks.com

Cover design: Paul Hodgson
Front Cover Photographs: The SPORT Collection;
   Basketball: Jessica Hill

Back Cover Photograph: The SPORT Collection
Interior design: Greg Oliver
This book is set in Bembo.

ISBN: 1-894963-49-0

Library of Congress Cataloging-in-Publication Data

Keiderling, Kyle.
   Shooting star : the Bevo Francis story / Kyle Keiderling; foreword by George M. Steinbrenner III.
      p. cm.
   Includes bibliographical references and index.
   ISBN 1-894963-49-0 (hardcover)
   1. Francis, Bevo. 2. Basketball players—United States—Biography. I. Title.

GV884.F68K45 2005
796.323'092—dc22

                                                    2005013724

      Printed in Canada

For Ky,

My son

My hero

My best friend

Shooting Star is dedicated in memory of Bill Ripperger, Carl Benner, Al Schreiber, and my friend Jack Fritz, all of whom left the court far too early in the game.

Bevo Francis

CONTENTS

Foreword

B evo Francis was born too early. When he was playing basket-ball, the game was practically in its infancy. There were no shot clocks, no baggy shorts, no "Air Jordan" shoes, and definitely no jewelry-wearing players or multimillion-dollar contracts.

In 1951 this gangly 6-foot-9 (that was considered extremely tall in the 1950s) kid from Wellsville High, an obscure school in eastern Ohio, came shooting onto the basketball scene. His has been called a Cinderella story—and that may be so, but I'd prefer to call it providence.

To me, there's no other way to explain what happened. When Bevo was a high-school senior, he played his only year of varsity basketball under Newt Oliver, an alumnus of little Rio Grande College in Ohio. Oliver knew immediately that he was looking at a real talent and began the grooming process straight away. And groom he did: Bevo scored 776 points in 25 games, for an average of almost 32 points per game. Then providence struck again: the coaching position opened at Rio Grande and Oliver was offered the job. (That he could deliver Bevo Francis didn't exactly hurt Oliver's prospects.)

I remember the first time I laid eyes on Bevo. I was coaching at Lockbourne Air Force Base in Columbus, Ohio. We had a fine basket-ball team made up of many experienced college players. Out comes this really tall kid—all arms and legs—so much so that you didn't think he would have the coordination to play basketball. But once he hit the court, his physical grace dispelled all such notions.

For such a big man, he had a very soft touch. He could always find a spot to shoot from, and he shot often. He was also quick and adept at driving. But it was his jump shot that left you speechless. We played against him three times, and during that period I got to know Bevo pretty well. He was a really nice kid, very humble, very small town, and very team oriented, always giving plenty of the credit to his team-mates—he was just a very nice kid.

That was the essence of Bevo Francis: a talented, gentle man. I am convinced that had he been born later and reaped some of the riches that players now enjoy, he would remain the same humble, hard-working person that he still is today. In Kyle Keiderling's book you will learn why his name will always be prominent in my memory, ranked with the early greats of basketball.

George M. Steinbrenner III

Introduction

I was in the fifth grade, at my desk in Flemington (N.J.) Elementary School, when I first read of Bevo Francis in *My Weekly Reader*. The story of his extraordinary feats made a particularly strong impression on an average but enthusiastic YMCA youth league basketball player who struggled to average eight points per game for Coach Paul Huffman's Flemington Knickerbockers.

Over the next season and a half, along with countless others, I monitored Bevo's progress, fascinated by the romance and improbability of it all.

My next recollection comes from my eighth-grade year when I was approaching a height of six feet but still averaging only a pedestrian eight points per game for my local CYO league team.

My best friend, Jack Fritz, and I were watching a telecast of a Harlem Globetrotters game in his living room. What intrigued us was that the camera caught a hand-lettered sign held aloft by a fan that read "Let's Go Bevo." How unusual, it seemed to us both, that anyone would be rooting for someone playing against the fabled Globetrotters. He must be, we both agreed, someone very special.

I remembered that sign about seven years later, when the Air Force had me stationed in California and I picked up the latest copy of *Sports Illustrated*. In a column called "Yesterday," the writer recounted the spectacular and controversial career of Francis ten years after he left Rio (pronounced Rye-oh by area residents) Grande College.

I found myself wondering what had happened to the man who had been such a dominating force, only to vanish almost overnight, and I resolved to find out some day when I had the time.

Fifteen years later I decided that the time had come. It was 1978, and I was managing a growing list of investment banking clients on a full-time basis while simultaneously leading the fortunes of my political party in my home county of Hunterdon (N.J.), hosting a weekly radio interview show, and attempting to keep pace with my thirteen-year-old son's various extracurricular activities.

Undaunted by the heavy schedule, and imbued with the vigor of youthful exuberance for a new challenge, I set out to get the answers to the questions about this intriguing man that had swirled in the back of my mind for decades. I contacted Bevo Francis and arranged to meet with him at his Ohio home. Once I had assuaged his fears that I was not acting on behalf of his former coach, from whom he was estranged, he agreed contractually to participate in the production of an authorized biography of his life.

A year later I finished the first draft of a manuscript. Bevo Francis approved it, and I placed it with a literary agent. Several rejection slips from publishers and a television network executive followed. Faced with the realities of managing the various facets of my busy life, I reluctantly and embarrassingly packed the tape recordings, notes, and manuscript in a cardboard box and stored them in a closet. I was discouraged but not defeated. When I had more time, I thought, I would revisit the project that my agent and I, if no one else, thought was of value.

During the intervening years something or someone would occasionally prompt me to retrieve the box from the closet. Once in the early eighties, at the request of the writer Dave Diles, I made a copy of the manuscript available to a candidate for a master's degree at Rio Grande who sought it for her thesis on the era. Then I wistfully put it back into the closet.

A few years ago I ran into George Steinbrenner at a dinner in New York; I jumped at the opportunity to review again with him his experiences with Bevo, which he had related to me when I interviewed him years earlier. He was enthusiastic about the prospects for a book on what he called "one of the greatest stories in sports" and urged me to pursue its publication.

Encouraged by his infectious enthusiasm, and a subsequent flurry of interest sparked by my friend Bill Raftery's contact with a film producer who expressed interest in the story, I hauled the box out of the closet in California, where it now resided among other artifacts of my life, and began to rework and edit the original manuscript. The literary agent who had represented me the first time around, Lawrence Jordan, still shared my belief in the project and agreed to try once more to find a publisher that shared our enthusiasm.

With much more time to devote to the project, I immersed myself in the task of bringing the story up to date and answering the question that inevitably was asked by everyone I contacted: "What ever happened to Bevo Francis?"

While it may have taken an inordinately long time to provide the answer, I hope that you will find it in the pages of the book that you hold in your hands.

Kyle R. Keiderling
Flemington, N.J.
September 2005

Prologue

The Butler University Fieldhouse rocked and reverberated with the thunderous ovation as it rolled over the Indianapolis court. The largest crowd ever to witness a single college basketball game was demonstrating its approval of an athlete, just as crowds have done since gladiators took the field in Rome.

This crowd, mostly Hoosiers, was cheering the performer who had just smashed the arena scoring record while leading his team to a stunning triumph over the nationally-renowned Butler Bulldogs. The 11,593 people who had come to scoff and jeer at him had witnessed something special and stayed to cheer his name.

The ovation continued for three or four minutes, until the vast throng was hoarse and drained from the sustained act of adulation. Minutes later, when the final whistle blew at the end of the game, the roar rose yet again. Sound cascaded down over the hardwood—and its amplitude and intensity swept the center and his teammates toward the sanctuary of the locker room. There the walls dulled the sound but not the thrill that he felt. The wide grin on his angular face reflected his own sense of accomplishment and well-being. An Indiana sportswriter's account the next morning told readers:

> Cheering Butler avidly at the outset, the throng gave evidence that it had come to see the home town boys prove that this hulking, nationally-ballyhooed idol had feet of clay. But his feet looked more like the smoothly pirouetting extremities of a ballet dancer as he deftly maneuvered Bulldog after Bulldog out of position and floated gracefully into the air to arch another two points through the hoop. In so doing, he restored confidence to

the cynical and made believers out of the non-believers. A skeptical Hoosier crowd in the tradition-shrouded Fieldhouse who had come to see a legend debunked remained to see history made. It was a thing you could feel—that gradual change of emotion which spread throughout the crowd and culminated in the greatest standing ovation in the arena's history

The scenario that the reporter described in early January 1954 was far from unique. It unfolded many times, in arenas from New York to Miami and from Buffalo to Omaha. The crowds were showering affection on a young man whose name was the best known and most controversial in American sports: Bevo Francis.

The magnitude of his scoring efforts defied credulity. When 20 points per game and 1,000 points over a three-year career were the standard measures of excellence, this twenty-one-year-old from the Ohio hill country had scored 116 points in a single game and had amassed 1,954 points in his first college season.

His exploits and exploitation led college basketball coaches to urge the National Collegiate Athletic Association (NCAA) to change its rules retroactively, stripping Francis of his 1952-53 records in a move that evoked the International Olympic Committee's treatment of Jim Thorpe forty years earlier. But the NCAA's actions simply whetted the public's already-ferocious appetite for more pyrotechnics by Bevo Francis and his team, and they did not disappoint.

The next season Bevo and his teammates from tiny Rio Grande College, with an enrollment of just 125 students, sallied forth on a mission that most experts thought was suicidal: to go head to head with the national college basketball giants, instead of playing the smaller colleges that usually filled Rio Grande's card.

Arenas that had stood half empty because of the college betting scandals of 1951 now filled to overflowing. Thousands fought to see the impossible dream realized, through Rio Grande and Bevo.

For the 1953-54 season the Rio Grande schedule included games against North Carolina State, Wake Forest, Villanova, Providence, the University of Miami, and Creighton. The Rio Grande Redmen didn't win them all, but they won many, acquitting themselves proudly on the national stage.

Bevo regained all the records that had been taken from him, including a 113-point performance that the NCAA, swallowing hard, was forced to accept as the highest score by an individual player in a single game.

Then, just as abruptly as Bevo's run had begun, it was over. He and Newt Oliver, his Svengali-like coach, left Rio Grande amid still more controversy to tour the country as the token opposition to the Harlem Globetrotters.

Today, more than fifty years since Bevo Francis first became a basketball marvel, his records remain unbroken. Will Michael Jordan, Magic Johnson, and Larry Bird be able to say as much fifty years from now?

Part 1

An Unlikely Beginning

The scoresheet from Bevo Francis' 116-point game
against Ashland J.C. February 9, 1953.

1

The Game

Show me a hero and I'll write you a tragedy.

— *F. Scott Fitzgerald*

January 9, 1953

The cold steel-gray winter day was not uncommon in the hills of southern Ohio. Now, as the light faded rapidly before the encroaching darkness, the temperature plummeted and a chill wet wind swept across the snow-covered campus. The sounds of spectators arriving for the evening's basketball game occasionally punctuated the eerie stillness. As the fans piled out of their cars, they were welcomed by the two frosted white globes that framed the entrance to the largest of the four buildings that comprised the campus of Rio Grande College.

The visitors from nearby Gallipolis and Pomeroy joined others who had read of the exploits of a sensational freshman center in that day's *Gallia Times*. According to the article, the statistical service of the National Collegiate Athletic Association had found Rio Grande's Clarence "Bevo" Francis well in front in the individual scoring derby for the 1952-53 season, with an incredible average of more than 40 points per game. Rio Grande also was among the national leaders in team offense.

Although it numbered fewer than two hundred, that night's crowd would be the largest of the season for Rio Grande. The Redmen had breezed through their first seventeen contests without a loss, but they had failed to generate as much fan enthusiasm as most high school teams. Similarly, the major Ohio papers had largely ignored the Redmen, much to the consternation of their fiery coach, Newt Oliver.

3

Despite his vigorous efforts, Oliver had managed to get the metropolitan dailies to print little more than a paragraph or two about his high-scoring center and the team. Sportswriters ignored the press releases that Oliver mailed, and they seldom returned his telephone calls.

As his charges went through their pre-game warm-up, Oliver surveyed the crowd that was rapidly filling the three rows of folding chairs on either side of the hall. He flashed a relieved smile. At least tonight, he thought, the gate would provide enough money to pay the officials.

His team's opponent, Ashland Junior College of nearby Kentucky, was not to be taken lightly. Although Ashland was only a two-year school, the Thoroughbreds had been a fixture on Rio Grande's schedule for years and more often than not had prevailed. As Oliver issued his final instructions to the starters, he felt that this year would be different.

From the opening tip-off it was evident that Oliver's hunch was right. Rio Grande was far superior in talent; after the first several minutes the only suspense was how wide the margin of victory would be.

Francis, in the pivot, was superb. He scored at will despite the efforts of two—and sometimes three—Ashland defenders. When the defense forced him out to the top of the key, guards Wayne Wiseman and Bill Ripperger sent him high, crisp passes that sailed over the outstretched arms of the cadre shadowing the center's every move.

Faking right and then whirling left with an uncommon grace for a man who stood six-foot-nine, he would leap high into the air and launch a soft, deft jump shot that would swish quietly into the net, as if drawn by a magnet.

Using a fast-break offense, Rio Grande dominated the fan-shaped backboards at both ends of the floor and soon had twice as many points as its opponent. At the end of the first quarter the Redmen led 40-20. The second period was much the same, and Francis continued to hit with ease. At the half the contest was already a rout. The score stood at 68-38, and Bevo Francis had single-handedly matched the output of Ashland's entire team.

The crowd milling about outside during the break buzzed excitedly. Inside, Oliver used the intermission to address his players in serious tones. "This game is far from over!" he snapped. "We have two things yet to prove tonight, and you all know what they are." Earlier in the season Francis had garnered 72 points against California State of Pennsylvania. Now Oliver reminded the team that Francis had a real crack at breaking the national scoring mark of 87 points in a single game. That, he said, would get the Redmen the publicity that they deserved. But he had a second reason for being so stern. During the Christmas break a player who was miffed at Oliver's plan to build the offense around Francis had left school and returned to Kentucky. "That player lives in Ashland," Oliver told the team, and "we have to send him a message."

As the Redmen headed back to the floor for the final twenty minutes, Oliver screamed, "Nobody quits on me, and don't you quit on me now!"

Those expecting to see a lackadaisical Rio Grande effort in the third quarter were never more surprised. Instead of coasting to an easy win, the Redmen starters stayed on the floor and played as if they were 30 points behind.

At the end of the third period Francis had 61 points and needed only 26 in the final ten minutes to tie the national record. As the fourth quarter got underway, the pattern was clear. The Rio Grande players were intent on only one thing: getting the ball to Francis. Passing up open shots of their own, they fed him in the pivot.

Following Oliver's orders, whenever Ashland would put the ball into play after a Francis bucket, the Redmen would immediately foul the first Thoroughbred to touch the ball, sending him to the free-throw line and—more important—stopping the game clock. These tactics made the period seem interminable but were essential if Francis were to have a shot at the record. The Ashland coach was livid, infuriated by Oliver's defensive tactics, and he protested loudly to the referees.

With five minutes remaining, the bespectacled Carl Benner, the Redmen's student manager, looked excitedly at the statistics that he was keeping and shouted over the din to Oliver: "He has seventy-seven now, and it looks like he could drop-kick one in if he wanted to."

The Thoroughbreds were thoroughly frustrated. They failed in their every attempt to thwart the Francis assault. Earlier in the game two players had guarded him, front and rear. Now, as the score mounted and Francis became the sole offensive threat, three and four at a time surrounded the lanky center. Raking his arms and shoving him to throw him off balance, they succeeded only in drawing more fouls, which sent Francis to the line and halted the clock yet again.

The number of men on Francis seemed to matter little as he continued to feint and jump high over the surrounding players to fire yet another shot at the fraying nets, which barely rippled as the ball dove home. /

With less than five minutes left, he had 80 points. The crowd tensed, sensing that the record was within reach. Several Rio Grande starters had to leave the floor, disqualified by the fouls that they had picked up while trying to stop the clock's relentless ticking.

Scoring with every shot in his arsenal, Francis pushed on toward the record. He tied it on a free throw. When he regained the ball on a fast break, he dribbled the length of the court at a dead run, leaped high in the air, and laid the ball softly in the net. The dramatic flourish and broken record brought the crowd to its feet, but three minutes remained.

Then the frantic pace began to take its toll. Francis, with 94 points, failed to convert his next four attempts. But then he got a second wind, notching his next two shots and bringing the tally to 98. Then he faltered again, with a jump shot that rebounded off the iron. Retrieving it, he whirled, fired, and missed again. But he gathered the ball off the boards, and his third attempt went up and in. He had 100 points.

He added five more field goals and two foul shots. With fifteen seconds on the clock Francis had 112 points. A final field goal and two more free throws and it was over. The score: Rio Grande 150, Ashland 85.

Bevo Francis had scored 116 points.

Never in the sixty-two years since James Naismith, the game's creator, had nailed two peach baskets to a wall in Springfield, Massachusetts, had a college or professional player scored so many points in a single game. Nor had any one team scored so many points in a single game.

Francis' teammates and other students mobbed him, hoisting him onto their shoulders and carrying him from the floor. His long weary legs dangled loosely toward the court as a shy grin spread across his wan and chiseled features. At the entrance to the dressing room they gently put him down, and the team let out still another cheer and embraced him as he slumped on one of the long benches.

Oliver burst into the room and made his way directly to Francis. Waving the scorebook aloft, the coach pummeled the exhausted center on the shoulders. "We did it! We did it! I told you we could do it! Now maybe those sons-a-bitches will listen to me! One hundred sixteen points! One hundred sixteen!" he screamed. "Lordy, boy, they'll have to listen to me now." Francis smiled up at the animated and youthful face of his coach and quietly asked to see the book. He calmly surveyed the maze of 2s amassed in uneven rows next to his name and the circles to the right. Only a few circles were hollow, marks signifying the missed free throws. Slowly shaking his head with incredulity, Francis looked up and told Homer Alley, the reporter for the *Gallia Times*, "I owe it all to my teammates. I couldn't have done it if they hadn't fed me the ball."

The players roared as the reticent Francis fell silent again. Oliver retrieved the score book and hurried toward the tiny cubicle that served as his office. There he picked up the phone and called a familiar number—Capitol 8-4306.

On the night desk of The Associated Press in Columbus a hand reached forward to grab the receiver and silence the persistent ringing of the news desk phone. Automatically cradling the phone between his chin and shoulder, the young night reporter said, "Dave Diles speaking."

"Dave, we did it! I told you we were gonna do it, and by God we did."

Diles immediately recognized the rapid-fire voice of Newt Oliver.

"Newt, what happened? What did you do now?" Diles asked as he reached for a pen.

"Bevo scored 116 points, that's all. I told you he was going to get one hundred one of these days, and tonight he did it. Lordy, Dave, you should have seen it—he was beautiful. He couldn't miss. They had four guys all over him, and he still made everything he threw up there. It was beautiful. A real work of art. Dave, you've never seen anything like it in your life. I mean ONE HUNDRED AND SIXTEEEEEN! Now those sons-a-bitches in Cincinnati will have to print the story.

"Dave, make sure you get this in all the papers. I mean, I called you first. You know you've always done right by us, and I'm giving you first crack at this one."

Oliver's rat-a-tat monologue had given Diles no break in which to ask questions. Now, as the coach paused for air, Diles said quickly, "Newt, are you serious? Did Bevo get a hundred and sixteen?"

"I'm telling you, Dave, it was INCREDIBLE. A hundred and sixteen. A new national record. This has got to be the biggest story in sports, Dave, and I gave it to you first. I've told you all along he was going to get a hundred, and tonight he did. He did it!" Oliver screamed hoarsely.

"Okay, Newt, now calm down and give me the details. I want to get this out over the wire as fast as possible. Now, tell me, HOW did he do it?"

When Diles hung up, he swiveled around to face his typewriter. He inserted a yellow sheet of copy paper and began to type the lead for the story that would go out to newsrooms across the country:

Rio Grande, O. (AP)—A modest young man who once feared he would never be strong enough to play basketball today held the nation's individual scoring record with the amazing mark of 116 points in a single game.

He is Clarence "Bevo" Francis, 6-foot, 9-inch freshman center for tiny Rio Grande College. Francis amassed 116 points last night on 47 field goals and 22 free throws as Rio Grande toppled Ashland (Ky.) College here 150-85.

The exhausted Francis was in a deep sleep when the knocking on the apartment door awakened his young wife. "Frank, wake up, honey," Jean said as she tried to rouse her husband. "Newt wants you to talk to some newsman from New York. He's calling on the phone and he wants to talk to you." Francis slowly shook the sleep from his brain and made his way down the stairs to take the call. He spoke with the reporter and tumbled back into bed. But before he could doze off again, Oliver's voice was urging him back down the stairs: "It's a paper from Detroit, Bevo—they want to talk to you. Come on down and talk to them, will you?"

By now he was awake and reluctantly obeyed, taking the call. He would get no more sleep that night. The phone rang incessantly with callers from as far away as Alaska and Seattle. The activity awoke the Francises' infant son. As Jean fixed a bottle for him, she looked at her husband's troubled and tired face. "Frank, are you all right?" she asked gently.

"I guess so, honey. It's hard to explain." He paused and looked at her before softly adding, "It's like a stick of dynamite has gone off."

2

Before the Storm

On September 4, 1932, Herbert Hoover was desperately attempting to assure the nation's voters that prosperity was just around the corner. The Democratic presidential candidate, Franklin Delano Roosevelt, was railing against Hoover, who had been the unfortunate occupant of the White House when the roaring twenties ended with a bang on Black Friday three years earlier. The country was in the cruel grip of the depression, and Americans in unprecedented numbers would turn to Roosevelt to answer their mounting problems.

On this day and into these troubled times came Clarence Franklin ("Frank") Francis, born to Clarence Franklin Francis and the former Ann Cronin on a small farm in an area known as Maple Heights, just outside the hamlet of Hammondsville, Ohio. (Although their names were identical, the son never has used "junior" in his name.) Both parents had been married previously and both had been widowed. With the arrival of the infant, their combined family consisted of seven children.

The farm was small, "less than six acres in all," Francis recalled, but it provided the family's staples. "My mother tended a vegetable garden, and we had a few hogs, chickens, and a cow—that was about it." With hard work the farm, never prosperous, provided subsistence-level support for the Francis brood, which was augmented by wages that their father earned at the McLain Fire Brick Company clay mines. The wooded area of the farm property was an additional source of income. "We'd cut maple trees from the woods in back by hand and shape them into posts," Bob Francis, young Frank's half-brother, remembered. "They were sold to the mining company and used in the same

9

mines where Dad worked. We didn't make much doing it, and it was hard work, but every little bit of money we could get helped."

While long soup and bread lines formed in every major city, in Hammondsville the effects of the depression were much more subtle. Because life in the little town had never been that good, the stinging deprivation that the economic collapse visited on others evoked little empathy. For those who worked in the clay mines, loading clay by hand, as young Frank's father did, the national calamity was simply a matter of enduring yet another of life's hardships. Although millions were now experiencing hunger and hardship for the first time, they were all too familiar to people in and around Hammondsville.

The senior Francis was born in Parkersburg, West Virginia, and had been working since he was fourteen. He never completed elementary school, dropping out in the fifth grade to help support his family. "The only real education my dad ever got was from the school of hard knocks," his youngest son asserted. When the senior Clarence was eighteen, he suffered what his family termed a nervous breakdown, which his relatives attributed to the long hours of back-breaking mining and the attendant pressure of contributing to the family. He recovered rapidly, and fully, and returned to work in the mines.

"It was hard work," Bob recalled of his father's early years. "He worked in miserable conditions. The mines were cold, damp, and slippery from the wet clay they hacked out with a pick and shovel. The shafts were so low he could barely stand up. His back was always bothering him, but he seldom complained."

A warm, friendly, and humorous man, Clarence Francis had a penchant for a soft drink, Bevo, that St. Louis-based Anheuser Busch turned out during Prohibition. "He developed a liking for it, and he drank so much of it his friends started calling him 'Bevo' or 'Beeve,'" recounted his youngest son. "The nickname stuck, and when I came along with the same [first] name, why naturally everyone started calling me 'Little Beeve' . . . and that's how I got the name." The "little" was discarded as the youngster grew nearly a foot taller than the six-foot "Big" Beeve.

The birth of Little Beeve, who was also called Frank within the family and Clarence by acquaintances, had brought his mother great joy. The young widow had married Clarence Francis after a short but proper courtship and found in him a hard-working and sober man who provided her and her children with a home and security. The birth of a son made the marriage seem complete.

The only child of their union, Little Beeve was surrounded by four half-brothers and two half-sisters. The size of the blended households exceeded by far the capacity of the three-bedroom farmhouse that Clarence owned when he and Ann were married. Bob said, "There just wasn't enough room or food for us all. Our parents would send some of the kids off to stay with aunts and uncles who had spare rooms. Everyone tried to help each other out." Although they would have preferred to keep all the children at home, the Francises found it impossible to do so and used the only solution available to them.

From birth Little Beeve was a frail child, and his mother was especially protective of him. The other children were all of school age, and she welcomed the child-rearing experience again, as if for the first time. Ann found that her little boy brought a sense of stability and permanence to the family unit that had been missing because the other children were shuttling among relatives.

As was typical of those times and that part of the country, Ann had not gone past the third grade. She was much more valuable to her family for her assistance with the chores at home. Education was a luxury that few rural families could afford.

She married as a teenager, again in the tradition of the region, and devoted herself to raising a family and tending to the household. Tempered by the hard times and the loss of her first husband, she instilled in the young boy a strong sense of honesty and integrity.

The work ethic was part of his mother's training, and Little Beeve exhibited it from an early age. Although never destitute, the family was never affluent by any standard. The Francises made do with what they had, and if that wasn't enough—and all too often it wasn't—all would sacrifice a little more.

When the depressed economy took its toll on the finished products of the clay mines, the family scrimped some more, and the elder Francis found work with one of the New Deal projects in the area. He would never earn a great deal of money, no more than $5,000 a year in the best of times. An automobile was an unattainable luxury, and he walked the two miles to and from work in the mines each day.

Bevo remembers that "we didn't have anything in the way of extras. We just scraped by with what we had. Times were tough. We never went without food, but we often ate the same thing for dinner over and over. My mother would use whatever was available in the garden and what she'd canned to feed us."

Entertainment was limited to the radio and social events at the local Grange Hall. Movie shows were a special and infrequent treat. The arrival of a traveling evangelical show was a welcome diversion, and the tent preacher's promise of salvation struck a responsive chord in the hearts of people who knew, instinctively, that they would never be free of their burden until the time came "to go up yonder."

Hunting and fishing were not sport but a way to put much-needed food on the table, and local boys learned early to shoot game, mostly rabbits, squirrels, and raccoons. Bob, eight years older, was Little Beeve's mentor: "We'd hunt in the fields around the farm, and I taught him to shoot as a youngster. He'd tag along whenever I'd go out, and by eight or nine he was a pretty decent shot." Little Beeve, then about five years old, thrived on this outdoor life: "I took to it right away, and as a teenager I'd spend hours in the fields hunting." The game he bagged provided his mother with the ingredients for a succulent stew. "I showed him the best streams and catfish holes, and we would fish throughout the spring and summer," Bob said. "It wasn't long before he was a better fisherman than me."

School interrupted the long care-free days of idyllic walks in the hills. The Hammondsville school system educated about two hundred students in the first through eighth grades in three classrooms. The school was two miles from the Francis home, and six-year-old Little Beeve walked both ways each day.

Soon after the school year started, Little Beeve began to complain of tiredness. He continued to make the daily four-mile trek, however, and the fatigue grew progressively worse. Finally, he simply could not summon the strength to get out of bed one morning. The family sent for the local physician, and he determined that the ailment was anemia. The prognosis was good, but he ordered Little Beeve to bed until his strength returned.

Ann nursed her child back to health. She tried her best to provide a diet that would build his strength, but her means were limited by what she could afford. According to Bob, Little Beeve "was so weakened at times that we would have to lift him out of bed and carry him to his bath. His legs just wouldn't support him."

After several months of bed rest the boy's health steadily improved, but it would be a full year before he could resume school and the normal pursuits of a seven-year-old. The poor diet would cause another episode of anemia a short time later, and the ravages of the condition would cause him to miss two years of school before his health stabilized.

Bevo remembers that at the Hammondsville school "the first through third grades were in the same room with the same teacher, fourth through sixth in another, and the seventh and eighth grades were in the third classroom." The school had no gymnasium and no organized physical education program. "We used the field surrounding the school as the playground." Long since denuded by hundreds of active feet, the dirt field had several basketball backboards with rusted iron rims. Although he was smaller and skinnier than his classmates, Little Beeve was an eager participant in the pickup games that were always in progress. As in the rest of the country, the playground games shifted with the seasons, from football to basketball to baseball. In these unorganized roughhouse surroundings Little Beeve acquired a love of sports: "No matter what the sport was, I loved to compete."

As he grew older, he and several school friends who shared his zeal for athletics began to focus on basketball. It required little more than a ball and basket and could be played with as few as two players—or even alone.

"I was always messing around with a basketball," he remembered. "As soon as my chores were done, I would go shoot baskets. There really wasn't much else to do. I would shoot until it was too dark to see."

When they were about twelve, the boys coaxed a friendly neighborhood farmer, Pete Cope, into permitting them to convert his barn into a makeshift year-round basketball court. Pete agreed to remove some discarded farm equipment from storage on the barn floor and even helped to install some lights for the boys. They put up baskets at either end and fashioned a rough-hewn court. On that foreshortened and crude court in Pete Cope's barn, Bevo—for he now was too tall for anyone to call him "little"—began to hone the skills that he would later display in spacious arenas before thousands of spectators. For now, the only audience was Pete.

"We'd play all day," Bevo said. "When we got tired, we'd lay down in the hay and take a little nap. Then we'd get up and play some more."

The games in that barn were nonstop affairs, and the boys often spent an entire weekend there. With sacks of fruit and sandwiches and icy-cold well water close at hand, they had all they needed to sustain themselves until Sunday night. To repay Pete for his kindness, they would do chores around the farm. But mostly they were occupied with basketball.

Chuck Cronin was one of the players. "In that cold drafty barn Bevo displayed a passion for the game that was remarkable," he said. "And it got deeper as he refined his skills."

As different as their rustic environment was from the steaming asphalt courts of New York that would later spawn so many greats of the game, the basics remained the same. To excel at basketball you had to eat, drink, and sleep basketball, and that is what Bevo Francis did. The barn was where he developed the soft shooting touch that would astound critics and fans alike. "Chuck Cronin would say to me back then, 'You're gonna be an All-American,'" Bevo said. "I'd just laugh at him."

Years later, after he had achieved national acclaim, Bevo Francis would return to Pete Cope's barn to play basketball simply for the fun of it. Away from the crowds and the glare of the spotlight, it became a game again, just a game played for bragging rights with boys from the neighborhood, no national press hounding his every move and critiquing each performance. Pete Cope's barn was his home court; he would never feel as comfortable anywhere else.

Despite the recurrent bouts of anemia that caused him to miss classes for extended periods, Bevo graduated in 1949 from Hammondsville Elementary School, where he had been an average student. The following fall he entered nearby Irondale High School. From the first day the seventeen-year-old freshman intensely disliked the school and its faculty. Irondale, which had about 250 students at the time, was an institution of strict discipline in the tradition of "spare the rod, spoil the child," although that approach was largely discredited by then. The slightest infraction brought noontime detention, and Bevo became a frequent attendee.

"I didn't want to go to Irondale. I really didn't like it there," he said. "The teachers seemed to show a lot of favoritism, and I just felt I wasn't treated fairly. I told my father [that] if I had to stay at Irondale, I'd rather quit school altogether." The situation became so acute, and his threats to quit school so emphatic, that his parents did not know what to do. They desperately wanted him to have the education that they had been denied and pleaded with him to reconsider. He would have none of it. Either they would allow him to transfer or he was through.

Convinced that their son was not going to stay in school any other way, his parents relented. But where could he transfer? Bevo had the answer. Wellsville High was only twelve miles away. He did not make that choice capriciously. Earlier that fall Irondale had played football against Wellsville. Because Irondale was not large enough to field a team that could play a competitive varsity schedule, its opponents were mostly the junior varsities of the larger area schools, including Wellsville. During the game a Wellsville assistant coach, Frank Solak, couldn't help noticing the play of a tall rangy end. "He made several outstanding catches that went for long gains," said Solak, who was also

Wellsville's varsity basketball coach.

Bob Curry, then a reporter for the *East Liverpool (Ohio) Review*, later also saw the lanky end at the East Liverpool-Irondale game. "That evening a group of us were gathered at our favorite hangout, Heimi's Cigar Store, and I casually asked, 'Did you guys get a look at that big guy who played for Irondale? I wonder if he plays basketball.'"

The player whose ability and size had impressed both Curry and Solak was Bevo Francis, of course. The once small and frail youngster had grown nearly six inches in the year before he entered Irondale and stood taller than six feet three inches as a freshman.

"I talked to some of the people at the game from Irondale and through them learned that basketball, not football, was Bevo's game," Solak said. Solak sought Bevo out after the game and complimented him on his performance. Bevo did not forget those kind remarks.

"During the Thanksgiving break I went up to Wellsville and worked out with the basketball team," Bevo said. "I'd had my fill of Irondale by then and was on the verge of quitting school." Solak counseled the boy to stay in school, stressing the need for an education. "But," the coach added, "if you should decide to transfer, let me know. You'll always be welcome here."

That was all the encouragement that Bevo needed. Now he could satisfy his parents' desire for him to complete school, and he could leave the aptly named Irondale. Better yet, he would be able to play basketball for the kindly Solak, whom he genuinely liked. The family soon found a small house to rent in Wellsville, and the elder Francis began making the ten-mile trip to work by bus. It seemed that all their problems were solved.

3

The Wellsville Tiger

I knew I had come upon the chance of a lifetime.
— Newt Oliver, on seeing Bevo Francis for the first time

Wellsville is a blue-collar town that sits on the Ohio River where it runs between Ohio and West Virginia. During the middle of the nineteenth century it had been a hub of river commerce. It also had the dubious distinction of having been the site of the northernmost penetration of Confederate troops during the Civil War, and Gen. John Morgan had surrendered near there, at an area called West Point, in 1863. By the early 1950s, when the Francis family moved there, Wellsville had fewer than five thousand residents. Most worked in the clay mines and the related pottery industry that dominated the economy of the area. The principal local entertainment was high school basketball.

The town did not open its arms to the Francis family. As in many small towns, the natives viewed the newcomers with suspicion. And newcomers was a term that applied to anyone who had not lived in the town for at least a quarter century (and even that did not guarantee acceptance). Neighbors were likely to treat newcomers with reserve, if not hostility.

Word of Bevo Francis' prowess on the basketball court spread rapidly through the school and community. The fathers of some boys who had counted on starring roles as Wellsville Bengal Tigers took steps to ensure that the arrival of some interloper would not bench their sons for the 1949-50 season. Before Bevo Francis ever suited up as a Wellsville Tiger (the team was known alternately as the Tigers and the Bengals), the men filed a complaint with the Ohio High School

Athletic Association (OHSAA) in Columbus. They claimed that the exertion of "undue pressure" had induced Bevo's transfer to Wellsville—that Clarence Francis had been offered a more lucrative job and financial assistance in securing a home. The Wellsville fathers insisted that something had to be done.

"None of it was true," Bevo Francis said. The family found the rental house by going "to the office of the local paper in Wellsville and look[ing] through the classifieds for houses to rent. Someone from the paper took us around town and showed us some places, and my dad rented one. He paid the rent. No one assisted him at all. It just wasn't true."

In Columbus the OHSAA's commissioner, Harold M. Enswiler, pondered the information that he had received. As commissioner, Enswiler was the sole interpreter of the rules and regulations promulgated by the board, which was comprised of high school principals and athletic directors from all over the state and served as the governing body for all high school sports. When Enswiler informed Coach Solak that there might be a problem with his player, Solak and Bevo drove the 170 miles to Columbus to tell their side. "I explained the circumstances as best I could," Solak said. "The allegations simply were not true, and I told [Enswiler] so. I could never prove it, but I always suspected [that] some of the coaches we would be facing had joined the parents in the complaint. Anyway, it was obvious to me that Enswiler was deeply concerned, and there was no doubt that the complaints were causing him a great deal of trouble."

Solak and Bevo made three more trips to see Enswiler, but nothing that they said changed his mind. "I had always expected that Bevo would miss several games as a result of his transfer, since those were the rules at that time," Solak said. "You were compelled under OHSAA rules to sit out one semester, but I fully expected he'd be available in January to play. Those complaints and charges were unfounded, and I was floored when the ruling was made." That November Enswiler ruled that Francis was ineligible for high school athletics on the basis of the allegations and suspended the player for one year. The decision was final. They could not appeal. Jealous Wellsville natives had succeeded where most players would fail: They had stopped Bevo Francis from scoring a point.

"I was really down in the dumps," Bevo said. "I was suspended from playing basketball, and right after that happened, I lost my mother. She was having 'routine' surgery to remove her gall bladder when she died on the operating table. I was really affected by the loss. I was about as low as I could be."

The darkness that enveloped the youngster began to lift, thanks to Mary Jean Chrislip, whom he had met early in his freshman year. Pert and pretty, Jean, as she was known, won the young man's heart. "She filled an empty spot in my life," Bevo recalled with feeling.

Bevo's classmates agreed that he and Jean were a perfect couple. "They were both backwards socially and very shy," classmate Bob Grimm told ESPN Classic for its *SportsCentury* documentary on Francis, which first aired in December 2000. "But they were just made for each other. You couldn't find two nicer, more decent people." Observed another classmate, Eugene "Buddy" Ceneviva, "from the start they were a twosome. That's the way they went through school. They matched up well."

"It all happened very suddenly," Jean said. "I started dating him as a freshman. Got married as a sophomore and by my junior year had a baby."

With high school competition denied to him as a seventeen-year-old freshman, Bevo turned to playing independent basketball. Each town throughout the Ohio Valley fielded a team, and the games were a popular form of entertainment for the rabid basketball fans of eastern Ohio in the pre-television days of the late 1940s and early 1950s. The competition and caliber of play were similar to those of the YMCA-sponsored leagues in urban areas at the time.

The area also hosted scores of tournaments populated with college teams that were playing under the innocuous name of some local sponsor. "Baldwin Wallace College might show up in the uniform of Al's Cigarette Service. Duquesne would play as the Iron Dukes, Geneva College would become Riverview Greenhouse," Bob Curry, the local reporter, explained. "While it shielded the participants from NCAA view, few in the crowds that they drew were fooled by the names on the jerseys. The teams would come from Pennsylvania, Ohio, and West Virginia, with college stars dotting the rosters of all the better clubs." Now Bevo faced his first real competition. Despite his youth and lack of experience, he was a standout performer from the beginning. He thrived on the challenge of facing better and more experienced college players, and his play steadily improved with each tournament.

Local sponsors bought the uniforms and paid some under-the-table expense money in return for the advertising that they gained from having their names on the uniforms and, if the team were good enough, in the headlines of the local sports pages. As Bevo traveled from tourney to tourney, his reputation spread. Solak remembered that "frequently, he would be the high scorer and more often than not would be named to the All-Tournament team. He was a gifted shooter."

All the other members of Bevo's team, the Eastern Ohio All Stars, were local boys who had recently graduated from Wellsville. "Whenever I could," Solak said, "I accompanied them. But often only the local sponsor or a parent of a team member came along, and then the team would play without any real coaching." It did not seem to matter. The boys continued to enjoy success, thanks to Bevo's torrid scoring. Although they really were nothing more than a pickup team whose players changed from week to week, they won whenever Bevo was playing center.

While Bevo and his ragtag teammates were prospering in independent play, the Wellsville Tigers and Solak were struggling. The town had an active and influential booster club that supported the team, and the boosters wanted a winner. Solak eagerly looked forward to the day when Bevo could join the Tigers and produce the victories that were so elusive without him. The irony was not lost on Solak that some impatient boosters were, no doubt, responsible for the star player's absence.

Both Solak and Bevo assumed that the young center would be permitted to suit up for the Tigers when the next season opened, and both waited impatiently for that opening game of the 1950-51 school year. "I spent the summer working in the pottery in town, playing basketball whenever I could," Bevo recalled. Certain that he would be playing for Wellsville when school began, he practiced nearly every day until the light faded.

He did not play football because the one-year suspension imposed by Enswiler would not end until late November, when basketball season started. Bevo continued to haunt the gym after school, playing for long hours, often shooting alone until the janitor locked up for the night.

When practice did begin in November, Bevo Francis was there. "I knew immediately that our fortunes were about to change. He was the best player I'd ever seen," Solak said. As was the custom, the school held a large pep rally before the first game that December. Solak introduced the players to the entire student body during an assembly, and Bevo, named a starter for that evening's game, received a loud roar of approval from the students.

That night, with the warm-ups concluded, the varsity players paced nervously in the dressing room in Beacom Memorial Gymnasium, the Wellsville facility where the Tigers played their home games. Fans packed the gym, eager to glimpse the lad who had earned such a fabulous reputation. Just before 8 o'clock, as play was about to start, Curry, on hand to cover the game for his paper, sidled up to the coach to ask a routine question: "Is the big guy going to play?"

The reporter was floored by the answer.

"You won't believe what that idiot [schools superintendent Seward E. Daw] just did!" Solak screamed.

"He went and called Enswiler! He was afraid he'd get into trouble if we played Bevo without permission," Solak said sarcastically. "I just can't believe he did it. They declared him ineligible again!"

The conversation between Daw and Enswiler had been brief, with Enswiler concluding by saying, "He must be guilty of something or other. He's suspended for another year."

Daw then had sped to the locker room, where Solak was giving final instructions to the Tigers. Motioning frantically through the doorway for Solak to join him outside, Daw delivered the news. "I was shocked," Solak recalled. "I explained to him that I'd already cleared the question of Bevo's eligibility with Jack Mills, the opposing Lisbon High coach. He was fine with it." And Solak demanded of Daw, "Why would you call Enswiler?"

Daw answered imperiously but not convincingly that he was just trying to get a definitive answer, to be sure that the school would not be penalized for playing Francis without permission.

Shaking his head in disbelief and resignation, Solak went back to his team. His face told the tale before he opened his mouth.

"I'm sorry, Beeve," he said softly, "but you've been suspended for another year."

The words and their simple finality hit the boy like a bombshell. He flew into a rage. "It's so unfair!" he screamed. "I have done nothing, and now they are keeping me from playing again! I've had it! I'm quitting school. They aren't ever going to let me play here." He hurled his uniform into the locker, dressed quickly, and left. The rage and frustration brought tears to his eyes as he plodded home alone in the brisk night.

Everyone who was there shared his frustration. "When they announced to the crowd that Bevo wasn't going to play," classmate Joe La Scola would tell ESPN, "the fans went nuts."

"I have never understood what prompted him [Daw] to make that call," Solak said years later.

After the game Solak went to see Bevo. "The youngster was still very upset and confused by the treatment he had received," Solak said. "I tried to reason with him to remain in school. His father also implored him to stay." Clarence had sacrificed so much to make the move; the least the boy could do, his father argued, was to stay in school. But Bevo wasn't budging.

"It was really hard. I'd see all my friends out there playing, yet I'm not allowed. It made me think someone had a grudge against me," Bevo said.

Solak visited several times in the next few weeks. "I told him he could still play independent ball and then play for me the following season," Solak said. It wasn't an easy sell, but finally Bevo relented: "I agreed to stay in school if I could play the following year. I was very bitter about the way it all happened." But he trusted and admired Solak. "He gave me his word I'd be able to play. So I stayed."

In the 1950-51 season Bevo and the Eastern Ohio All Stars again traveled across that part of Ohio to play basketball. They appeared in independent tournaments in Hubbard, Sebring, and Cortland, where Francis made the All-Tournament team. In nearby East Liverpool they played in the prestigious Tri-State Tournament, which drew more than seventy teams from Ohio, Pennsylvania, and West Virginia. In those days this was as good as it got in amateur basketball.

Tri-State was the largest and most highly competitive tournament of its kind. The Akron Goodyear team from the Amateur Athletic Union's Industrial League played in that tournament, as did most of the area's college teams, including the University of Dayton, Baldwin-Wallace, Bowling Green, Geneva, Duquesne, and Pitt, among others. All were thinly disguised by sponsors' names but instantly recognizable to the fans and the press.

Bevo Francis was named to the Tri-State All-Tournament team. Although he had yet to take the court in a high school game and was only eighteen, he stood equal to the best collegians in the area in first-class competition.

Meanwhile, the Wellsville Tigers' two lean seasons without Bevo Francis had taken their toll. The powerful boosters had seen enough mediocrity. They wanted a winner. At the end of the season Frank Solak was fired as head basketball coach at Wellsville High School.

The man who had meant so much to Francis and who had become almost a substitute father for him would not be around to coach him. But he could do one last favor for Bevo Francis before he moved on. "I called [Enswiler] to ask for . . . a written decision that Bevo would be eligible for high school sports when school opened in the fall of 1951," Solak said.

Bevo was hurt and confused by Solak's firing and believed that the same group that had conspired to keep the teen from playing was responsible for having Solak removed. Solak consoled Bevo and urged him not to dwell on the past. "I told him if he played as well as I knew he could, he would get a scholarship to college and an opportunity to continue his education. 'That,' I told the boy, 'should be your goal.'"

Francis worked again that summer and practiced even harder for the coming basketball season. He would turn nineteen in September, so 1951-52, his junior year, would be his final year of high school eligibility. He vowed to make the most of it.

As the school year began, Bevo Francis, free now to compete, immediately reported for football practice. Assisting the head football coach was the new varsity basketball coach, Solak's replacement. His name was Newt Oliver.

As the players filed out of the locker room for their first practice that warm September day, Oliver squinted through the slanting sun and sized up the prospects as they took the field. One of the last to emerge stooped low to clear the doorway. Oliver watched the tallest player as he ambled by, arousing the coach's instincts and curiosity. Oliver soon learned that "the big guy" was considered one of the school's finest basketball prospects. The coach quickly drew aside Principal Francis Gant and summoned the head football coach, Chuck Sell, to join them. They huddled for several minutes before calling Bevo out of the jumping jacks drill. Gant put his arm around Bevo and introduced him to Oliver.

"The first thing he said to me," Bevo remembers, "was, 'What the hell are you doing out here?' I said, 'What does it look like I'm doing? I'm practicing football!'" Then Oliver launched into an impassioned plea to Bevo to carefully consider the dangers of football and what any injuries would do to his ability to play basketball. The youngster at first respectfully resisted the entreaties. "I tried to explain that I'd just had to sit out two seasons of ineligibility and, now that I was eligible, I wanted to play everything I could," Bevo said. "I wanted to play football as well as basketball." Oliver and Gant persisted. Didn't he realize that the school needed his talent in basketball far more than in football?

"I told him basketball was his game and he was taking a terrible risk playing football," Oliver said. "Every time he went out for a pass and was tackled, I saw 30 points going down the drain. I knew the first time I saw him [that] I had come upon the chance of a lifetime."

Bevo Francis, of course, was not in the least interested in missing yet another season of any sport for any reason. He was, however, smart enough to know that defying his new coach was not a good way to begin the relationship. Oliver and Gant kept the pressure on, and soon Bevo realized that they were too powerful to fight. After a single game he reluctantly hung up his spikes. His gridiron career was over.

More important, it was the first of many decisions that Newt Oliver would make for Bevo. Now the standout athlete focused only on basketball, working out every day, often alone, for hours at a time. Sometimes Oliver joined him. As the days grew shorter and basketball season approached, the two would often stay in the gym, playing one-on-one long after everyone else had gone home. Newt Oliver was only twenty-six, not much older than Francis, and not long before had been a high-scoring collegian who had earned Little All-America honors on the court. He could still play.

"I could shoot the ball," Oliver recalled. "And in that gym I could see that he was an individual who had all the capabilities of becoming very famous, becoming outstanding. Everyone in town had told me about him. But I knew everywhere you go, you hear about some star, and then after you look them over, you find out they're not so great. In Bevo's case, though, it was all true." The years of independent play and tournament competition had given Bevo Francis the maturity and confidence that come only from competing against those older and more experienced. Only one ingredient was missing: a coach who could teach the finer points of the game and polish the obviously spectacular skills of a highly motivated athlete. Bevo had gotten no particular coaching or personal attention as an Eastern Ohio All Star. Now Oliver doted on him and schooled him in fundamentals, skills that were overlooked in the free-wheeling run-and-gun play of the independent league.

Oliver's constant attention and concern became increasingly important to Bevo. Here, at last, was a coach who not only could tell him what to do but, more important, could demonstrate the moves himself.

Their meeting came at a crucial time in the teenager's life. He was in a fragile and particularly vulnerable emotional state. He had lost his mother, suddenly and tragically, barely two years before, and he felt that loss deeply. The firing of the kind and gentle Solak, who had championed Bevo's cause and served as a trusted adviser to the youth, left him feeling even more alone and isolated.

For two long years he had suffered the unfair and humiliating persecution by the bureaucrats in Columbus who had prevented him from competing in sports. He was vulnerable and pliable when he encountered the self-assured, fast-talking Oliver.

Oliver filled the void. He became at once coach, counselor,

advocate, and protector. Those who would later seek to understand the hold that he had on Bevo would focus on the talented but shy young-ster's reticence and Oliver's eagerness to step in and promote him. But, in fact, their bond went far deeper than that.

"I didn't really know at first if Newt was a good coach or not," Bevo explained. "He was really the first coach I ever had. He was a tough disciplinarian and a stickler for conditioning. As far as his knowledge was concerned, I had nothing to measure him against."

The bond between a player and his coach often rivals that of parent and child. The relationship is one of respect, admiration, awe, and fear. A strong desire to please their coach leads many athletes to perform at a higher level. When it works properly, the player-coach relationship often is lifelong. Countless leaders in all fields credit a former coach for their success.

In the case of Bevo Francis, his parents were not much interested or involved in sports at all. Although their fathers often are role models for young men, Bevo's father had never played any sport. His mother was no longer there to counsel him.

Thus Oliver's constant attention probably meant more to Bevo Francis than it would have to other players. Although their ages meant they were nearly peers, Oliver never let Bevo forget who was boss. "One thing about Newt was that you always had to put out one hundred percent for him or he let you know about it," Bevo said. "You would be running laps until you were dragging if he felt you were doggin' it."

Although Oliver was in total command on the court, they were rapidly becoming friends off the court. One factor in particular drew the two even closer together: Both were newly married. Oliver had brought his bride, Maxine, to Wellsville with him, and the two couples spent much of their free time together. Bevo and Jean had gotten married at Jean's home in January 1951; he was eighteen, she was sixteen. They planned to live with the Chrislips until they graduated. Jean set about the task of housekeeping with the unbridled enthusiasm that only young love can produce.

The other players were somewhat in awe of their married teammate and treated him more like an adult than as one of the guys. For his part, Bevo found it difficult to relate to fifteen- and sixteen-year-olds who had never gone on a date, and they felt constrained in their locker-room chatter with a married man present. These factors slowly and steadily drew Newt and Bevo together from the start.

As the Wellsville Bengals prepared for their first game of the season,

Oliver drilled them extensively in basic ball-handling and passing skills. "It was not easy playing for me," he acknowledged. He was embarking on his third season of coaching after two years at Upper Sandusky High School, 160 miles to the west. There his teams had compiled a combined record of 27-10. "I was never happy there," the coach said. "There was too much pressure about playing certain individuals because they were from prominent families. I spoke to the local Lions Club once and told them all, 'Look, I won't come down to Main Street to tell you how to run your business. So don't come into my gym and tell me how to run my team.' I told them, 'The only things I have are my clothes, my automobile, and a rented apartment. I can leave just as fast as I came. Nobody is going to coach this team but Newt Oliver.'" And, he said, "We turned that team around. I wasn't running any popularity contest."

Although disquieting rumors circulated in Wellsville about Oliver's run-ins with officials and opposing coaches, the Wellsville boosters were optimistic about the team's chances. The parents who had conspired against Bevo were silent; their sons had graduated and moved on. The local fans were eager for basketball season to begin, and Bevo's debut was the prime topic of conversation in McGreenhan's Restaurant downtown. Everyone was expecting the most exciting season since neighboring East Liverpool High had streaked to the unofficial state championship at Delaware, Ohio, in 1906.

Reporter Curry was introduced to the new Wellsville coach as basketball season approached. "I asked Newt, 'What about the big guy?'" Curry remembered. "Newt snapped, 'He'll have to make the team like anybody else.'"

"Well," said Curry, "we all knew in that area of the Ohio Valley how good a player Newt had inherited, and I knew he was aware of it also. I recognized his bluster for what it was. From that point on, Newt used Bevo."

Oliver wasted no time in building the offense around Bevo, his tall center. The other players lacked height and experience, and only two lettermen were returning. The coach shrewdly told his charges that the player with the most assists at the end of the season would be named the most valuable player. "I did it by design to get them to feed Francis," Oliver said. While the local papers naively interpreted this move as a noble and laudable incentive for team play, it really was Oliver's way of getting the ball to Francis as often as possible, instead of letting the other players try their own shots.

"While Newt was handing out the uniforms, he tossed one at me with number thirty-two on it," Bevo said. "'Here,' he said, 'this is what I want you to average.'

"I just looked at him and laughed."

But Oliver was not kidding.

Wellsville opened against Canton Lehman on November 30 at the Canton Memorial Fieldhouse. More than twenty-three hundred fans saw Wellsville squeak by the more experienced Polar Bears, 56-54. Bevo Francis led all scorers with 23 points, but more important was that the close contest proved to be an early and well-learned lesson for Oliver. With the Bengals in command by seven points in the last quarter, Bevo had fouled out of the game. During his days of independent play he had been an active and aggressive rebounder and defensive stalwart, and playing like that had often sent him to the showers early. It was no different against Canton Lehman. Bevo's absence from the game in the final minutes led to a late surge by Canton Lehman that saw the Bears pull within two points before missing a final attempt to tie at the buzzer. Oliver's team, mediocre without Francis, had nearly blown the game. The young coach would make absolutely certain that it would never happen again.

To do that, Oliver would have to harness his star's defensive instincts. After the game he impressed upon Bevo his value to the team and underscored what had happened while he was on the bench. Bevo remembers the lecture well: "'You can't be so aggressive,' he told me. 'You are too important to this team to be sitting on the bench.'" Bevo reluctantly accepted Oliver's advice.

But now that Oliver knew his team's capabilities, Wellsville rolled through its opposition with ease. To stop Francis, opposing coaches would often assign as many as three players to guard him. Often, all of them ended up on the bench, the result of the personal fouls that they accumulated as they tried to stop Bevo from scoring. After Wellsville's second win, the papers in East Liverpool and Wellsville were describing Francis as sensational and spectacular. Their preseason reporting had never failed to mention his two-year suspension. Now the tone shifted noticeably. Sportswriters were speculating about a district championship and never mentioned the two-year hiatus again.

In Wellsville's third straight victory, over East Palestine, Francis shattered the school scoring record when he matched the total output of his opponents with 41 points.

That record would stand for only two nights. On his home court in Beacom Memorial Gymnasium, playing before a capacity crowd for the first time, Bevo scored 44 points against Mingo Junction, whose entire team scored only 41 points. The following day Curry began his game story by asking, "Who can stop him?"

The reporter soon got his answer. The Big Red of Steubenville High handed the Bengals their first defeat, 64-42, in a game marred by sixty-two personal fouls. Francis managed only 22 points in the slugfest as three Steubenville players blanketed him, only to rack up fouls that benched each of them.

But Wellsville got back on track and rolled to an easy victory over Chester. With five wins and only one loss, the Bengals prepared to face Newell, West Virginia, which had won its last game 85-24. Twelve hundred fans expecting a high-scoring duel packed the Wellsville gym. But instead of a pyrotechnic scoring display, the fans got a dud.

The Newell coach was the first in a long line of coaches to see that his only salvation was in a stalling offense. Opposing coaches reasoned that denying Bevo the ball was the best insurance that he would not score. In the early 1950s the rulebook gave a fouled team a choice: It could take the ball out of bounds, maintaining possession, or it could use the free throw. And the shot clock did not exist in those days. Time and again, Newell chose to take the ball out of bounds—and lost anyway, 33-17, although the West Virginians held Bevo to 12 points. But instead of the high-scoring game that fans expected, the strategy gave the sellout crowd a slow-motion ballet of inactivity.

The coverage of the Wellsville-Wintersville game, which the Tigers won, included a sidebar that alluded to a sensational performance by a Cincinnati senior, Robin Freeman, who had scored 56 points in a game for Hughes High School while averaging 37 points per game through eleven contests. "I had seen the coverage that he had attracted with that scoring mark and just filed it away," Oliver said.

As the season rolled on into January, the Bengals had earned an impressive 11-1 record, and Bevo was maintaining his torrid scoring pace. He was achieving the Oliver-mandated quota that was embla- zoned on his jersey.

Oliver escalated his efforts to gain press coverage for his team and Bevo Francis, sending clippings and game accounts to the major papers. Bevo's scoring average caught their eye, and they began to monitor his progress more closely.

At about this time Oliver took three of his players, Bevo, Bob Mundy, and John Viscoglosi, to a game between Oliver's alma mater, Rio Grande College, and Steubenville College. Rio Grande was clearly out-manned and poorly schooled in fundamentals, which embarrassed Oliver, who had been a star player. Only one player on the

Rio Grande team that evening showed any potential, a ball-hawking guard who made deft behind-the-back passes. The Redmen lost badly.

"We all agreed that our high school team could have beaten them," Bevo said. "They had only one player on that team that would have been able to play with us, and that was it. For a college team they were really bad."

By now his scoring exploits were attracting the attention of college coaches. Bevo began to receive feelers from a number of schools, and the frequency of their arrival escalated as the season wore on. Although this was his final year of eligibility, he was only a junior because of his transfer and would lack the credits necessary to graduate in June.

Nonetheless, he received more than sixty inquiries from schools all over the country, including the major basketball powers. But Bevo had no interest in staying at Wellsville for another year and then having to sit out yet another season as a freshman at some school that kept freshmen off the varsity. That eliminated virtually all the major schools, and he never considered any of them seriously.

"In those days in that part of the country," Chuck Cronin told ESPN Classic, "kids followed their fathers into jobs. If your father was a coal miner, you became a coal miner. If he worked in the pottery, chances were pretty good you would end up in the pottery. College wasn't something we even thought about in those days. It just wouldn't enter our minds."

Throughout the second half of the season Oliver talked to Bevo incessantly about Rio Grande and his experiences there. The young coach skillfully played up the college's small-town atmosphere and informality, qualities that he knew would appeal to Bevo. Bevo's time in the independent league had taken him to several of the larger Ohio colleges, and he had found their sprawling granite campuses to be intimidating.

Oliver had not told Francis or the others, but the road trip to the Rio Grande game was no whim. "I had been in contact with Doctor Davis about the possibility of returning as coach," Oliver said. J. Boyd Davis, who had been the superintendent for Upper Sandusky schools when Oliver was hired, was now president of Rio Grande.

"The Baptists down there were always saying Doctor Davis had been sent by God to save the school," Oliver said. "If so, then I must be God, because I was instrumental in getting him that job. I had called Don Allen, the school's wealthiest and most influential alumnus, and recommended that they hire Davis the prior year." Allen, a Rio Grande native, was then the biggest Chevrolet dealer in the country, someone

Oliver knew from his own years at the college.

Now Davis "asked me about coming down there, and I told him I'd consider it," Oliver said. But he would take the job only if the school admitted Bevo Francis and could supply enough scholarship money to attract other high-caliber players.

The plan that Oliver had been formulating since he first set eyes on Francis was beginning to take shape. He cooked up a scheme to get Bevo's eligibility certified, although the player would be entering college without completing his senior year of high school or obtaining his diploma.

"I told Doctor Davis to write an innocuous-sounding letter to the Ohio College Association officials inquiring about the eligibility of an unnamed student enrolled at Rio Grande that wanted to participate in the Drama Club," Oliver claimed. "Then I told him to go on and ask about eligibility for the same unnamed person or persons to participate on the debate team. Finally, I said, 'At the end of the letter ask about eligibility for intercollegiate sports.'"

The unsuspecting officials who received the inquiry replied in due course that if "the student met Rio Grande College's criteria for eligibility then that student would be deemed by the Conference to be eligible." One obstacle had been removed.

Then, Oliver recounted, "I set up an appointment to meet with Allen in his office in Buffalo, New York. I told him that I knew he'd wanted all his life to see Rio Grande College on the map. I said I had the player, and the ability to do just that, but I needed his help. I told him about Bevo and the plan to bring him down to Rio Grande with me, [adding,] 'But I need some money to recruit a supporting cast of players, and the school has no money to give me for scholarships.'"

Allen had been born at home, on land adjacent to the campus, and his parents still rented out rooms to students. Allen was painfully aware of the school's faltering finances, both because he had been a Rio Grande trustee since 1947 and because the administration was constantly putting the touch on him; he listened patiently as Oliver outlined his plan to make Rio Grande a basketball powerhouse. "I said, 'You give me six thousand dollars, and I'll put the name of Rio Grande in every newspaper in America.' He probably thought I was crazy," Oliver said. "But before I left, he agreed to give me three thousand dollars to use for scholarships. It was half of what I'd asked for but more than I expected to get. There was no way I was going to go down there without the scholarship money to bring these players in."

As the two men parted, Oliver pledged to bring Rio Grande to

Buffalo to play in the arena that was visible in the distance from Allen's office window.

With Allen's commitment secured, Oliver advised Davis that all his concerns had been met and that he was accepting the offer. He'd be coming to Rio Grande in the fall and he'd be bringing Bevo with him.

"Doctor Davis once said about me, 'Newt Oliver is undoubtedly one of the finest basketball coaches I ever knew, but he scares me to death,'" Oliver reported. Scared or not, Davis formally offered Oliver the job.

Meanwhile, the Tigers still had several games remaining in their season. In the game against Youngstown-Chaney, Bevo managed 35 points despite being knocked senseless for several minutes. His season point total now stood at 460, and he was approaching the season record of 642 held by Dave Legett. Wellsville was now 15-1 for the season.

As eighteen hundred fans flocked to the final home contest, against Alliance, they were looking ahead to the state championship. For Oliver and Francis the setting was perfect.

In his final appearance on the Wellsville court in the Beacom gym, Bevo put on a dazzling scoring display that the hometown faithful would long remember. He made 57 points against Alliance High, which featured a starter, Len Dawson, who would go on to the Pro Football Hall of Fame. Dawson fouled out while trying to stop Francis from shattering the mark set earlier that year by Robin Freeman. The wire services picked up the story and retold it in detail to fans across Ohio and as far away as Korea, where freezing GIs read in *Stars and Stripes* of the scoring sensation back home. By now Bevo held the state Class A record for scoring in a single high school game and had maintained a 30-point average through seventeen games.

At last Oliver was getting the kind of coverage that he felt he had deserved all along, and college offers continued to pile up in the Francis family mailbox. None received a reply.

Two more easy victories followed. Entering the final regular season game, against Canton Central, Bevo Francis had 562 points. That game concluded what Bob Shaffer of the *East Liverpool Review* described the next day as "the most sensational season ever recorded by an individual in the history of district scholastic basketball." Bevo had burned the nets for 50 points in an easy 86-42 romp. With 612 points in twenty games he trailed only the 716 points racked up by Freeman in eighteen games.

The Class A district tournament was conducted in two brackets. Through the luck of the draw Wellsville and Steubenville—the only team to defeat the Tigers—were in different brackets. If all went as expected, they would meet again in the sectional championship game. Indeed, they marched through the single-elimination tournament as scripted. In advancing to the sectional finals, Wellsville had gone further than any team in the school's history. Along the way Francis had smashed the tournament scoring mark with a 54-point outburst against Barnesville. The division final against the Big Red of Steubenville sold out in minutes. Scalpers were hawking tickets at twice their face value to spectators eager to see the rematch.

But there was no joy in Wellsville that evening. The Big Red eliminated the Bengals from the tournament by a score of 65-61. Francis managed 29 points in a rough-and-tumble contest that saw the three players assigned to guard him ejected on fouls. One, Vic Edinburgh, lasted but five minutes against Bevo before leaving with five personals in the third period. The Big Red had four players who would later go on to star in college football, including Calvin Jones, who earned All-America honors at Iowa as a lineman. Steubenville was a physically intimidating team, and its muscle proved too much for Wellsville to overcome. Yet at the conclusion of the game Steubenville resorted to a slowdown. As the clock wound down, tempers flared and a scuffle broke out. Both benches emptied, and Oliver and the Steubenville coach, Ang Vacarro, and about twenty-five spectators scuffled on the court before police restored order and allowed the game to continue. Wellsville's most successful season ever ended at 23-2.

Ohio sportswriters ranked Wellsville eighth in the state, its highest ranking ever. The honors for Bevo Francis included selection to the All-Ohio team of the International News Service. Of the three thousand cagers competing at the Class A level, he finished second only to Robin Freeman in the balloting. (In the agate listings of the All-Ohio honorees, Dick Barr appeared among the Class A honorable mentions. LeRoy Thompson, a Junior from Waynesburg, was listed among the Class B honorable mentions. All would meet at Rio Grande.)

Oliver's incessant promotion of his star player had paid off. "I promoted Bevo from the first day I had him as a player until the day I left him," Oliver said. "Of course, I had a vested interest. Why would I tell you different? I saw in him my own chance, a chance to come out of oblivion. If I had it to do over again, I would."

Oliver's efforts paid off again when the Helms Foundation of Los Angeles selected Bevo for a special award for basketball excellence. Oliver triumphantly showered the state with press releases touting the award that he had induced the foundation to make, describing it—

accurately—as the "first of its kind ever awarded to a high school cager."

A friend of Oliver's, the promoter for the North-South All-Star Classic at Murray State College in Kentucky, invited Bevo to play in that game. The classic was a showcase for the finest high school talent in the nation and a smorgasbord for recruiters. Among those selected that season were Tom Heinsohn of New Jersey and Robin Freeman, both of whom joined Francis on the North squad. After a week of practice scrimmages, Heinsohn gained the starting position over Francis. Even so, Bevo tallied 13 points against the high-quality competition. In a limited amount of playing time, he hit six of seven shots from the floor.

For the week that they were at Murray State, Francis roomed with Freeman, who would go on to Ohio State and All-America honors. They were polar opposites, an urbane seventeen-year-old from a major city and a reticent newlywed farm boy of nearly twenty. "He was this real country bumpkin we'd all read about," Freeman said. The only thing they had in common was an ability to shoot baskets with exceptional accuracy, and that transcended the many sociological differences between them. Freeman remembered Bevo as a superb shooter with a deadly jump shot who "lacked rebounding strength. But he had a beautiful soft touch with his shot and was surprisingly fast for a big man. After the game I told him how much better he'd played in the game than in the practices." Freeman got to know Francis well enough to understand that his new friend was no scholar. "I couldn't imagine how he'd ever get into a real college," Freeman said. "He hadn't even graduated from high school yet."

Oliver had taken great care to assure Bevo that his missing 1.5 high school credits—enough to preclude his admission to any other college—were nothing more than a "minor technicality" that would not be a problem at the coach's alma mater. He had also arranged for Bevo to receive a scholarship, thanks to Allen's largesse. By the end of the season Oliver had Bevo's future scripted. He'd be going to Rio Grande College, and Newt would be there with him. "I said, 'OK, I guess I'll give it a try,'" Bevo said. "Of course, I had no idea everything was going to break loose like it did."

Part 2

The 1952-53 Season:
Not Rio—Rye-oh!
Not Texas—Ohio!

From the moment of his arrival Bevo Francis was
the center of attention at tiny Rio Grande.

4

Rebirth of the Redmen

The real test of a man is not when he plays the role that he wants for himself, but when he plays the role destiny has for him.

— *Vaclav Havel*

By 1952 Americans needed a break. They had struggled valiantly against the stranglehold of the Depression and won. They had survived two global conflicts that had claimed and maimed their sons. But before they could savor victory in World War II, their boys again were asked to fight and die, this time in a seemingly interminable conflict for an uncertain purpose in Korea. Tired of war and strife, Americans wanted peace and harmony more than anything. They found what they wanted in the grandfather-general whom everyone called Ike, whose calm demeanor was just the tranquilizer that the jangled nerves of the nation needed.

Although the Eisenhower administration would be criticized by political scientists as lackluster, that was precisely what the war-weary public wanted. Turmoil, riots, strikes, political assassinations, and yet another war would follow. In the meantime Ike brought at least the veneer of a much-needed pause and peace.

But the fabulous fifties had their troubled moments. The decade spawned Joe McCarthy and Richard Nixon, marking its early years with suspicion and doubt. Not even college sports were immune to the unsettled feeling that hung over the nation, and events soon proved there was genuine reason for concern.

The basketball decade began with the Cinderella double victory of the City College of New York (CCNY), which captured both the NCAA championship and the National Invitation Tournament (NIT) in

35

the spring of 1950. But the team that wrought that never-duplicated feat soon was testifying about point shaving before a grand jury. The story broke after a player approached by two former players to throw a game went instead to the New York district attorney; the scandal severely tarnished the sport and reduced the disgraced CCNY team to minor-league status.

In his 1977 book on the scandals, *The Game They Played,* author Stanley Cohen summarized the devastation that followed the 1951 indictment of several CCNY players: "By the time the grand jury was dismissed it had heard testimony implicating thirty-two players [among them, seven players from the victorious CCNY team] in the fixing of eighty-six games from 1947-50. Twenty of the players and fourteen men charged with bribing them had been indicted and convicted. What had begun as a New York City scandal, with Madison Square Garden its center, had spread across the nation. Games had been fixed in at least twenty-three cities in seventeen states, most of them in local gyms and field houses." Sports fans had seen nothing like it since the 1919 Black Sox scandal.

The scandals of 1951 were like a cancer that had grown silently on the game of college basketball. When finally discovered and exposed to the world by the industrious Manhattan District Attorney, Frank S. Hogan, the effect on the nation's psyche was profound. The fans who lived through the long dark winters vicariously with each triumph of their adopted teams were numbed by the shocking revelations. Presented with the undeniable facts that their heroes had sold them out for several hundred dirty dollars to a group of seamy underworld gamblers, they felt betrayed—and then they abandoned the betrayers.

Before the scandals, college basketball had become a showpiece sport in New York City. The doubleheaders instituted by Ned Irish at Madison Square Garden were deemed the best test for teams from all across America. They traveled to the bright lights of Manhattan to enjoy an all expenses paid trip and a share in the gate receipts as much as to prove themselves on the most famous court in the land. Once there, they competed against the local powerhouse quintets located throughout the metropolitan area that called the Garden their home.

City College, coached by Nat Holman, Long Island University, whose Blackbirds were led by Claire Bee, St. John's, where Joe Lapchick held sway, and nearby Seton Hall University, coached by Honey Russell (all future Hall of Famers) led the array of talented national powers. In addition, Brooklyn College, Fordham, Manhattan, Iona, and St. Francis College were available to serve as local host teams.

Columbia, while located in the city, avoided the Garden but still managed to produce one of the most notorious fixers, Jack Molinas, in a later scandal.

This vast array of talented teams all enjoyed a strong loyal following whenever they served as the host team for the popular series of twin bills. Crowds of 15,000 were commonplace. The games were also broadcast from the Garden to a wide-ranging listening audience that was treated to the distinctively sparse patter of announcer Marty Glickman, who described the action punctuated by his trademark "*Swish.*"

In addition, it was the Garden that hosted the premier postseason tournament of the time. The NIT was invitational, and only the very best in the land were invited to participate. The NCAA, with its smaller regional format, was decidedly second rate. It was limited to an eight-team regional event in venues as far removed from the Garden as Kansas City. Even when they moved the East-West Final to the Garden, it was still an inferior drawing card.

Accordingly, when the point-shaving and dumping scandals were announced in New York it shook the sport's very roots. Madison Square Garden, the Mecca of the sport, was found to have been the wellspring of college basketball's near-fatal destruction. The reaction to the revelations finished the NIT as a major postseason tourney, and led to a massive de-emphasis of basketball at the schools that had once dominated the sport in New York City.

The scandals were much more shocking than the Black Sox affair in major league baseball. Those players were professionals and had already left the amateur ranks to accept money. The college basketball players of the late 1940s and early 1950s were amateurs (their paid scholarship status not withstanding), and were seen as student athletes, with the emphasis on *student*. Their purity of purpose was unquestioned, and when it was revealed to have been a sham the effect was immediate and dramatic. Attendance and attention plummeted as the indictments, arrests and convictions mounted.

"It had a disastrous effect on the sport here and elsewhere," George Faherty of Adelphi College recalled. "[College basketball] had lost all credibility with the public."

The venerable *New York Times* ran an editorial pointing a long finger at the universities. "Too many of our colleges nationwide have themselves chased the easy buck (just as these basketball players did) or passed it on. Proselytizing of good players, the soft campus job for the star who can produce on the court; the building up by dubious means of a 'name' team for the aggrandizement of the college, the unearned passing mark on the report card, the glorification of a game and the devaluation of principle through the failing to put first things first—these are the crimes that finally beget crimes."

The National Association of Basketball Coaches added their interesting assessment of blame. "We believe the recent gambling expose has grown out of a laxity on the part of college administrators to actively uphold the standards which would discourage such practices. Entirely too much emphasis has been placed by the schools on income and winning the game."

Had it been confined to New York and the Garden, where it started, perhaps the blow would have been less severe. But quickly, the revelation that players at Bradley (in Peoria, Illinois), and at tradition-cloaked Kentucky, where the imperious Adolf Rupp had declared that "gamblers couldn't get within a ten foot pole" of his players, showed just how widespread the cancer was. When his former stars were later found to have been inextricably involved, Rupp snorted: "Their point shaving hadn't kept them from winning." It took strong action by the Southeast Conference to suspend him and his Wildcats for the 1952-53 season.

The realization that clean-cut All-American boys had opted to accept dirty money from sleazy underworld characters to enrich themselves (sometimes less than $250 bought a player's cooperation) and appease the gamblers was almost more than the fans could believe. But it was true, and it devastated the public's confidence in the game and those who played it.

The resulting de-emphasis of the sport in New York stripped the Cinderella double champions of CCNY of their major league status. LIU, Brooklyn College and Manhattan soon followed. Only St. John's, where the intercession of Cardinal Spellman had kept the school from being ensnared in Frank Hogan's net, survived as a major college basketball power.

The Garden felt the blows directly. Denied their local host teams' presence and tarred with the brush of the scandals genesis, attendance dropped dramatically. The once-packed Garden stood half empty and subdued in the aftermath. The NCAA announced that they would never again hold their tournament there, and urged all their members to follow their lead and boycott the once hallowed venue.

As the string of indictments and arrests spread across the pages of the newspapers, the scandals became America's favorite soap opera. But Jimmy Cannon of the *New York Post* was not entertained by the drama. Instead, he voiced a sorrow that he shared with countless others. "The tall children of basketball have been consumed by the slot machine racket of sports. They are amateurs exploited by a commercial alliance of culture and commerce . . . It is not because I am a sports writer that I have compassion for the arrested players. They have forfeited honor at an age when the dream of life should be beautiful. We should weep when we come upon a boy who has been fleeced of principles before he is a man. What made them special has destroyed them. Their youth has been slain. The assassin of youth is the most repulsive of criminals."

Basketball fans fled in droves from the arenas they had once filled to overflowing on those long winter nights that bridged the gap between the end of football season and the beginning of baseball in the spring. The stench of the scandals permeated the atmosphere at the Garden and elsewhere. Newspapers announced that they would no longer carry scores of the games or point spreads that were once prominent on all sports pages. The game that columnist Jimmy Cannon had called the "slot machine of sports" was on permanent tilt.

Clouds of suspicion and doubt hung ominously over the game, dampening all enthusiasm for it. Madison Square Garden, which fans had packed to see college hoop stars, not pro players, became anathema to the midwestern teams that only a season earlier had coveted a Garden appearance. As the sportswriter Bruce Lowitt told his *St. Petersburg Times* readers in a 1999 story about the scandal, "Playing the Garden was, to basketball, what playing the Palace was to vaudeville." Pious college administrators throughout the country rushed to announce a de-emphasis of the sport that had so tainted America's scholar-athletes.

The Garden wasn't the only sports venue to suffer; arenas across the country stood half-empty as fans stayed away in disgust. College basketball was reeling from the body blows of the betting scandals and desperately needed something or someone to resuscitate it.

The monotony of flat northern Ohio is broken abruptly as one travels southeast along Route 35 from Chillicothe. The hills of southern Ohio rise up to greet the traveler as the road twists and turns as it makes its way toward the Ohio River, which separates the state from West Virginia. But the hills of southern Ohio, which have no respect for the cartographer's boundary line, are a continuation of the mountainous terrain on the far side of the river. Southeastern Ohio is much more akin, culturally and socially, to its rural neighbor to the east than it is to the urban northern and western parts of the state to which it belongs.

Weathered barns, their sides heaved outward under the weight of sagging rusted roofs, flank the highway. Faded hand-painted signs adorn the sides of the more strategically located outbuildings, urging, "Now that you've tried the rest, why not try the best? Chew Redman."

This is tobacco-chewing, fiddle-playing, hard-working country. The farms in the area are known as side-hill farms. Although most of the tillable land is rich and fertile, much of it is also hilly and difficult to cultivate.

The unmistakable drawl in the speech of the locals echoes nearby Kentucky and West Virginia and is downright alien to the ear of more urbane Ohioans, who look down on their poor country cousins, whom they've dubbed *Hillians*.

During the Great Society years of the mid-1960s, when the United States would have a fit of social conscience and attempt to aid its least fortunate citizens, this poor, pious land would be included in the area called Appalachia. It was perceptibly poorer in the fifties, only back then no federal official came around to announce that it wasn't supposed to be that way.

In 1876, here in the hills of Gallia County, the Baptists had founded a college that they named after the blink-of-an-eye town called Rio Grande. The founders immodestly and effusively referred to their college as "the Lamp of the Hills." But by 1952 that lamp was flickering, its wick burned nearly clear through. The Baptists had maintained the school for nearly seventy-five years, but it had never flourished, even in the best of times. The church affiliation saddled the school with seminarians, whose tuition was subsidized by what the college charged its other students. As enrollment declined after the World War II vets reentered the workforce, the school became a losing proposition. Awash in red ink, it had turned to its alumni and friends for the money to stay open. Local businessmen responded: Don Allen, the hometown boy who was then the biggest Chevrolet dealer in the country; the farm operator Stanley Evans; Dr. Charles Holzer, a physician who started the nearby Holzer Medical Center; Dr. Francis Shane, a medical doctor who was the physician for the college's athletic teams; and others. Their largesse went to meet the payroll and to fend off a growing list of creditors. But the situation continued to worsen. Finally, in 1951 the Baptists withdrew their support. The Korean conflict had taken away many college-age men; enrollment was down to ninety-four students. As the 1952-53 school year began, the school faced a bleak and uncertain future. "A creditors' meeting had been held over the summer,"

recalled Shane, a former trustee. "We had just received a $25,000 dona-
tion from Don Allen, and the place was packed with creditors who
wanted their money. I asked them to take fifty cents on the dollar or
wait for payment since we only had $25,000. Or, I told them, just take
the school. Most accepted the offer, but things were really bad. Those
of us who had supported the school financially were in agreement that
it was just a matter of time before it folded. We had done all we could."
Only a miracle could save the school now, they believed.

Oliver, a 1949 graduate of Rio Grande, was well aware of the problems, and college president J. Boyd Davis had fully apprised him of the
situation when he first offered Oliver the coaching job. "He told me I
might just be the last coach the school would ever have," Oliver
recalled. "I was to receive $3,500 as a coach and teacher, and the
contract was for twelve months." Oliver would have full control of the
basketball program, including scheduling.

Armed with the $3,000 from Don Allen for scholarships for other
players, Oliver went off to the University of Wyoming to complete his
master's degree during the summer of 1952. While there he began to
assemble the supporting cast that he knew he needed to execute his
plan for the Rio Grande basketball team.

He used his coaching contacts to find likely prospects and began to
recruit them by mail from Wyoming. The first player he sought was Bill
Ripperger. An All-City selection at Sycamore High School in
Cincinnati, the six-foot guard had been a two-year starter for Chase
College in his hometown and competed against Rio Grande College.
"[Wayne] Wiseman [a Rio Grande standout] had guarded me,"
Ripperger remembered. When Chase disbanded its basketball program
after Ripperger's sophomore year, he needed a place to play.

"I got a letter from Newt Oliver asking me to come down to Rio
Grande and try out for the team. I had asked my former coach at
Chase for help in finding a place to play and he'd contacted Oliver,"
Ripperger recalled. "My parents were divorced and my mom rented
out rooms to make ends meet. I worked all summer as well. I needed
a scholarship if I was going to continue my education, and he offered
one, so I grabbed it. Besides, I didn't have a lot of other choices.

"My Mom and I drove down there in the fall, and it was just like
Podunk Junction," Ripperger remembered. "There was a cow pasture
behind the gym. You can imagine the impression that made on a city
kid."

Oliver remembered what the place looked like that first fall. "The
rooms weren't clean. The college couldn't afford a janitor so they were

just deplorable. [Ripperger's] mother wanted to take him right back home."

But the boy told her no: "It was my only chance to get a college education. I'm staying."

As he settled in, Ripperger learned of the financial problems plaguing the school. "Everywhere I go, the school is in trouble. Maybe I'm jinxed," he thought.

Other coaches at Wyoming told Oliver about a prospect from Ashland, Ohio: Dick Barr. The six-foot-two forward had been an honorable mention All-State selection for Ashland High School. Ashland had an outstanding program, and Barr was not a starter until his senior year. But he displayed enough talent to receive several scholarship offers. "Both Kent State and Ashland College had contacted me," Barr recalled. "I just felt like I wanted to get away from the area a little, so when Oliver's offer arrived, I decided to take it." Oliver was dangling a full scholarship but for only one year. "He told me if I produced, he would get me another year." Confident in his own abilities, Barr decided to accept as soon as he had time to visit the school. "We called several times to schedule a visit, but after agreeing to a date Oliver would call back and reschedule. This happened several times, and it was just about time to report for classes and we still hadn't seen the place," Barr remembered. "Finally, with classes about to begin, my parents and I went on down there without an appointment. When we arrived at this sleepy little village, my mom just about collapsed. There was just a filling station, general store, and post office. Ashland, with a population of fifteen thousand, looked like a metropolis by comparison." After his mother recovered, she urged him to turn around and go back home with her. "I told her the surroundings were just what I was looking for," Barr said. "But even I couldn't believe those four shabby buildings were a college. They call it Appalachia now, but it was worse then." Failed in her efforts to convince her son to reconsider, Vera Barr and her husband headed back to Ashland.

During a telephone conversation, Jim McKenzie's mother told him, "Jim, you've got some mail here from Texas." That was how he learned of Oliver's interest in him. The former All-State performer from nearby Catlettsburg, Kentucky, took a circuitous route to Rio Grande. "I was at Marshall [in Huntington, West Virginia], where I'd enrolled and was a member of the freshman team," McKenzie said. "I went there after visiting Adolf Rupp at Kentucky and he about scared me to death. The place was so big, and he had the walls of his office lined with All-Americans. I was just overwhelmed by it all. I got out of there as fast as I could." After considering and rejecting Moorehead State, McKenzie had enrolled at Marshall. "When I got there I found out that they only had about five or six freshman games scheduled. The rest of the time I was going to be shagging balls for Walt Walowac, their senior star. He had led the country in scoring the prior year, and I was expected to be a ball boy for him." It was about then that his mother called to report the arrival of Oliver's letter, which she mistakenly identified from its letterhead as having come from a Texas school.

"I went on down there [to Rio Grande] and worked out with the team," McKenzie remembered. "We had a scrimmage game and [Bevo] Francis scored about 70 points. Wayne [Wiseman] and I played the guards. I had never even heard of Francis before that. I was amazed at what I'd seen. After the scrimmage was over, Oliver asked me, 'Are you gonna come or not?' I said, 'I guess so,' and that was that." McKenzie went back to Marshall to collect his belongings and returned to enroll at Rio Grande.

Although Oliver had had little time in which to gather a supporting cast, the three he snared, Ripperger, Barr, and McKenzie, turned out to be superb finds. Joining them were two other players already at Rio Grande: Roy Moses and Wayne Wiseman.

When he got back to campus in September, Oliver had learned that one of his former Upper Sandusky players was already enrolled. "Roy Moses was a hard-driving, no-holds-barred-type player for me in high school and I admired his style," Oliver recalled. "I always called him 'Bull' because he'd charge right on through you or over you to get to the basket." In fact, Moses, a rising sophomore, had not played the year before but accepted Oliver's invitation to go out for the team.

Wayne Wiseman turned out to be the flashy ball-handling guard whom Oliver and Francis had admired at the Rio Grande-Steubenville game the year before. "Newt would be the third coach in as many seasons that I would play for at Rio Grande," Wiseman said.

He had grown up in the hamlet of Waterloo, Ohio, not far from the Rio Grande campus. In the mid-1930s a colorful high school team known as the Waterloo Wonders had taken the state by storm. With fancy dribbling and ball-handling tricks, the unsophisticated kids from the village of 150 took on all comers and racked up more than one hundred wins while losing only twice. They earned back-to-back state Class B titles while setting Columbus on its ear with their wizardry. Wiseman was related to a team member and copied the Wonders' flashy style while observing them on the local courts. "My mother was a schoolteacher and she had attended Rio Grande. I had received offers from one or two other schools, but Rio Grande was only twenty miles from my home so I decided to go there," he said.

Wiseman, with his geographic and genetic connections to the Wonders, had developed a slick ball-handling and behind-the-back passing style that rivaled that of the originals. His first two coaches at Rio Grande had no appreciation for his considerable prowess and urged him to abandon the flash for the more traditional and deliberate approach favored in the fifties. "They told me to save my tricks for the schoolyard," Wiseman said. Although he was far and away the most talented performer on the Rio Grande team during his sophomore year, as Oliver and Francis had witnessed, Wiseman nonetheless was anxious to learn how Oliver would regard his skills. "I had endured two miserable seasons with my skills under wraps and didn't know what to expect," Wiseman said.

With Ripperger, Barr, Moses, McKenzie, and Wiseman, Oliver thought he had a pretty fair ball club to support Bevo Francis and his scoring wizardry. The young coach added John Viscoglosi from his Wellsville team, along with Bill Frasher, a raw six-foot-eight recruit from Lucasville. Delbert Davis and Jack Gossett rounded out the team as substitutes. Only Ripperger and Wiseman had played college ball.

Bevo, Jean, and their infant son left Wellsville for Rio Grande in an old battered car with a full gas tank, thanks to Bevo's father. They didn't have a dime between them as they headed south toward Rio Grande. "We drove right on by it and ended up in Jackson about twenty miles down the road," Bevo recalled. "It was so small I didn't even see the sign for the town. When we got there and saw the campus, we were surprised it could be a college. There wasn't really much there compared to the other colleges I had seen playing ball."

Jean and Bevo settled into a small second-floor apartment that Oliver had secured for them next to the one that he and Maxine were renting in the neat white-and-green house that belonged to John and Edna Wickline, who lived on the first floor. The Francises and the Olivers each had a small kitchen-dining area, a bedroom, and a living room. The two couples shared a bathroom.

When Bevo asked about the returning players from the previous year's squad, Oliver told him, "I'm gonna run 'em off."

"You mean it's gonna be tough?" Bevo asked.

"You bet it's gonna be tough," Newt replied.

Because Rio Grande was only an associate member of the Ohio College Conference, it did not have to follow any rules specifying when practice could begin. Oliver instructed the team to meet at

Community Hall, Rio Grande's gym, for a scrimmage in the lingering September heat. The equipment Oliver found there said as much about the condition of the school as it did about the magnitude of his task: a few yellowing rolls of adhesive tape, a half-empty first aid kit in an old trainer's bag, and mismatched uniforms that had faded from scarlet to a sickly pink mottled by bleach spots. Two badly abused basketballs completed the equipment list—and a large bubble protruded from one of them.

"I arranged to sell the old football uniforms and supplies that were a relic of a time when the school still had enough students to field a team," Oliver said. "I managed to get enough for them to buy some additional balls and some training equipment and little else. I was able to shake loose $25 from the school to forward to the NCAA Service Bureau in Shawnee Mission, Kansas. That fee made us eligible to have our statistics and records kept and compiled by them." It would prove to be a shrewd investment.

During the scrimmage Bevo racked up 70 points. His teammates were stunned. Most had found their first several weeks at Rio Grande traumatic once they understood that their college campus had but four buildings and a cow pasture. Now they had just seen a six-foot-nine teammate throw in more points than they could count. Their biggest shock was yet to come.

"I told them all about Bevo's high school records and his ability to shoot and score," Oliver said. "Then I told them to take a good look around them to see the shabby conditions in Community Hall, where they would be expected to play."

"We called it the Hog Pen," Wiseman said.

The building, erected at the turn of the century, served as an auditorium, convocation center, theater, and banquet hall as well as home court. But it did not have a hardwood floor. "The floor was black floor tiles, badly worn in places and laid over unyielding concrete," Ripperger said. At one end the stage jutted ominously out toward the court. At the other, the entrance was just to the left of the basket, and the wall stood within a few feet of the end line. The playing surface measured thirty by eighty-five feet. On either side were three tiers of steps upon which rested folding chairs for spectators. Several inadequate globes suspended from a peeling and flaking ceiling provided what lighting there was. Rust-stained patches from roof leaks formed crazy patterns overhead. The building had no shower facilities, and the small cramped dressing rooms offered only a long bench along the wall.

Now Oliver's shrill voice rebounded off the walls in the empty gym. "Before you graduate we are going to be playing in Madison Square Garden," Oliver announced, his jaw jutting forward.

Wiseman, who had endured two losing seasons at Rio Grande and had seen scant few fans in attendance at the Hog Pen, remarked in a stage whisper, "The only Garden this team is ever gonna see is one you work in with a hoe."

"We all thought he must be crazy," Ripperger said of their new coach. "Here we were, in the middle of nowhere, at a school no one ever heard of, and this coach is telling us we are going to play in Madison Square Garden. We were all sure he was nuts."

Oliver continued to regale them with future possibilities: "If we go undefeated with Bevo getting 50 points a game and the team averaging one hundred, we will get out of this dump we're in." He explained to his astonished audience, "If you all are averaging about 20 points per game, nobody will ever take any notice of us. I am not about to stay here in the woods in this gym with twenty or thirty people around. We are going big time. One way or another we're going to the top."

Oliver recalled, "I had seen this [publicity] happen when I was playing here and led the nation in scoring. I knew what would happen if I could produce a super scorer [with Bevo]. It would open all the gyms in America. Above all, and beyond, I'm a promoter."

As he had in Wellsville, Oliver outlined his plan to award the MVP designation to the player with the most assists. And he would give a second MVP trophy to the runner-up in assists. "I wanted them to know that I appreciated what they were doing," he said. He didn't say that it was the only way to ensure that his plan would succeed.

Afterward, the players trudged back to their dorm rooms over the cafeteria. With Oliver's exhortations still ringing in their ears, they mulled over what they had seen and heard. The consensus, recalled Ripperger, was "that Francis was the best thing they had ever seen on the court and that Oliver was certifiable." In the "Animal Dorm," as it was known to the students, the players decided to make the best of a very strange situation. They had little choice.

Practice sessions under Oliver were long and intense. "Newt was a strong disciplinarian. You knew immediately that he was the boss," Wiseman said. "The first two weeks he worked on fundamentals, and we had long sessions of calisthenics and medicine ball drills. Games are won in practice." Wiseman, who would become a successful high school coach, came to appreciate the method to Oliver's madness: "We were in excellent physical condition. Compared to those practices Newt put us through, the games we played were a breeze."

Ripperger, who also became a coach, said, "Newt knew his basketball. He coached and stressed fundamentals. He was also a PR man. He knew what he wanted to do: He wanted to win."

Oliver wasn't kidding about running the returning players off. "He would run us until we were ready to drop," Bevo said, "and then he'd run us some more." Before long most of the returnees were gone, leaving a team that Oliver had assembled through determined recruiting, fortuitous happenstance, and, in the cases of Wiseman and Moses, inheritance. The squad, headed by Francis in the pivot, was as good a college team as could be assembled, given the time and circumstances in the pre-shot clock era of slower, more deliberate play.

"It wasn't long after we'd started practicing that we came to realize that we were going to have a good team," Ripperger said. The sixth man at the outset, Ripperger observed from the sidelines that "Bevo's shooting percentage was phenomenal. He impressed me as much with his ability to run with us as he did with his shooting. He never slacked off."

After the experience of his first two seasons Wiseman found the new circumstances to his liking. "I wasn't a scorer. If I could contribute defensively and utilize my passing and ball-handling skills, it [the plan] was fine with me. I knew right away that it was a great opportunity to play with improved talent."

After Oliver and Francis arrived, Wiseman's residential situation improved as well. He had managed to scrape by the first two years with help from his parents. Oliver's arrival provided him with a scholarship and meal tickets. Although his apartment rent was only $40 a month, he needed the help.

Bevo settled into the college routine easily. He maintained a full college schedule and completed the course he lacked for his high school diploma. He too was on full scholarship and received $50 a month in grocery money from Don Allen. He also had a part-time job: custodian at Community Hall. For sweeping out the gym he would receive 50 cents an hour to help make ends meet.

Through the early months of school the grueling practice sessions steeled the players for the long season ahead. The scrimmages reassured them that Bevo was every bit as good as Oliver had said he was. A quiet optimism was building in the Animal Dorm.

In his cramped corner office in the Hog Pen, Oliver spent all his free time trying to schedule games for his developing team. "Nobody wanted to play us," he said. "I called every college in the tri-state area and tried to schedule games, and they wouldn't play us. I kept calling and scheduled anyone who said yes. We played service teams and junior colleges and anyone who would take us on. Later [critics] would say, 'They don't play anybody.' Well, we tried and they wouldn't have us."

Eventually, he constructed a schedule of forty-two games against twenty-one challengers, one to be played at Rio Grande and the other at the campus of the challenger, with a gate guarantee of $50 per game. Three would be canceled before the season started, leaving the Redmen with a slate of thirty-nine games, an ambitious undertaking for any school. For one with but thirty-seven male students, it appeared to be sheer madness. For Newt Oliver it was a calculated gamble yet one he felt certain he would win. After all, one of those thirty-seven students was the best pure shooter he'd ever seen.

5

A Star is Born

On most college campuses football dominates the early days of November. At Rio Grande it was basketball.

As at many schools in that era the traditional home opener for the Redmen was the alumni contest. This usually proved to be an easy warm-up against older, less well-conditioned players, and it provided an opportunity for the coach to assess his team under less-than-pressing conditions.

On November 8, a Saturday night, the Redmen squared off against the alumni for the first game of the season. The Redmen rolled to an easy 116-50 win over the graduates. The score was not indicative of the caliber of play, and Oliver was not pleased. Although Bevo Francis managed to ring up 44 points in his first college game, the team had not gelled. "They didn't look too good. They were a little tense and the passing was bad," Oliver told Homer Alley of the *Gallia Times*. Gate receipts of $19.75 did nothing to improve Oliver's mood; the sum didn't even cover the costs of the officials.

With a week off before the Redmen's next game, against Cumberland Junior College, Oliver drilled the team relentlessly in an attempt to correct the weaknesses he had observed.

The visitors who arrived at Rio Grande on Saturday, November 15, from Williamsburg, Kentucky, represented a school of about 350 students, nearly four times the size of the Rio Grande student body. Playing much more smoothly, Rio Grande turned back Cumberland, 84-73. The game was close throughout the first half, with Cumberland pulling within a point near the end of the second quarter. Francis and Dick Barr dominated the boards at both ends against their smaller opponents, setting up numerous fast-break opportunities for the

49

Redmen off Cumberland misses. Francis scored 45 points with ease against the undersized defenders, four of whom left the contest with five personals in a vain effort to stop him.

Oliver was more pleased with this effort and told his players that they had performed well when pressed.

Their next game, again at home, was against a school whose name the Redmen soon became sick of hearing. Sue Bennett College, a junior college in London, Kentucky, had an enrollment of about two hundred students and was in fact a coeducational facility and not a girls' school, despite the snide claims that would come later.

The Sue Bennett game on November 18 marked the first explosion by Oliver at his team's performance. At halftime his team held a 10-point lead, but he launched into a tirade of threats and criticisms. "I said, 'If you don't beat this team by 20 points, I'll practice you until the damn sun comes up in the morning. By God, I'll run you off this campus.'" He referred to his players' lackluster performance against "some girls' team" and warned, "You better really go this last half, because if you don't, all hell's gonna break loose. You'll wish to hell you never saw a day like today."

As the chastened players headed back onto the court, Bevo said, "Hey, fellas, he means every word of it."

The Redmen defeated Sue Bennett, 121-99.

Bevo scored 58 points in that game, only one shy of the total that his coach had racked up against the same school three years earlier. Bevo was amazingly accurate, hitting on 68 percent of his shots from the floor. McKenzie and Moses added to the scoring with 24 and 15 points, respectively.

After three games the Redmen stood 3-0 and were averaging 107 points per game. Bevo's average stood at 49. The impossible didn't look so crazy after all.

Now, for the first time, Oliver sensed that his players could be all he asked them to be. "After that game, when they blew that team away in the second half, I knew right then we had a team that would be able to win against anybody," Oliver recalled. "I told them that next week that they had the potential to be the greatest small college team of all time."

But no one was writing about the team's early successes. So far, Oliver's ultimate goal of gaining publicity and recognition was a dismal failure. But not for lack of trying. "I would sit in that unheated office and call all the papers in the area, trying to get some coverage, and they all ignored me," Oliver complained. With his battered typewriter and the overworked mimeograph machine that he'd used four seasons earlier to garner coverage for himself, Oliver pounded out press releases by the score, to no avail. For the most part, the major papers in Ohio considered Rio Grande unworthy of precious news space.

Oliver continued to refine the schedule and now had his team playing nearly every other night. With Sue Bennett out of the way, the Redmen would meet Waynesburg College of Pennsylvania on Thursday, November 20, and the University of Dayton freshmen on Saturday, all at Community Hall.

Against Waynesburg, which had an enrollment of 550, Rio Grande took an early 18-9 lead and steadily built the margin. The Redmen led 45-32 at the half. Bevo Francis again was amazingly accurate, once more hitting 68 percent of his shots from the floor, and Jim McKenzie zeroed in from the corners. In its attempt to halt Bevo and his team-mates, Waynesburg picked up numerous fouls. The Redmen, emulating their coach's success (Oliver's free-throw percentage had led the nation in 1948), made 23 in a row at one point and missed only six of forty-six attempts for the game. Rio Grande triumphed 108-70, with Bevo accounting for 46 points. McKenzie, improving steadily, added 24. Afterward, Homer Alley wanted to know whether Newt felt guilty about running up the score. "We only beat them by thirty-eight," Oliver snapped. "That's not much when you consider they beat us by more [60-0] in football."

Later, the Waynesburg coach, Jim Haddick, would claim, "Bevo can do everything Mark Werkman [West Virginia All-American in 1952] can do—and better."

With four straight wins behind them, the Redmen prepared to face the University of Dayton's Freshmen Flyers, who were led by their seven-foot center, Bill Uhl. In fact, the Flyers' average height was six-foot-five. They would be a stern test for the Redmen.

Francis, facing Uhl for the center jump to begin the contest, thought, "I didn't know they made them that big." Despite the mountainous Uhl's advantage in size, Francis controlled the tap, and Barr converted an easy lay-up to give the Redmen the lead. The game was a battle throughout. The Redmen built a 15-point lead early in the second half before a Flyer time-out and subsequent adjustments brought the Dayton team back into contention. With Uhl bottling up the pivot, Rio Grande found success from the perimeter, with Barr, Bill Ripperger, and Wayne Wiseman contributing key buckets. Roy Moses found the lane blocked time and again as he charged through like a bull, eventually drawing enough fouls to add 11 points from the free-throw line. Francis, double-teamed throughout the contest, scored on 40 percent of his attempts from the field while sending four Dayton players, including Uhl, to the sidelines with personal fouls. Bevo finished with 35 points while holding Uhl to 10. The most exciting moment of the contest was supplied in the first half by Ripperger, who made "an impossible shot," Alley declared. "With one man hovering on his back and one in front of him, he faked a pass, thrust the ball in front of him, made a sort of underhanded throw into the air, [and] the ball came through the rim, tying the score at 28." Dave Demko and Arlen Bockhorn added 21 points each to the Flyers' effort as the Redmen prevailed, 93-89.

For the next three seasons Uhl, with Bockhorn and Demko, would form the nucleus of the Flyer Five, an alliance that would take them to the NIT three times, with two appearances in the finals. Uhl was impressed by Rio Grande. "Bevo was an excellent shooter," he recalled. "We lost five players trying to stop him. I was very surprised by the later [negative] publicity. I followed his career closely. He was definitely an excellent player." It was not a one-man show, noted Uhl. "We were a nationally ranked team each of the next three seasons and featured several All-Americans," he said. "Rio Grande was for real."

With only Sunday off after the Dayton contest, the Redmen faced Wilberforce College on Monday, November 24, in a game that Oliver had moved up from December 8. Press accounts of the game mention that Wilberforce was a Negro college, which says more about social conditions in the years before *Brown v. Board of Education* than it does about sports. But Wilberforce was not the sports powerhouse that Grambling and Jackson State were and proved no match for the Redmen.

In notching their sixth straight win, the Redmen mauled the visitors 111-71 before a sparse crowd. Bevo, who garnered 69 points, nearly matched the Wilberforce team's combined effort. At one point he scored on nine consecutive field goals, finishing with 46 from the floor and adding 23 from the line. His total was the second highest ever recorded by a Rio Grande player (Jack Duncan had tallied 71 in 1941). Bevo erased his mentor's 59-point performance from second place on the college scoring roster. Homer Alley noted that Oliver sent in every player on the team as he prepared his ten-man squad for its first road game against Bluefield, West Virginia, on the following evening, November 25.

Leaving the friendly, if rudimentary, surroundings of Community Hall behind at last, the Redmen took to the road for the trip to Bluefield. But Rio Grande did not own a bus. The team was forced to travel in two battered and worn station wagons that Don Allen had donated to the college some years earlier.

Oliver drove one wagon and student manager Carl Benner piloted the other. "Since none of the players wanted to ride with Newt if they could avoid it, my wagon was always jammed full," Benner remembered. "Oliver's wagon was always the one that held the latecomers and scrubs, and while less cramped, they were forced to endure Newt's nonstop monologues on the long trips."

"The school had no money to pay for lodging for the team," Wiseman recalled. "Unless the host school provided rooms for us, we were forced to make the ride back to school right after the games. We'd pool our meager funds and buy something to eat on the way back. It was a Spartan existence." But a winning streak and youthful exuberance can overcome many hardships, and the players seldom complained about their plight.

Bluefield forced Francis to the bench early with four fouls. Forced to pick up the slack, McKenzie accounted for 21 points and Moses hit for 23. Barr added 16 to make the game, despite Bevo's prolonged absence, a 93–63 romp. Bevo managed only 21 points after playing less than half the game, which marked the first and only time that Francis was outscored by a teammate. Predictably, Oliver left grumbling about the poor officiating.

Thanksgiving break was scheduled to begin when the Redmen returned to the campus. The players were ready for a much-needed respite. But Oliver felt that the team needed some extra practice before dispersing for the holiday and called for a late Wednesday afternoon session.

Francis had planned to leave with his family to make the trip back to Wellsville to spend the holiday with Jean's parents. He was not pleased with Newt's decision. Bevo's displeasure was only thinly masked as he reported for practice and began running the laps that Oliver required before each session. As Bevo loped easily along with the rest of the players, displaying a marked lack of enthusiasm for the exercise, he was struck from behind by a blow to the head that sent him sprawling forward. Turning quickly, eyes blazing, to see who had knocked him down with a basketball, he found Oliver pointing an accusing finger and yelling, "You deserved it! You were doggin' it!"

Francis, his face flushed with rage, stood over his taunting mentor, barely in control of his emotions and shocked at the treatment and humiliation.

"Both of them had strong wills and were fiercely stubborn at times," Wiseman recalled. Bevo said nothing and returned to his laps. As the scrimmage started, he exacted his revenge by refusing to shoot the ball. "Each time we'd throw it in to him, he'd toss it right back out," Wiseman said. Again and again, Oliver screamed at his star to shoot. Bevo stubbornly refused. Whistling the practice to a halt, Oliver ordered Bevo to run ten more laps as punishment for not shooting. The rest of the team scrimmaged without him as Bevo circled Community Hall. When he rejoined the scrimmage, he again failed to shoot. Oliver, growing more and more irritated by the moment, whistled the play to a stop and screamed at Bevo, "Twenty-five more laps, and this time run them outside the building."

"It was freezing cold out and Bevo went right on out and ran those laps in his sweaty uniform," Ripperger remembered.

Back at practice once more, Bevo steadfastly ignored Oliver's instructions to shoot. The sentence was repeated and he ran twenty-five more laps around the gym.

"It was getting late and everyone was on edge," Ripperger recalled. "What's worse is, I had a date, and I was going to miss it if one of them didn't give in soon."

"Newt was a very emotional guy who tried to be tough on us all the time," Barr remembered. "He had to have his way all the time. Bevo could be temperamental too, and when the two went at each other's throat, the rest of us just stood around with our mouths open. We couldn't believe what we were seeing."

"We had gone into the gym at three, and now it was close to seven, and still neither one would budge," Ripperger said. "I begged Bevo to shoot the darn ball so I could meet my date."

Finally, Newt sent Benner over to the cafeteria. "He told me to bring him back some sandwiches," Benner said. "It was obvious he wasn't going to back down."

Oliver dismissed the rest of the team with a wave of his hand, while Francis continued his stolid traverse alone around the gym in the freezing night air. Finally, his legs would support him no longer and he dropped to his knees on the frozen ground. The confrontation ended, and Francis and Jean headed for home.

It was the first of many clashes of will that would mark Francis and Oliver's time together. Theirs was a strange relationship that was often dangerously close to ripping apart but somehow always managed to survive. They maintained an uneasy, disquieting truce, frequently punctuated by more incidents that the others regarded as foolish and childish but were very serious to Francis and Oliver.

Oliver was a domineering disciplinarian who expected unquestioned subservience to his every whim. Francis, the object of his attention to a far greater extent than the others, was increasingly disgruntled
by the authoritarian attitude of his coach. While the younger players
meekly acquiesced, Francis rebelled. Those willful acts of disobedience
and independence amazed the players. "The constant give-and-take
created an air of tension that was always present," Ripperger said. The
three players who became coaches after college (Wiseman, Ripperger,
and McKenzie) all agree that Oliver was strict, inflexible, and stubborn
to a fault. "He was not one for compromise," Wiseman observed.

After the Thanksgiving break Rio Grande traveled to Granville,
Ohio, on December 2 to meet Denison University, which had an enrollment of more than twelve hundred students. The Denison team was
making its first start of the season. Rio Grande had for some time been
Denison's traditional opening game opponent. In the past the Redmen
had provided little opposition and served as a convenient tune-up game
for Denison, whose schedule was filled with tougher opponents.

This season would be different.

"We knew of Bevo's reputation as a scorer," guard Ted Bosler
remembered.

"Our strategy was to post our center [Jim Emanuelson, who was
six-foot-nine] behind Bevo and a six-six forward, Jim Cope, on one
side and a six-five forward, Bob Jones, on the other," said guard Bob
Laird. "But the supporting cast, especially their guards, were
outstanding."

Using a 1-2-2 zone defense that deployed its height to best advantage, the Denison team battled the Redmen. Denison managed to
contain Bevo—he scored only 26 points for the game. But Denison
lost anyway, because Moses and McKenzie scored at will by taking
advantage of the breathing room afforded by the collapsing Denison
zone. Moses tallied 23 points and McKenzie 20, accounting for much
of the final score, 88-78.

Oliver allowed his players a day off, but then they took to the road
again to meet the Pioneers of Marietta College in Marietta, Ohio, on
December 4. Although smaller than Denison, with an enrollment of
about seven hundred, Marietta proved to be a much tougher foe for
Rio Grande. Shuffling fresh players into the contest throughout the
evening, Marietta used twelve in its attempt to untrack the Redmen
and nearly succeeded.

Rio Grande had a narrow 19-15 lead after the first period and built
it to 43-34 at the half. But the Redmen were only nine points ahead

as the last quarter began, and in short order they lost both Wiseman and McKenzie to fouls. Barr and Moses played the last period, hampered by four fouls each, as Rio Grande struggled to hang on for a win. Outscored by six points in the final quarter, they resorted to a stall to preserve their winning streak and finished the game ahead by 76-73. Francis was back on the scoring track with 37, but the Redmen were happy to have escaped defeat. "It was a rough game and their guards just kept coming at us," Ripperger said.

With only Friday to recover from the scare thrown at them by Marietta, the Redmen prepared for Saturday's game against Beckley, a West Virginia junior college. Located just north of Charleston with about six hundred students, Beckley provided a breather for the Redmen. Rio Grande breezed to an easy 90-71 win, the tenth straight.

After several sub-par performances Francis seemed to be back on the pace established for him by Oliver's preseason edict that he score 50 points per game. Bevo was averaging 42.7 points per game, and after the first ten contests the Redmen were averaging 98 points per game.

By now Wiseman knew that he was part of something special. "I knew with certainty that when I led the break down the court, the lanes would be filled. If the center was denied me, I knew that I could always count on a trailer to be there to receive a pass over my shoulder for an easy lay up," he said. The games were even becoming predictable: "If the defense sagged on Bevo at the start, I would get the ball out to McKenzie or Barr, and they'd have uncontested shots. When the outside shooting forced the defense to come out to pick them up, I went in to Bevo." A special chemistry was building between the flashy guard and Bevo. An arched eyebrow or nearly imperceptible head or eye movement would tell Bevo where Wiseman wanted him to go. Wiseman seldom failed to deliver, and Bevo almost never missed. "It was like the ball had radar," Wiseman said. Finally, Wiseman found that basketball was fun again.

Because Oliver had moved up the Wilberforce game, the Redmen now could take a break from their grueling schedule. After the Beckley game on December 6, they were not scheduled to play again until the evening of Friday, December 12, when they would host California State College of Pennsylvania.

⊕ ⊕ ⊕

Although the players had followed Newt Oliver's seemingly far-fetched blueprint to perfection, they had yet to derive the benefits that Oliver had predicted. The press had all but ignored him and the team, despite Oliver's frantic efforts to get the papers to look and listen. Even the local paper, the *Gallipolis Daily Tribune*, gave more prominent coverage to the local high school team than to Oliver's undefeated squad.

The exception, Dave Diles, reported for work at the Columbus Bureau of The Associated Press. Diles and Oliver were not strangers. While still in his teens, Diles had covered Oliver's career at Rio Grande for the *Gallia Times*. He had begun as a local reporter, covering Meigs County, and later reported on the local college basketball team under the watchful tutelage of editor-publisher Harold Wetherholt. Diles had covered Oliver during the season that he set the national record for free throws and scored 725 points to earn Little All-America honors.

While Oliver's brusque and overbearing style turned off many reporters, Diles recognized it as the same style that Oliver had used to promote himself as a player at Rio Grande. Because his tactics were familiar, Diles was not as turned off as most by the coach's strident drum beating for Francis and the Redmen of 1952-53.

The lack of attention and local support for Oliver did not surprise Diles. "They are people who are pious and poor," he said of Rio Grande residents. "They have a basic simplicity to their lives. They are not dumb. But neither are they conniving. They are much more suspicious than the people in Cleveland, for example. And they do not like hustlers and promoters there."

Oliver, the self-proclaimed promoter, never would understand the lack of acceptance by Gallia County residents and resents it to this day. "I can never understand why we were never accepted there," he said.

Diles had long been the recipient of Oliver's almost nightly phone calls about the team and its scoring star, Bevo Francis. "He would call me regularly and tell me what had happened and ask me to get him coverage," Diles recalled. "'I sure hope you can get this in the Cincinnati papers,'" he'd say, "while he'd regale me with statistics. 'The world's got to know about him,' he told me as he pleaded for some coverage for Bevo. 'Make him look good,'" he'd say.

Although he was using every device he could to court the press, Newt was never very comfortable with Ohio's big metropolitan papers and their writers. With Diles he felt a certain kinship for an old acquaintance who didn't look down his nose at the school as a country oddity or object of derision. Diles, after all, was a boy from the hill country himself, a native of nearby Middleport. Oliver felt a special connection with Diles that was lacking when the coach courted the writers for the larger urban papers whom he desperately needed.

As a young reporter on the news desk in Columbus, Diles found himself trying to establish a reputation in the highly competitive world of Ohio journalism. With its numerous major population centers Ohio was fertile territory for The Associated Press, United Press, and International News wire services. All sought to develop fresh and novel stories that would attract editors' attention and result in their using the story.

Diles had listened patiently as Oliver regaled him with what seemed like fantastic claims about Francis. Unlike most writers, though, he was somewhat sympathetic toward Oliver and the plight of the struggling school from his own area of the state. As the season unfolded and Bevo's point production escalated, Diles began to give Oliver's star some attention. At first it was only a paragraph or two. As Oliver spewed forth more and more information, the coverage expanded somewhat. "My boss at the AP was Fritz Howell, a gifted and respected writer," Diles said. "As the story progressed, he asked me to stay on top of it. Inevitably, as I'd come into the office for the three-thirty-to-midnight shift, he'd ask me about 'my boy Bevo.'"

After the Beckley game Howell suggested to Diles that he go on down to Rio Grande "to check things out."

"[Howell] had a great nose for news," Diles said. "But he wanted to be sure that everything we were hearing was legitimate." If so, they agreed, it might make a nice little human-interest piece.

"I took along a stopwatch to use," Diles said. "I didn't have any reason to suspect Oliver was extending the games to allow Bevo to score, but I wanted to be absolutely certain."

✦ ✦ ✦

Diles was on hand for the game against California State of Pennsylvania on December 12.

Earlier in the day a sleek modern bus had delivered the visitors, nattily attired in blue blazers and slacks, and they had boisterously voiced their disdain for the condition of the "cow pasture" campus. The Redmen overhead them. "We decided if they thought we were a bunch of hayseeds and farmers, we'd dress up like farmers and take them down a notch," Ripperger said. Carl Benner scurried around the campus to come up with bib overalls for the players to wear over their uniforms. "I found some straw hats and a pitch fork or two as well," he remembered.

Diles, who arrived later and was unaware of the plan to masquerade as farmers, sought Bevo out for an interview. "Here was this painfully shy kid in bib overalls with a shirt whose sleeves came half-way down between his elbows and wrists," Diles said. "I thought to myself, 'This can't be the sensational star Newt is talking about.' It was difficult to get any reaction from Bevo. He was truly shy. His answers to my questions were monosyllabic and barely audible. He was very polite, but I got the impression that he would just as soon be left alone."

Beneath the bib overalls, Diles found a painfully thin youngster who stood six-foot-nine and sported a crew cut. His features were chiseled and his complexion gym-rat pale. Large brooding blue eyes dominated his pleasant angular face. Diles thought that Bevo was hardly a striking physical specimen capable of scoring 50 points per game.

Diles was having serious misgivings about the viability of his feature story as the reticent youth attempted to respond to his questions. Oliver, who arrived almost immediately after the interview began, filled the awkward gaps with his machine-gun patter of hyperbole about his star. "Tell him about that guy the other night, Bevo. Tell him about how he was hanging all over you and grabbing at you and elbowing you and how the refs wouldn't call anything. Tell him about how they had three guys on you all the time. Go on, Bevo, tell him about that," Oliver coached.

"They were on me pretty good," came the soft reply.

"You'll see for yourself tonight, Dave. I'm telling you, here and now, this boy is gonna get a hundred some night. You'll see. Make him look good, won't you, Dave? Those damn city boys won't print a word I send them about him, and you can get them to do it for us. You'll see tonight. He's every bit as good as I told you he was. You watch and see. You'll believe me after tonight," Oliver declared. With his stopwatch concealed beneath his overcoat, Diles took his seat among the approximately 150 spectators for the game.

Oliver's locker-room pep talk was a simple reminder of their opponents' derisive and scornful remarks. As the Rio Grande players took the court in their farmer costumes, the California State players hooted at their appearance.

Rio Grande led 27-15 after the first quarter. The Teachers fought back to narrow the gap to 49-42 at the half. But their efforts to contain Bevo were taking the inevitable toll: California lost three starters to fouls, and four others earned four a piece as they swarmed Francis from all sides.

Shedding their overalls for the second half, the Redmen surged ahead by a dozen points in the third period. Francis, profiting from his opponents' problem with fouls, scored 35 points in the final period alone. For the game he tallied 72, only one point less than the visitors' total output. Rio Grande garnered its eleventh victory, 105-73.

Refusing Oliver's offer to put them up on campus for the night, the visitors dressed quickly, piled into their bus, and sped away into the night. They were not laughing.

Diles, sneaking a look at the scorebook, checked his stopwatch. It had all been on the up-and-up. In a regulation forty-minute game Bevo Francis had poured in an unbelievable 72 points on 27 field goals and had sunk 18 of 27 attempts from the line. His field goal shooting percentage was more than 60 percent by Diles' reckoning.

"He just took all the oxygen out of the room. He was it. You didn't watch anyone else," Diles said. As the AP man prepared to drive back to Columbus, he thought, "Newt, you really *do* have something here."

Back in Columbus, Diles made his way to his desk as his colleagues made cracks about the California team that wasn't from California and other lighthearted jibes that they had aimed at him as he prepared the Bevo story.

"I reported my findings to Fritz Howell and assured him everything was legitimate," Diles said. With a savvy veteran's nose for news, Howell urged Diles to write a feature that would go out on the AP wire. Diles readily agreed because he figured Bevo "might make a nice little human interest story."

Others were taking note as well. The Gallipolis radio station, WJEH, announced in the *Gallia Times* that it would rebroadcast the California State game for listeners on Saturday.

The next day the Redmen traveled to London, Kentucky, for their rematch with Sue Bennett College.

The Redmen triumphed again, this time 114-68. Bevo, scoring from all angles, accounted for 59 points. Although Rio Grande's point total was smaller than the 121 from the first foray against Sue Bennett, the margin of victory widened to 46 points from the 27 in November. The team was steadily improving in all facets of the game and was growing more confident with each win.

Returning to the campus on a frigid windswept night, the two-vehicle caravan traversed roads slicked by ice. Suddenly, a car skidding wildly out of control crashed into the station wagon that Oliver was driving. It would be forever remembered by the players as "The Night Ripperger Went Blind" because the bespectacled player, cut above both eyes by his broken eyeglasses, kept screaming, "I'm blind! I'm blind!" Head wounds usually are bloody, and it was the blood from two minor cuts flowing into his eyes that caused his panicked reaction. Ripperger was the only one injured, and eventually another car was dispatched to the accident scene in Salt Lick, Kentucky, to retrieve the coach and players.

Homer Alley's coverage for the *Gallia Times* of the Sue Bennett game (which now eclipsed the space devoted to the local high school team) included his perceptive prediction, based on the early results, that Rio Grande "was a cinch for national recognition."

Thanks to Oliver's schedule switching, the team was facing a busy week. The Redmen would meet Steubenville College at Community Hall on Tuesday, December 16, and then travel for games on Thursday, Friday, and Saturday in Kentucky.

As the third week of December began, the Redmen had twelve victories. They had managed to score 1,199 points to their opponents' 877, and they were right on target for reaching their goal of 100 points per game. According to Oliver, Francis was scoring on 72 percent of his shots from the floor and had tallied 558 points, for an average of 46.5 per game.

Back in the bleak surroundings of the Hog Pen, the Redmen turned back Steubenville, 107-58. The game was marred by the failing lights in Community Hall, which several times required that play be halted. Oliver sent Carl Benner to fix the problem. "Here it was, the middle of a game, and all of a sudden there are no lights," Benner recalled. "I went scurrying around the building as fast as I could to find new fuses. I had to do it two more times before they finally stayed on."

The darkened gymnasium mirrored Oliver's mood as he railed against the inadequate and archaic facility and wondered aloud how long his team would have to play in virtual and literal obscurity. Francis scored 50 points against the Barons, whose school was nearly four times the size of Rio Grande and had whipped the Redmen soundly the year before as Oliver and Francis watched.

With Wednesday off, the Redmen climbed back into the tired station wagons for their trip to Kentucky. They figured their first contest there would be their sternest test of the season. Pikeville, a junior college with about 350 students, had a high-scoring, free-wheeling team that had handed Bluefield a worse beating than Rio Grande had inflicted. Pikeville came into the contest on an eight-game winning streak and had yet to taste defeat. A large crowd, attracted to the battle of the undefeateds, assembled in the Pikeville gymnasium on December 18.

'Posting one man in front of and another behind Francis, Pikeville was able to contain him throughout most of the game. Rio Grande took a slim four-point lead after the first period and stretched it to 32-27 at the half. With Francis effectively bottled up by Pikeville defenders, who benefited from local referees' indifference to their mauling of the Rio Grande center, the Redmen turned to Barr, Moses, and Wiseman for offense. They combined for 37 points. Rio Grande gained its 72-52 win through tough, in-your-face defensive play and a balanced scoring attack that made up for the loss of Francis. Pikeville would be the first of many teams that would learn that Rio Grande was far from a one-man team. The supporting cast was more than capable of picking up the scoring slack when the forest of defenders surrounding the Redmen's center was too thick to penetrate. With few exceptions, they would overcome.

Continuing their jaunt through the bluegrass, the Redmen traveled to Jackson, where they took on the Generals of Lees College on Friday, December 19. Displaying none of the attributes of its legendary namesake, Lees felt the full brunt of Francis' frustration as he unloosed a fusillade of baskets. After ending the first quarter with a tally of 31-9, the Redmen coasted to victory. Rebounding from his Pikeville performance, Bevo made up for it with a stunning 76-point effort that eclipsed his season-high mark against California State. With 27 field goals and 22 of 26 free throws from the line, Francis alone scored 12 more points than the combined effort of Lees' shell-shocked squad.

In Columbus, Diles had been receiving regular reports from Oliver after each contest and the promise that even better was yet to come. "He would call me after each game, spouting off statistics and claims about Bevo's talent. He also kept me posted on the ever-changing schedule that shifted from week to week," Diles remembered.

"While the team was on the road, Newt would call me and he'd ask me to contact various reporters for him with the game results," recalled Jean Cooper, the Rio Grande archivist who worked in the college administration office in those years. Wherever he went and by whatever means he could, Newt continued to pound the drum of publicity.

Diles was still working on the feature story on Francis. Now Bevo had topped the performance that Diles had seen and verified as real. Diles felt his story was ready to go out on the AP's national wire.

The story bearing Diles' byline moved to papers around the country on December 20, the day after the Lees College game, ready for publication in the Sunday papers of December 21. With Howell's blessing and "let's see what kind of reaction we get" attitude, Diles waited nervously at his desk.

❀❀❀

On the evening that the AP moved Diles' story to its subscribers, Rio Grande was taking the floor for the Redmen's return game against Cumberland College, in Williamsburg, Kentucky. This game would mark the end of the Kentucky swing that had seen them play Pikeville, Lees, and now Cumberland on successive nights.

As they had throughout the southern trip, the Redmen jumped out in front and never looked back. By the half they had more than doubled their opponent's score, holding a commanding 46-22 edge. They coasted home from there and finished with a 78-49 win with substitutes on the court. Francis scored 34 points on eight of twelve shots from the floor and went 18 for 21 from the stripe. Barr and Wiseman had 11 points apiece, and McKenzie and Moses each chipped in 8.

When they returned to the campus late that night, a small contingent of students still on campus greeted them warmly. The Christmas recess had just begun. Rio Grande was not scheduled to see action again until after New Year's, when classes would resume. Aglow with their many triumphs, the players scattered for the holidays to be home with their families. Before they left, Oliver told them to return to campus early so that they could resume practice. "I don't want you to lose your edge," he told them.

Despite some grumbling, they would, with one exception, be back on the floor in Community Hall the day after New Year's 1953.

❀❀❀

The response to Dave Diles' story was immediate and astonished everyone involved. Hundreds of AP subscriber papers across the nation picked up and ran in its entirety the thousand-word piece entitled "Siege Gun of the Rio Grande." Diles, delighted to see his byline on his first major feature, was as surprised as anyone. "At the time I was unaware of the impact the story would have on the readers," he said. "I felt it was a nice, little, somewhat offbeat human interest story on a small college basketball player. Now, in looking back, I can see the appeal it held. It was legitimate. It was honest. It was romantic, and it was small-town Americana."

Now Diles was concerned that a senior writer with an established reputation would pirate what Diles had misjudged to be a sports story of limited interest. Howell, equally stunned by the almost universal interest in the Francis piece, assuaged his young reporter's fears. "It's your story," he said. "Take it and run with it. But stay on top of it. I think you've really got something special here."

Bevo Francis was now national news, and the INS and UP news services frantically sought to catch up on the story that had been right under their noses all along. From now on they would take those calls from the peppery coach with the attitude. Beaten out of the box by the AP, they would make certain that they weren't scooped again. Both dispatched seasoned reporters to follow the Francis saga.

Newt Oliver found out about the reaction to Diles' story when he called Jean Cooper back at the school. "Reporters have been calling here," she told him excitedly. "They want to talk to you!" she exclaimed, as mystified as anyone about the sudden shift in attitude.

For the first time since the season began, Oliver began to believe that it might just all work out the way he'd planned.

While Diles' story had reported accurately the facts of Francis' bouts with anemia and the days in Pete Cope's barn, the other wire services—in their rush to catch up—dramatized the anemia with poetic license that had the youngster "near to death" on two occasions. They would use that same license to expand the barn games to include "crowds of spectators that exceeded those at high school games." So many stories repeated both canards that they ultimately were accepted as factual.

Reporters at the major Ohio papers began to take a second look at the Rio Grande story. The first to convert from disinterested skeptic to believer was Earl Flora of the *Ohio State Journal* (which, despite the name, had no connection to the university). Flora was the sports editor of the widely read and respected paper, which was housed in the same building where Diles worked. Flora had a large following of loyal readers. When he ceased his merciless ribbing of Diles about "Bevo and that Texas school," Francis and Rio Grande gained instant credibility. But the skeptics still far outnumbered the believers. Their conversion, when it came, was slow and grudging. Some would never accept the story as more than a P.T. Barnum hype, and they steadfastly refused to legitimize it.

"Some people embraced it immediately. Some refused to believe it and never did accept it. They still don't to this day," Diles said.

⊕ ⊕ ⊕

When Jim McKenzie arrived at his home in Catlettsburg,

Kentucky, for Christmas, he was greeted as anything but a returning hero. There exists a less-than-friendly rivalry between Kentucky and Ohio in all sports but in none more so than basketball. A Kentucky native who elects to wear the uniform of an Ohio school is viewed with almost as much animosity as were carpetbaggers during Reconstruction. The pressure on McKenzie to leave Rio Grande began almost immediately. "The people there would get after me about feeding that 'big guy' and letting him grab all the headlines," McKenzie recalled. "They told me that they [Rio Grande officials] were just using me."

McKenzie, who had been the star performer for his Morgan County High School team, had bent to Oliver's will, albeit reluctantly, and subjugated his potent offensive talent to Oliver's plan. Yet like all athletes, he possessed a certain degree of ego and self-confidence that, while under Oliver's tutelage and part of the Rio Grande team, he had held in check.

"After the first two or three games we played," Bevo remembered, "there was some jealousy that surfaced on the part of Jim and some others. Newt called a meeting then and told them all again that the only way we'd ever get any place was if we had one guy doing the scoring. Up until that meeting, I think we were really nothing more than a one-man team. You can't win like that. After the meeting, the attitude improved and the team came together."

"I don't think Jim ever really bought it," Wiseman said.

So McKenzie was ripe for the old one-two from his friends, neighbors, and family—accusations that he'd been duped into going to Rio Grande accompanied by flattery for his own talent. "Jim came here not really knowing anyone," Bevo noted. "About the only people he had become acquainted with at school were the players. Really, there wasn't anything about the school that you could look at it and say, 'This is what I want.'" He added, "I think Jim didn't really know what he wanted."

During the holiday break Bill Carter, the coach at nearby Ashland Junior College, visited McKenzie more than once, urging him to leave Rio Grande and enroll at his school. "He told me I'd be a star down here, while 'up there' I'd be nothing more than a feeder for the big fellow. They kept the pressure on me throughout the entire time. I didn't have much of a mind of my own then, and they impressed me," McKenzie recalled. "I also had a girlfriend back home at the time and that helped make the decision not to return a little easier."

McKenzie finally succumbed to the local pressure. Instead of returning to Rio Grande at the end of Christmas break, he remained at home in his native Kentucky.

⊛ ⊛ ⊛

During the holiday break the NCAA Service Bureau reported on December 27 that Bevo Francis held a wide lead in the individual scoring race among small college players: He was averaging 47.3 points through fifteen games (the report did not include the Cumberland game). Walt Walowac of Marshall was runner-up with 29.3. Francis also led the nation in rebounds, with 324 caroms, an average of 21.6 per contest. Among teams, Rio Grande trailed only Arkansas State in scoring. Walter Dukes, Seton Hall's All-American, led the major college scorers with an average of 29 points per game, fully 18 points behind Francis.

With a skein of sixteen victories behind them, the Redmen prepared for the remainder of the season. Practices were even longer and harder than before. "Newt ran us and ran us," Ripperger remembered, "and then he'd run us some more." On more than one occasion, the conditioning would prove to be the difference in the outcome of a game.

The post-holiday schedule began with a trip to Findlay, Ohio, on Wednesday, January 7, to play Findlay College, which boasted the presence of six-foot-seven Herk Wolfe, who had averaged 31 points per game the previous season. Traveling north for the game, the Redmen were eager to resume action. They would get all they could handle.

"They had Wolfe at center and the Marquette twins [Ron and Leroy], and they were three fine ballplayers," Wiseman said.

The Findlay College Oilers came out with guns blazing. Their two guards, Ron Marquette and Jerry Brown, couldn't miss. "Everything they threw up was going in," Ripperger remembered.

While Bevo managed to contain Wolfe inside, the Oilers' outside shooting kept them in the game. The lead see-sawed back and forth, with neither team able to gain the upper hand.

"Ripperger and I struggled all night trying to keep up with their guards," Wiseman said. Ripperger recalled that "it didn't seem to matter where they were—they just threw up these long-distance rainbows and they went in."

Frustrated in their efforts to halt the barrage, Ripperger and Wiseman found themselves in foul trouble on the bench. They were joined there by Barr, who'd also been disqualified. Without McKenzie,

Rio Grande was forced to use players who had seen little action under fire. Rio Grande led 79-77 with time running out when John Viscoglosi fouled Wolfe in desperation, sending the Findlay star to the line. Wolfe converted both shots, sending the game into overtime. With three starters on the bench, Francis assumed the scoring burden in a makeshift lineup. The teams matched buckets in the overtime period, and the score remained tied at 89 with five seconds to play. Then little-used Rio Grande reserve Delbert Davis heaved a long overhead shot from the far corner. Francis and Wolfe jockeyed for position as the desperation shot went up. "On the bench we were all moaning, 'Oh, no!'" Ripperger said. "I don't think he'd taken more than one or two shots in a game before that."

There would be no rebound to grab. The last-second buzzer beater swished through hoop. Rio Grande had escaped with the victory.

In his personal battle with Wolfe, Francis accounted for 44 points while holding Wolfe to 27. Findlay, however, had managed to get 42 points from its guards, Ron Marquette and Brown, which kept the Oilers within a bucket of victory all night.

Relieved to still be counted among the ranks of the undefeated, Rio Grande was more than happy to escape back to campus. The team's improbable hero, Delbert Davis, smiled all the way home.

With but a single day to recover from their adrenaline-sapping win, the Redmen were scheduled to meet their next foe in the snug confines of Community Hall. That day, January 9, the NCAA released its statistical update, which showed that Francis was maintaining his position as the nation's leading scorer. This time, with the Cumberland game included, his average stood at more than 46 points per contest. His field goal accuracy was 54 percent, good enough for seventh place. Rio Grande still trailed only Arkansas State in scoring.

Impressive laurels, to be sure, but what the Redmen, especially Bevo, did next all but wiped those statistics from the minds of legions of sports fans and brought new readers to the nation's sports pages.

That was the game against the Thoroughbreds of Ashland Junior College on the cold, gray evening of January 9, when Bevo scored his unbelievable 116 points, and the Redmen cruised to victory, 150-85.

6

America Falls
for Bevo

The story of Bevo Francis, which had been a nice little oddity, was transformed overnight into a national phenomenon. When *Life* magazine ran its spread a month later, the headline read: "BEVO GIVES A LITTLE OHIO COLLEGE A BIG LIFT: RIO GRANDE RISES WITH THE FIRST BASKETBALL PLAYER EVER TO SCORE MORE THAN 100 POINTS IN ONE GAME." (His score remains unchallenged to this day. Pete Maravich, the major college record holder, scored a career high of 69 points. Larry Bird had a college career high of 49 points, while Kareem Abdul-Jabbar [known in his college days as Lew Alcindor], scored 61 points at his college best. Magic Johnson's college best was 31 points, and Michael Jordan's was 39.)

"What Bevo represented, in his innocence, was a radical departure from the smelly and tainted atmosphere of college basketball," William Nack, the long-time writer for *Sports Illustrated*, declared during the *SportsCentury* documentary. "Bevo Francis represented a broom, sweeping the sport clean."

Nack was not alone in his observation or conclusion. Millions of readers had seen a wire service photo depicting a tall, gangly youth in a plaid flannel shirt and jeans wielding a long-handled push broom in the dank and dingy Community Hall. The image of Francis and the message it conveyed subtly, perhaps subliminally, was implanted firmly in their minds. Bevo Francis, the aw-shucks simple farm boy from rural Ohio was literally and metaphorically sweeping the vestiges of scandal away from the sport. It was a message that resonated with fans who had been turned off by the greed and avarice of those caught up in the scandals. Legions of fans, entranced by the purity and romance of his story, returned with renewed interest to the sport of college basketball.

For Bevo, Newt Oliver, and Rio Grande the transformation from unknowns to household names was immediate, and its scope and impact overwhelmed both Francis and the college. Bevo fever swept the country, and all in its path would be affected. Of the principals involved, only Newt seemed able to comprehend the magnitude of the public relations potential that Bevo's scoring feat had placed in his hands. He would not waste the opportunity to seize and shape it.

"The most amazing thing about that game," Newt would insist, "was not the 116 points. It was that he scored 55 points in the last ten minutes. That's a 220 points-per-game clip."

With the news of Bevo's feat splashed across the sports pages of the nation, Oliver was in his element. The writer Danny Faulks, co-author of Oliver's 1995 memoir, remembered, "Newt just loved it."

That he did. "There weren't a whole lot of people there that night," Oliver recalled. "But from that night on, there weren't any more greasy hamburgers or those two old wagons. We moved into first class. From that day on it was filet mignon."

Virtually every AP subscriber in the United States ran Dave Diles' account of the Ashland game, usually devoting several columns to the story under a banner headline proclaiming, "116 POINTS FOR BEVO FRANCIS" or a variation thereof.

Some confused editors mistakenly placed the school in Texas instead of Ohio, and virtually none knew that the correct pronunciation was "RYE-OH," not "REE-OH." But that mattered little. Bevo Francis had done something no one had done before—or even come close.

He became the biggest story in sports and captivated a nation that wanted someone or something to believe in. The damage inflicted on the sport by the scandals had reduced college basketball to a game played in front of half-empty arenas. Now, suddenly, a genuine hero was playing basketball in an incorruptible tiny town in the hills of southern Ohio. The sheer improbability that a player from a school with ninety-four students could achieve such a scoring record, coupled with his genuine aw-shucks shyness, captured the hearts and minds of Americans.

Eisenhower's pending inaugural, Korea, and Sen. Joe McCarthy's alarming charges about communists in government all took a backseat to the story of Bevo Francis and Rio Grande College.

"The phone started ringing and never did stop," Diles remembered. "People were calling from everywhere to find out more about Bevo and Rio Grande. With Oliver's constant schedule juggling, it was impossible to get straight answers from him on where Rio Grande would be playing next. Of course, all those callers wanted to send reporters to cover the games. Getting answers for them wasn't easy."

In the neatly trimmed home of the Wicklines, the phone in the hall downstairs never stopped ringing, either. As the day wore on, the calls continued. "I went without sleep for twenty-four hours," Oliver recalled. Everyone, it seemed, *had* to talk to Bevo, "for just a minute, please."

The sleepy crossroads village of Rio Grande, population 203, was under siege. Within three days of the Ashland game the college campus was overrun with reporters and photographers, as well as television and newsreel crews. Cables snaked in and out of Community Hall, and the camera crews crushed out their cigarettes on the gym floor and trampled through the bushes.

Phone lines into the tiny hamlet were woefully inadequate to handle the heavy volume of calls routed to the Wicklines' home and the college. Service was often disrupted entirely when the overworked operators and overtaxed routing system simply collapsed under the avalanche of calls.

While the media flocked to town, the Redmen took to the road to meet Mayo Vocational School in Paintsville, Kentucky, on Saturday, January 10. True to form, Rio Grande grabbed an early lead and never looked back. In a game that saw Mayo lose four starters on fouls, Francis scored 63 points as Rio Grande rolled over its host, 119-91. Bill Ripperger had replaced Jim McKenzie in the lineup and was becoming more familiar with his teammate's style now. He accounted for 21 points and Dick Barr added 16. It had been a spectacular week for Francis and the team. Rio Grande had established a new national team scoring record with its 150-point tally against Ashland. Bevo owned the all-time individual scoring mark and had scored 223 points in the three games that week. In an era when 1,000 points in the span of a career was considered the mark of excellence, he'd scored a year's worth of points in a single week.

The account of the Mayo game in the *Gallipolis Daily Tribune* that Sunday revealed the altered state of affairs at Rio Grande College. In a sidebar outlined in bold black was an announcement that *Life* magazine would arrive on campus at 10 a.m. the next day, January 12, and would spend two days in the area. Another notice on the same page alerted the few Gallia County residents fortunate enough to have television sets that Bevo and Newt would be appearing on Jack Bradley's popular evening sports show on WSAZ-TV out of Huntington, West Virginia.

The team had two days to rest after the Mayo game before returning to action against Wright-Patterson Air Force Base in a game that would benefit the March of Dimes campaign against deadly polio. The home game, shifted hastily from the cramped confines of Community Hall, was now slated for the more spacious Washington High School gym in nearby Gallipolis that Monday.

While Oliver reveled in the attention that he was finally receiving from the media and attended to the numerous requests for interviews, the team hunkered down in the Animal Dorm over the cafeteria to try to figure out what had happened. "We had been on the road to play, and we were not aware of the uproar that had been created by the Ashland game," Ripperger recalled. "When we got back to the campus, the place was swarming with reporters and photographers who hounded us everywhere we went."

Unaccustomed to attention and somewhat uncomfortable with it, all the players retreated to their dorm. "We would kid among ourselves a bit nervously about being 'stars' and such," Wayne Wiseman said. The playful banter masked their uncertainty about what had happened to them, literally overnight. But the peace and quiet that they found in the Animal Dorm didn't last long, and on the tiny campus of Rio Grande, they had nowhere to hide.

For Bevo the tumultuous atmosphere on campus was not pleasant. "The lid blew off. They just flocked in," he remembered. "From then on it was never the same. There was absolutely no privacy. Newt liked it, and at first I went along with it. But I never did like it."

Oliver recalled that "I explained to Bevo, when he complained about all the demands being made on him, that this was the price of glory. This is what we have been working for." But Bevo thought it was "like being in jail."

Instead of making his star center run laps in Community Hall, Oliver was urging him to speak to every reporter who called or visited. When *Life* arrived that Monday, the magazine's reporters and photographers were determined to document Bevo's day. From the time he arose until he joined the team for that evening's game, they were in his face or shadowing his every move.

"I got up for breakfast and they were there taking pictures. I'd go off to class and they followed me there. When I came home for lunch, they were there taking more pictures. I couldn't move without running into them. Someone was always at my elbow, sticking a mike in my face. It was a rat race," he said.

Jean was drawn into the maelstrom too. "They would show up and tell me to fix Bevo a meal. So I'd fix him a meal," she said. "Then they'd decide to take pictures of the baby, and they'd tell me to fix him a meal, and I'd get a meal together for him. It didn't matter to them that he needed to have a nap or that I'd just fed him. They just ordered us around and we followed their orders. We were young and dumb."

Of course, the only person to whom they could turn for help and advice was Oliver, and his interests were not theirs. Reluctantly, they went along with all of it.

By the time the *Life* crew was finished, it had more than a thousand shots of Francis eating, attending class, strolling across the campus, feeding his son, visiting the gym, sweeping floors, shooting pool and baskets, and huddling with Oliver. In short, the magazine chronicled a contrived record of his day that omitted only the most personal moments.

Bevo simply "wished it would all just go away," Diles recalled. "He just wanted to play basketball."

⊕ ⊕ ⊕

The Washington High gymnasium, while far more spacious than the Hog Pen, was sorely strained to accommodate the crowd that began to arrive early for the January 12 game against the team from Wright-Patterson Air Force Base and continued to grow as game time approached. Designed to seat approximately 750 people, the hall was packed with more than a thousand by tip-off. Outside, hundreds more impatiently waited in line in an attempt to gain admittance. People were everywhere—in the aisles, on the stairs; even in the corridors leading to the court, fans were jammed shoulder to shoulder in an effort to get a glimpse of Bevo Francis. Police stationed outside finally closed the doors, turning more than four hundred fans away.

The Wright-Patterson Kittyhawks were no pushovers. Their lineup included such recent collegiate stars as Joe Genaro of Akron and Pete Boyles from the University of Dayton. Former Georgetown star Tony Durmowicz and Rutgers standout Ben Roesch, along with All-Ohio selection Bob Armstrong from Portsmouth, added to the Kittyhawks' strength. In Wright-Patterson, Rio Grande would be meeting a fine, seasoned team that had been competing at a level that the Redmen had never been exposed to.

Gallipolis City Manager J. Roy Bartlett proclaimed Rio Grande Day in Gallipolis and presented a trophy to the Redmen to mark the occasion. In other pre-game ceremonies he presented Bevo with a key to the city and named him honorary city manager as newsreel cameras whirred and the omnipresent *Life* photographers shot their lightguns.

But the *Life* photographers weren't the only ones armed with flash-guns. Scores of other photojournalists were on hand to record the events of the evening, and hundreds of fans had brought their own flash-equipped cameras. As a result, the first time Francis went up for a shot, he was nearly blinded by the explosion of flashbulbs whose combined effect turned his gym-rat pasty pallor a shocking alabaster white. "The glare from those flashbulbs was so intense I couldn't get the blue spots out of my eyes for a while," he recalled. He retreated to defense, stunned by the intensity of the flashes.

The Kittyhawks concentrated their efforts on Bevo in the early going. Recognizing the now-familiar pattern, Wiseman calmly shifted his sharply thrown passes to Ripperger, Barr, and Roy Moses, who found themselves open for easy baskets. The success of the talented but unsung Rio Grande performers forced the Kittyhawks to loosen the shackles on Bevo. He responded in his usual fashion as Wiseman darted through traffic again and again to find his center and deliver the ball.

"Bevo could go either way," Wiseman recalled. "He preferred to go to his left, though. He would play a high post with his back to the basket and receive the ball and turn in one smooth motion. He'd be jumping and turning all at once, and he'd loft the shot with the softest touch I had ever seen. He wasn't getting any easy uncontested lay-ups, either. He had two or three guys on him all the time. Still—he would score."

At halftime the score was 61-39, and the Redmen coasted, more easily than most thought they would, to their twentieth straight win, 113-85. Wiseman led the Redmen through a ball-handling and passing display that brought a roar of approval from the crowd. "With three or four minutes to play we decided to put on a poor imitation of the Globetrotters for all those fans. They seemed to really enjoy it and so did we. It gave the rest of us a chance to shine a little," he said, "and I think Newt saw that and allowed us to continue to do it from then on whenever we had the game under control."

"Later on, we started to do the same thing in our pre-game warm-ups as well," Ripperger added. "Carl Benner painted a ball with red, white, and blue panels, and we used it to do our fancy ball handling and behind-the-back and under-our-legs passing. The fans all loved it."

Despite his slow start, Bevo had tallied 55 points, aided by a solid 17-point effort from Ripperger. Moses had 14 points, and Wiseman and Barr contributed 13 each before the largest crowd ever to see a game in Gallia County.

After twenty games Bevo Francis had 1,021 points and was within easy striking distance of the national season scoring record, set the year before by Seattle's Johnny O'Brien with 1,051 points. Rio Grande still topped the shrinking list of thirteen schools that had yet to taste defeat.

The Redmen risked that position as they traveled to Columbus three days later to meet Bliss Business College in Aquinas High School's gymnasium on January 15. The chaotic scene at Gallipolis was repeated in Columbus. The gym, which could accommodate a crowd of twelve hundred at most, in seats at court level and in an overhanging balcony, was packed. "When we took the floor to warm up, there were people sitting on our bench," Oliver remembered. "I told the officials there that I didn't mind the promoters' making as much money as they could, but I wasn't going to coach my team from the stands."

Protesting the playing conditions—which his hype had helped to create—Oliver threatened not to take the court until something was done. Eventually, the bench was cleared enough that Oliver and the reserves could be seated, but the crowd pressed tightly in behind them. Outside, some of those denied seats scaled trees to peer in through the windows.

Later, the press would estimate that twenty-five hundred had gained admittance with just as many turned away. Photos of the game reveal not an inch of empty space—people were standing five deep on the perimeter of the court. In their enthusiasm they had even torn the back door to the gym off its hinges.

When play got underway in the raucous and steamy gym, the assembled newsreel and television crews included one from Dave Garroway's popular *Today Show,* which telecast coast to coast. With the news crews' powerful flood lamps illuminating the floor, the jammed gym grew oppressively hot. After only a few minutes of play, the Bliss coach called time-out and threatened to walk out with his team unless the lights were extinguished. After a lengthy argument the crews agreed to use fewer lights, and play resumed.

Francis struggled through the first half. He failed to hit a field goal during the first quarter, and it wasn't until midway through the second that he canned his first basket from the floor. He ended the half with only 13 points. Bliss had assigned four players to converge on Bevo whenever the ball moved to his side of the court. The strategy proved effective in blunting his firepower through most of the half. But it failed in its ultimate objective of containing Rio Grande. The Redmen took a 39-21 lead to the locker room at the half.

"People don't realize that those boys were good," Bevo said. "A lot of times when I was covered up like that, they'd just take over, and they could score. Moses was deadly from the corner, and Barr and Ripperger could hit as well. McKenzie had a terrific two-handed set shot that he threw up from way outside. Wiseman, we called 'Garbage Man.' He had a knack for picking up the ball around the basket and laying it back in. A lot of times they won the game. Sure, I got my points, but they were responsible for a lot of those wins and never got any credit for it."

In the second half against Bliss, Bevo got on track when Bliss was forced to spend more time guarding Ripperger and Barr. "That freed up the middle some, and I was able to get the ball in to Bevo, and that was all it took," Wiseman recalled.

Bevo quickly made up for lost time, pleasing the camera crews in the process, as he accounted for 38 points in the second half to finish with 51 points. Ripperger had another outstanding game, hitting for 18 as Rio Grande dispatched the pencil pushers 102-53. Bevo's output enabled him to easily pass O'Brien's single-season scoring mark. His performance in the second half kept the overflow crowd on its feet in an uproar. He finished with a creditable 19-40 from the floor.

In retaliation for what he felt were deliberate stalling tactics by Bliss at the start of the game, Oliver allowed Wiseman to lead the players through their ball-handling and dribbling show with about three minutes left in the contest. The performance delighted the packed house, and the camera crews happily recorded it.

Bevo's surpassing the single-season scoring mark, coupled with the airing of the game on national television later that week, set off another blizzard of stories about him.

Writing in Columbus after the game, Tom Keys, who had been part of the huge press contingent, observed, "No doubt about it, he's a great one."

And after the Wright-Patterson and Bliss games, Rio Grande was the hottest attraction in Ohio—and the cheapest. Promoters from across Ohio crowded Oliver's cramped office day after day, convincing basketball's heir to P.T. Barnum that he held the upper hand. And, of course, he was right. "I'm upping the ante," declared Oliver. He publicly vowed to ask henceforth for $1,000 guarantees against sixty-five percent of the gate receipts.

Jack Myers of the Hobart Arena in Troy, Ohio, found "lines of promoters waiting to see Oliver" when he made the trek to Rio Grande to try to secure a date for his facility. Myers, whose seven-thousand-seat arena won the nod from Oliver, declared upon leaving, "Rio Grande should walk out of Troy with a check for $4,000!"

Although Newt had been juggling game dates and locations since the season began, he now had a scheduling nightmare on his hands. He was being offered dates with large payment guarantees in major city arenas, only to find that he was locked into a contract for that same date at the old Rio Grande rate of $50 or $75. Usually, he was able to dissuade the schools from holding him to the preseason contracts. He dealt with some contracts simply by voiding the contract and sending the school $50 to cover the gate receipts guarantee.

But in one well-publicized instance, he failed to smooth-talk his way free. City College of Oakland, Indiana, was not happy about missing out on what it felt certain would be its biggest payday ever. The administration was intent on holding Oliver to his agreement to play Oakland on the original date and at the same terms. Newt, however, had already scheduled another game for that night in Cleveland and for much bigger stakes than the minuscule guarantee that he had eagerly grabbed in the fall. "I have no intention of playing them," he declared when the Indiana school threatened legal action for breach of contract. When Oakland Athletic Director Del Dissler pressed his case further through the sports pages, Oliver wryly agreed to play them: "In mid-March. Without Francis."

"What kind of a deal is that?" Dissler moaned. Oliver sent off a check for $100 and announced he'd honored his guarantee. An enraged Dissler sent the check back.

"Later, I learned that Doctor Davis [Rio Grande's president] had sent them a check for $500," Oliver said. "I hadn't even been consulted."

7

Under the Microscope

Press coverage of Rio Grande, which only a few weeks before had consisted of dispatches from Homer Alley and Dave Diles, now carried the bylines of the best basketball writers in the country. At each Rio Grande game the number of reporters grew as they gathered first-hand information on the freshman phenom to pass on to their readers.

"I couldn't even move without bumping into them," Bevo remembered. "They would follow me around from the time we got to the game until the time we went on the floor."

In his column in the *Pittsburgh Post-Gazette* Al Abrams told his Steel City readers, "This Clarence 'Bevo' Francis is a fabulous guy any way you look at him. There are some who look down their noses at his 50 point average because it was made against Class C and D competition. . . . Even if Bevo played against Class Z competition, his 116 points in one game and the ability to swish the nets at 50 per contest is the most amazing thing to hit the sports pages in years."

Hy Turkin of the *New York Daily News* told Gotham readers that "the most exasperating and astounding basketball player in the world today is a shy freshman named Clarence 'Bevo' Francis." Turkin, in an uncanny display of fortune telling, cited four reasons why he felt Francis was drawing as many "ows as oohs." One was the dilemma facing the keepers of the record book in deciding whether Bevo's record-shattering performances would be recognized because he was, technically, still a high school student. The second reason was the disappointment of the pro teams, which would have liked to approach Francis immediately; instead, they would have to wait until his class graduated from college before they could sign this sure-fire winner and box office magnet. (Under the NBA rules of the day a team could not sign a college player until his class graduated, whether the player stayed in school or not.) Then there were the victims-in-waiting, the teams on Rio Grande's schedule that had yet to face the rampaging Redmen. Finally, Madison Square Garden officials had realized only belatedly that they could have turned their failing Holiday Festival tournament into a success by inviting Rio Grande. But Turkin was convinced that mistake would be rectified in March when the Garden would invite Rio Grande to its National Invitation Tournament.

Turkin continued, predicting that "if Francis were to stay in college for four years, he would surely rewrite the record book." He did speculate, however, "that a lucrative AAU contract offer just might be too much for the young father and husband to resist."

In a sidebar to Turkin's column, Oliver was quoted as saying that his Rio Grande team "would be a well-trained unit by the time the 1956 Olympic tryouts roll around." This implied, in typical Oliver overstatement, that the Redmen would win the right to represent the United States in the Olympic Games.

Olympic gold for the Rio Grande College Redmen? The same Rio Grande that nearly folded only a year before? Somehow it didn't sound so incredible anymore.

But not all the coverage was so kind.

Murray Olderman, syndicated columnist for the Newspaper Enterprise Association (a Scripps Howard feature service) and a cartoonist, saw it differently. In an article that bore the headline "BEVO BEING EXPLOITED," and accompanied by a less-than-flattering cartoon of the player, Olderman was mildly critical of Bevo's talents. But he reserved his most stinging rebuke for Oliver, whom he termed "skittish." Olderman conceded that, "allowed to round out his game, Bevo could probably become a great player. Right now he is a product of exploit."

As evidence for his charge, Olderman reported that Oliver had said, "We need a new gym. We want to go to the Garden. Tell that to Ned Irish [the Garden's basketball promoter] in New York."

Proof enough, Olderman concluded, that Oliver was far more concerned about gate receipts than he was about the development of his star player.

After a caustic column in which he noted the poor quality of Rio Grande's opposition, Al Bricker, a Columbus sportswriter, learned that Bevo had more support than he had imagined. Nine Rio Grande coeds wrote a letter taking Bricker to task for his comments and defending Francis and Rio Grande. Bricker printed their letter in full in his column and then, still unswayed, added yet another criticism of the schedule and media hoopla. Later, he would admit to being shocked by the volume of mail that arrived in defense of Bevo and Rio Grande, castigating the writer for his treatment of them.

The growing media coverage was particularly bitter for the major college coaches to swallow.

In California, Sax Elliot of Los Angeles State College staged a contest between his varsity and the Chapman College junior varsity that he had designed to mock and deride Bevo's 116-point performance. Stationing his six-foot-six center, John Barber, beneath the basket throughout the forty-minute "game," Elliot had his players feed Barber exclusively. Barber racked up 188 points in a game that ended 202-88. "There," Sax Elliot seemed to be saying, "that ought to kill all the furor about the 'greatness' of Bevo Francis." It didn't.

"You couldn't help but have a twinge of jealousy when someone playing against such poor competition was grabbing all the headlines," recalled Robin Freeman, the Ohio State All-American who had played with Bevo in the North-South All-Star Classic during their high school careers.

In Columbus, home of the Ohio State Buckeyes, Coach Floyd Stahl was doing a slow burn. As his squad struggled through a lackluster season, all Stahl heard or read about in the Ohio papers was Bevo Francis and backwater Rio Grande College. Unused to being upstaged and ignored, Stahl could take no more. He uttered some derogatory comments to a reporter that found their way into print. The reaction astounded Stahl.

Letters to the editor defending Francis and Rio Grande flooded in by the hundreds, criticizing Stahl for his remarks and characterizing him as jealous of Francis and the Rio Grande Redmen. Stahl hastily concluded that, as much as he disliked what was happening, he wouldn't say so publicly again. In his last public utterance on the topic, Stahl declared that he had been "genuinely surprised." He added, "I can't say anything bad about Francis again. He seems to be a sort of common man's All-American." If he meant the latter to be an insult, and he no doubt did, no matter. That backhanded compliment came as close as any to summing up the almost universal appeal of Bevo Francis and the public's fascination with him. And it had just begun.

✦ ✦ ✦

After the Bliss game on January 15, the Redmen stayed overnight in Columbus because they were scheduled to face the team from Lockbourne Air Force Base in suburban Groveport the following night.

But Bevo had no chance to kick back with the guys in Columbus. Newt led him through a nonstop schedule of interviews and radio and television appearances. "They went running from one place to the next all day," Carl Benner recalled. The hectic schedule and frantic effort to accommodate all the reporters would become commonplace for them wherever they went. As soon as they arrived in a city, the press was waiting. "Newt always insisted we do the interviews," Bevo said. "It was impossible to get any rest. I couldn't ever relax."

Like Wright-Pat, Lockbourne was a service team sprinkled with former college stars. Their schedule included a number of college teams from the area and they were 17-2 and had won nine in a row. But the Airmen had one advantage that most of the Redmen's other victims did not. Their coach, a young first lieutenant, had been one of the fortunate spectators to gain admittance to the Aquinas High gym.

"I had seen Francis and Rio Grande in action and was able to prepare the team for what they could expect," recalled the lieutenant, whose name was George Steinbrenner.

Eager to avoid a repeat of the calamitous scene at Aquinas, where traffic had ground to a halt and a near-riot had broken out when twenty-five hundred fans were turned away, the Columbus papers took an extraordinary step. The editions of Friday, January 16, included a large notice in bold black type in the sports section: "All 2,100 seats to tonight's game are sold," it warned. "There will be no tickets sold at the door."

Scalpers, however, did a brisk business with those who failed to heed the warning. Buying and reselling tickets, they were able to command as much as five dollars a ticket from people who just had to see Bevo Francis. In 1953 five dollars was an unheard-of amount for a ticket to a college sporting event. Big-city arenas priced their tickets at only fifty cents to one dollar each.

Steinbrenner figured that his scouting trip to Aquinas High just might pay off. "I devised a defense that used Bill McCollum at 6-foot-7 in front of him and John Brown behind to keep the ball away from him and hold Francis down. For the first half it worked pretty well," he recalled.

Steinbrenner's tactics soon began to take their toll in the form of fouls by the Airmen guards surrounding Bevo. "I think we lost three starters in the first half, and they just wore us down from there," Steinbrenner said.

The Redmen played the same game that had served them so well all season, going to the outside shooters when Bevo was tied up. That response eventually forced Steinbrenner's packed-in zone to come out and pick up Barr, Ripperger, and Moses. And Wiseman found the seams that allowed him to thread his passes in to Bevo. Bevo ended up with 36 points as Rio Grande eased out to an 84-50 win. Moses contributed 15, with Barr and Ripperger adding 11 each.

Although better prepared than almost any other team that faced the Redmen, Steinbrenner's charges became victim number 22, although they held Bevo to a personal score of 36 points, which was well below his average.

Back on campus once more, the Redmen had a three-day respite. They were not scheduled to play again until Tuesday, in a week that would see them play three times.

But Bevo and Oliver enjoyed no break. Photo shoots and interviews had backed up while they were away. Newt also scheduled another trip to West Virginia to appear on Bradley's television show. The coach also had arranged for the two to stop off at a high school gym on the way back so Bevo could put on a shooting exhibition.

"He was the only man I knew of that could [dribble] the ball between his legs and bounce it off his forearm into the basket on a dead run. And he'd do it every time," Oliver said. "The fans loved it."

On Tuesday, January 20, the well-rested team and a weary Francis piled into the wagons and made their way to Troy for their first game in a major arena. They would meet Cedarville College in the contest that promoter Jack Myers had secured for Hobart Arena on his earlier trip to Rio Grande.

While national press coverage of Francis had been extensive since the Ashland game, Rio Grande's torrid schedule had not allowed many reporters, eager to see the Redmen in person, to catch up.

In the seven-day period that followed the 116-point performance, Rio Grande had played four road games. Now the three-day hiatus had allowed the national sports press corps to track down the vagabond Redmen. Myers issued press credentials for sixty-six newspapers for the game. In addition, camera crews from *Life* and Paramount News of the Day were on hand.

Hobart Arena had a stated capacity of 7,000 for basketball. Myers sold 7,451 tickets before fire marshals forced him to shut down the ticket office. More than a thousand people waiting in line were turned away. Police urged another thousand stranded in a miles-long traffic jam to turn around and go home.

The overflow crowd and massive press contingent were all attracted by one thing: They wanted to see Bevo score. The Cedarville Yellow Jackets went to extraordinary lengths to see that he didn't.

The Cedarville coach was Floyd Rees. He had secured the position after being fired by Rio Grande the previous year. Rees harbored no love for the Redmen.

Although Cedarville was only slightly larger than Rio Grande, and therefore just as unlikely to play Hobart Arena, Rees refused to allow his team to actually play the game of basketball. A former player recalled, "He had issued explicit instructions to us in the dressing room. 'Do not shoot. Stall. Stall. Stall,' he told us. We followed his instructions. What else could we do?"

Those who saw it would forever after refer to the game as "the Deep Freeze."

At the outset Cedarville's tactics seemed to be little more than a deliberate effort to control the ball, a tactic not uncommon when underarmed teams faced the potent firepower of the Redmen. But the Yellow Jackets fell immediately behind—and still continued to stall without even attempting a shot. "We had faced stalls and slowdowns before and always handled them because our guards were so good," Barr explained. "But these guys weren't even attempting to play. They just stood there with their arms wrapped around the ball."

The record-breaking crowd swiftly grew impatient with Cedarville. After one quarter Rio Grande, which had averaged 100 points per game, led 10-5.

"In the second quarter it got even worse," Bevo remembered. The situation bordered on insanity, and Oliver, in disgust, ordered his players not to come out from under their basket to pursue the statue-like Cedarville guards. "He told them to go on down under the basket and to wait there until they decided to come out of their stall. Just wait," Benner said with a grin.

"Well, we went on down and sat on the floor after awhile and waited. And waited. And waited," Wiseman said.

Rees had told his players at the end of the first period not to pass, not to dribble, and, above all, not to shoot the ball. They obeyed.

The fans, who had become restless for activity during the first period slowdown, were now growing nasty in their anger. After all, they had paid record sums to see this farce. Bevo had managed only 11 points in the first half. Debris rained down on the court. "They started throwing things at the Cedarville team," Ripperger said. "Pop bottles and pennies were flying down from the stands."

The referees stopped the game and tried to clean up the playing floor. When they whistled for play to resume, nothing happened. The Cedarville guard stood embarrassingly still, both arms clutching the ball to his chest. He stared imploringly at Rees for permission to do something. Anything. Rees refused.

On the bench Rees was confronted by a frantic Myers. Only moments before, Jack had been basking in the realization that his promotion had attracted a record box office. Now he was facing a huge crowd that was dangerously close to becoming an uncontrollable mob.

A singsong chant of "We want our money back" began to replace the waves of booing and catcalls and spread rapidly through the arena. It was not what Myers wanted to hear. He begged Rees to allow his players to play. Still, Rees refused.

Growing more frantic by the minute, an enraged Myers found Cedarville Athletic Director Byron Hollinger. He enlisted Hollinger's aid in convincing Rees to change his mind. Hollinger, just as disappointed in the tactics as the fans—who were now trying to tear open the ticket booth doors to get their money back—readily agreed to intercede. With the clock stopped to clean up the debris, the period had now lasted twenty-five minutes as Hollinger argued heatedly with his coach. Finally, Myers stormed into the animated argument and sputtered an ultimatum: "Either you play ball or else." The livid promoter then stomped off to find more police to control the crowd that clamored angrily at the ticket windows.

On the court the Rio Grande players donned their warm-up jackets and lounged on the floor. "Wayne and I matched pennies we picked up off the court," Ripperger said. "Moses and Barr were stretched out on their backs with their hands locked behind their heads pretending to sleep. We figured if they were going to make a joke out of the game, we'd go along with it."

Francis, disgusted, took a seat in the stands behind the basket. "I just sat down there and started to sign programs and things. Then a reporter came up to me with a mike, and I did an interview with him right there—during the game!"

While Bevo did his impromptu interview, Myers was at his wits' end. There were, he knew, not enough police on hand to prevent what surely was going to become an ugly riot at any minute. After checking with the sizeable and now sizzling press corps, Myers grabbed the microphone for the public address system from the scorer's table. In desperation he issued his final ultimatum to Rees for all to hear.

"If you don't play an open game in the second half, I will personally recommend to every newspaper person and radio man here that they blast you and keep blasting you and Cedarville College until you're blown to oblivion," the frazzled, sweating Myers shouted. With that, the frustrated promoter slumped down into the lap of his startled announcer.

As the echoes from Myers' last-ditch threat died, Newt told Hollinger that he'd cancel the return home game with Cedarville if his team didn't play ball.

Play finally picked up again. Although still slower than usual, at least they were playing.

Oliver ordered his players to start the third period with a ball-handling and passing exhibition that had the crowd applauding.

Still playing deliberately, Cedarville had only 15 points to Rio Grande's 32 after the third period. In the fourth quarter Rio Grande was in a vengeful mood and tallied 34 points before beginning another Globetrotter-like display to amuse the crowd while totally frustrating Cedarville's desperate attempts to stop its public humiliation. Wiseman and Ripperger tantalized the hapless defenders with behind-the-back and through-the-legs passes. Their deft ball handling and feints had the Cedarville players lunging foolishly at empty air as they sought to stop the cagey duo.

The carnival act had the once-unruly crowd on its feet in appreciation at game's end. Rio Grande left the court to thunderous applause. The dark scowl that had clouded Jack Myers' face had finally become a smile.

Bevo had managed to score 38 points in the 66-29 farce, 27 in the second half before the Redmen shifted into entertainment mode. More important, the Redmen were bringing home a check from Myers for $4,785. All doubt about their drawing ability had evaporated. They could fill any arena that would have them and was willing to pay for the privilege. At last, Rio Grande College's financial future didn't look so bleak. Provided, of course, that Bevo kept on scoring.

Life featured Bevo and the Redmen in its first February issue, using pictures from the Cedarville game and others. It was a major story in the popular magazine and focused even more attention on the Redmen. "That was a real thrill. Seeing yourself in *Life* was just unbelievable to us," Ripperger said.

On Thursday, January 22, the team was back in action against Cincinnati Bible Seminary in a game that had originally been scheduled for Community Hall. Si Burick, sports editor of the *Dayton Daily News*, had called Oliver to try to get the game switched to Dayton.

"He asked me to come up and play a polio benefit game in the Dayton University Field House," Oliver said. Burick had approached other teams to play in the benefit, but they had turned him down. Oliver eagerly agreed.

The crowd, to Burick's delight, overflowed the hall.

The game was preceded by an exhibition tennis match between Pancho Segura and Ken McGregor. Members of the Cleveland Browns football team then played a preliminary basketball game against a local USO team. Pvt. Eddie Fisher, on leave from the army, performed at halftime as the bobby-soxers in the crowd swooned.

Amid the gala atmosphere of the fund-raiser, the Seminarians managed to play Rio Grande to a draw in the first period. Then the Redmen, led by Bevo, got on track and took a lead that they never relinquished in rolling to a 79-54 victory. Bevo had 42 points in the team's twenty-fourth straight win. Moses added 15 and Ripperger had 10.

Traveling on to Zanesville, the squad was hit with the flu bug and arrived feeling none too fit for the game against Mountain State College on Saturday, January 24. Promoted by the *Zanesville News,* this game also was a benefit to raise money for the March of Dimes. The paper's photographer took several photographs of the players receiving flu shots—after the fact and too late to help.

Flu or no flu, Mountain State wasn't going to stop the Redmen. With Bevo accounting for 68 points, Rio Grande, hacking and sneezing, fought its way to an easy 133-83 romp before yet another overflow crowd. Despite the paper's warning that day that no more seats were available, hundreds had stood six deep on the steps outside the Zanesville Auditorium in an attempt to get in to see the sold-out game.

In only a week more than fifteen thousand fans had seen them play.

The mounting national acclaim for the twenty-five-game winning streak and Bevo's scoring had brought the Redmen the attention that Oliver had sought since September. The Redmen and Bevo were the talk of the sports world. The crowds that they were attracting wherever they went were a promoter's dream come true after the two dark, bleak seasons that followed the betting scandals. Everyone, it seemed, wanted to see Bevo Francis and Rio Grande College.

Now it was impossible to read a sports page anywhere in the country without seeing some mention of Bevo Francis. Television was still in its infancy, so people got their information from the papers. And the papers were frantic to get profiles and feature stories about Bevo and the Redmen into readers' hands. Competition was fierce, and Francis and Oliver were constantly being interviewed and photographed.

Newsreel crews from Paramount News of the Day were among those jockeying for the attention of Francis and Oliver. The newsreels still delivered national and world news to movie audiences. Both MGM and Paramount had covered the Mountain State game, for example. The cinematic profiles that they compiled would appear on movie screens across the nation the following week. For 25 cents moviegoers could catch a double feature and the Cinderella saga of Bevo Francis and Rio Grande College at their local theater.

❀ ❀ ❀

When Newt Oliver returned to the campus from the trip to Zanesville, he found another sign that his team had arrived: College officials said that he could send the team uniforms out to be laundered. "My wife, Maxine, and Jean would wash those uniforms out by hand in the bathtub," he explained. "Then they'd hang them up to dry, still dripping, from a line in our tiny apartment. You can't imagine how happy they were when we were able to afford the laundry bill."

Bevo, on the other hand, was dealing with the publicity as well as he could, and that wasn't very well at all. "At times I'd get home and I'd ask my wife, 'Why'd this have to happen to me? Why can't I just play basketball and be left alone?'" he said. Jean didn't have the answer, but everyone else seemed to understand that you can't score 116 points and be left alone—no matter how much you want solitude and privacy.

"It was tough on him. He dealt with it, but it took its toll," Ripperger recalled.

A few months earlier Newt's declaration that "we're moving up and out of these woods" had rung hollow. Now it was a reality. The only question was, how far would they go?

One sure-fire measure of public sentiment is the reaction of politicians. Members of the Ohio State Senate and General Assembly were ever conscious of the tremendous popularity of Francis and Rio Grande among voters. Accordingly, the state legislature adopted a resolution congratulating Bevo Francis for the national prominence and acclaim he had brought to Rio Grande and designated the Rio Grande College Redmen as the Official Sesquicentennial Team of the state of Ohio.

In his office at Ohio State University, Floyd Stahl fumed silently.

Conveniently forgetting that he'd played side by side with Bevo, Ohio State's Freeman explained in an interview years later that Oliver had "taken this country bumpkin and made him a household name. We all felt he wasn't anything more than a creature of Newt's imagination."

Meanwhile, the darlings of the national media and of the solons in Columbus were engendering a less positive reaction back on the Rio Grande campus.

Davis and the administration simply were unable to cope with the overwhelming amount of attention that Francis and Oliver were reaping. "We just engulfed that little school," Oliver declared. The trustees and administration had begun to talk uneasily among themselves about the effect that all the attention and prominence were having on the school. Although accurate, many articles were less than flattering about conditions at Rio Grande. *Time* magazine, for example, reported in a short piece on January 26 that the gym was both "dilapidated" and known as the Hog Pen and observed that Rio Grande was an "obscure little" college that Bevo chose because "it was willing to overlook the fact that Bevo had not graduated from high school."

While the school sorely needed and appreciated the money that the team was earning, many in the faculty and administration resented how it was being earned. The situation was, they concluded, getting out of hand. "Some of the faculty didn't like all the travel we were doing, and made it plain they objected to a schedule that kept us out of class so often," Barr said.

Oliver had a different perspective: "It was just plain jealousy. That's all it was. The situation with the administration started to go down the tubes when *Life* magazine refused to use any pictures of the president or other administrators. They [*Life*] just wanted the team and games and such. I think we were just overshadowing everybody there. And some of them didn't like it. Of course, I didn't use a lot of finesse with the situation."

Others believe that the genesis of the strained relationship between Oliver and Davis was indeed related to the arrival of *Life* on campus but in a different way. "I remember we were all standing together, and the president came over to get into the picture with us," Ripperger said. "Newt turned to him and asked, 'What the hell are you doing here? We haven't seen you around before and we don't need you here now.'"

"Newt could be abrasive," Wiseman said. "Maybe, if he'd consulted others instead of just deciding we're going to play here and we're going to do this, it wouldn't have been so bad. But he just unilaterally made all the decisions. The administration never learned about it until they read it in the paper." Barr thought that "Newt was strident. He was a very demanding character. He had to have his way all the time. He was very stubborn and I think that's what caused it." Carl Benner agreed, noting that Newt "had a mind of his own. He was headstrong and at times arrogant. An outsider looking in would have said he's just an arrogant SOB."

Whatever happened, it was apparent to everyone that Davis and Oliver, who had been together at Upper Sandusky and now at Rio Grande, were no longer on good terms.

Nonetheless, the sudden and dramatic emergence of Rio Grande from near oblivion to national prominence presented the college's administrators with an irresistible opportunity to raise the money they needed to keep the school open. The opportunistic Davis parlayed the team's road trips to major population centers—the same trips his faculty decried—into speaking engagements. He appeared before local service clubs to plead his case for financial aid for the desperate school that was playing in their city. It worked. The trustees soon announced to the press that the college had nearly reached its goal—which a few months earlier had been only a pipe dream—of raising $350,000 over three years. Davis had converted the success of Bevo Francis and the Redmen on the basketball court into open wallets from an empathetic audience that admired their pluck.

In the win over Mountain State, Francis had added yet another season record to his credit: his fourteen free throws enabled him to establish a new single season mark of 368, erasing Johnny O'Brien's record of 361. Through the first twenty-five games Bevo had scored 1,254 points, and Rio Grande was one of only six teams nationally that remained unbeaten. Even today, for a college player to score 1,000 points in four years remains the standard by which basketball excellence is measured. It occurs so infrequently that when it happens, the game is always halted so the ball can be presented to the player to commemorate the achievement and to allow him or her to receive the plaudits of the crowd.

Wilberforce was next on Rio Grande's schedule. But Oliver canceled the game, which had been set for the evening of Monday, January 26, at Wilberforce. The Redmen would play, he informed stunned Wilberforce officials, but at a later date in a larger facility. They reluctantly agreed to the postponement.

Rio Grande instead traveled to West Virginia to meet the Beckley College Blue Eagles in a game that had been shifted to the spacious Huntington Memorial Field House. En route the road-weary wagon driven by Oliver had a flat tire.

"I always had to follow him when we drove to games," Benner said.

Oliver surveyed the flat and ordered Carl to change it. "I told him if he wanted it changed, he'd have to change it himself. I had my good clothes on and wasn't about to ruin them. Newt threw his arm around me and said, 'Benner, you and I are going to get along fine.' And we always did." Reserve Bill Frasher eventually changed the tire, and the two-wagon caravan moved on.

When the Redmen arrived in Huntington two full hours before game time on January 30, an eager crowd was already gathered. Although Walt Walowac of Marshall College was among the nation's top scorers, Marshall had never been able to fill the five-thousand-seat arena that served as its home court, but an SRO crowd of fifty-two hundred packed the fieldhouse to see Francis and company play lowly Beckley, a junior college that the Redmen had already defeated once.

The spectators got what they came for. Francis smashed Walowac's fieldhouse record of 43 points with a 46-point barrage that left the former record holder weeping and the crowd cheering. Rio Grande had little trouble dispatching the Blue Eagles, 102-68.

The game also marked the return of the wayward Jim McKenzie, who observed Walowac's reaction. It was McKenzie's first appearance since he had failed to return from the Christmas recess. Oliver, aware that the Redmen were lacking in depth beyond the starters, needed McKenzie and had gone to Kentucky to convince him to return. "Wayne and Newt and Ripperger and I all went on down with Newt to talk to him," Bevo recalled. "Newt told him again that with five guys scoring twenty a game, no one was going to pay any attention to us."

"I told him," Oliver said, "'Look, they'd all say, "Well, looky here, isn't that nice? That little Christian school downstate is doing just fine. Isn't that nice? Aren't they just a fine bunch of fellows?" Hell, Jim, if we did that, we'd never get out of this place. Can't you see what I'm trying to do here? I'm trying to get us out of here. I'm trying to get us to the big time. I told you we'd be the talk of the country. WE ARE. I told you we'd be playing in the Garden. By Jesus, WE WILL. We're gonna get there. But you have to understand that without Bevo scoring all those points, we'd still be playing in the damn Hog Pen for peanuts and NOBODY would give a hoot or holler about any of us.'"

Both Wiseman and Ripperger talked to McKenzie about the success they'd enjoyed and urged him to come back. The team had voted to have him back. McKenzie, the impressionable former Kentucky All-State star, was won over. The rebellion ended. He was once more a part of the Redmen and Oliver's grand plan. There would be no looking back.

Against Beckley both Barr and Moses had outstanding games as they tallied 19 and 16 points, respectively. Bill Ripperger, who had become a steady starter after McKenzie left, was improving with every game. He and Wiseman were developing a special chemistry and were comfortable with each other and their roles in the offense. Wiseman was the trigger, but Ripperger was always there to relieve the pressure on the point guard. McKenzie would now be the sixth man. Ripperger, who had endured Oliver's taunts and teasing to break into the lineup, wasn't about to give up his spot.

"I was pretty hard on Bill," Oliver acknowledged. "I kidded him about going back to that school he'd come from to play for them [Chase College in Cincinnati]. I told him he wasn't good enough to play here and maybe he could play there. Of course, I knew they didn't have a team anymore."

"It was motivation for me. The more he got on me, the harder I tried," Bill said. "I told him, 'I'm going to make the team.' And I did. Eventually, Newt took to calling me Shotgun. He said he did it because every time I got the ball and was in doubt about where to go with it, I'd shoot." Once in the lineup, Ripperger played with a fierce determination and skill that pleased Oliver immensely—though he never told Bill that.

The Rio Grande traveling show moved on up the Ohio River to meet Steubenville College in a rematch on Saturday, January 31. The game was played in a high school gymnasium in Toronto, Ohio, that could hold twenty-two hundred fans. It had been sold out for weeks. The local paper informed readers that three hundred standing-room tickets would go on sale at 6:30. More than fifteen hundred people turned out. Some arrived as early as noon to reserve a place in line.

Rio Grande had swamped Steubenville in their first meeting, the game that had been marked by the deficient lighting at Community Hall. The Barons had improved since then and in their recent game against Marietta had lost by only two points to the team that had extended the Redmen to the limit. Hometown fans expected a close contest.

At first, they were not disappointed. But, as usual, Rio Grande took command in the second half, and the superbly conditioned and road-hardened Redmen coasted to a 78-65 triumph. Francis rewarded the fans with a 41-point performance that had Steubenville fans out of their seats in appreciation.

Oliver had arranged for the next contest to be shifted, on short notice, to Wellsville and the familiar confines of Beacom Memorial

Gymnasium. The game against Pikeville was to be a triumphal home-coming for Oliver and Francis, who had left only six or seven months earlier and were making a heroic return amid national acclaim. The town had an elaborate reception planned.

Bevo arrived directly after the game in Toronto to stay with Jean's parents, the Chrislips. Jean and their little boy, Frank Jeffrey, were already there.

The next day they all attended a testimonial dinner for Bevo at the American Legion Hall. The speakers included Mayor C.C. Leatherberry, who presented Bevo with the keys to the city—a huge white plasterboard key nearly four feet long. He then proclaimed Monday to be "Bevo Francis Day" in Wellsville.

Myron Weiss, the Chamber of Commerce president, next praised Bevo for the attention he had brought to the town. Mrs. William Daugherty, representing the Women's Civic Club, inducted him as an honorary member. She was followed to the podium by the postmaster, the president of the Kiwanis Club, and schools superintendent S. E. Daw, who presented Bevo with his diploma from Wellsville High. Under the tutelage of John Wickline, the local high school principal and his landlord, Francis had completed his course requirements in Rio Grande some weeks earlier.

Bevo had scored more than 1,000 points in college while still, technically, a high school student.

Next came state Rep. Delmar O'Hara, who presented Bevo with a copy of the unanimous resolution that O'Hara had sponsored in the Ohio General Assembly, the resolution that had so ticked off Floyd Stahl. Finally, Ed Seaton, president of the local booster club, praised Francis for his accomplishments. He proudly added that the next day's game had sold out, turning away scores of disappointed fans.

When Bevo finally stood to address the assembled dignitaries and crowd, he thanked them all politely. "I am very proud to be from Wellsville. I just hope you'll all still be as pleased with me after tomorrow as you are tonight," he said and sat back down to a standing ovation.

On Monday, February 2, school was dismissed early so that students could view the parade that would go from Fourth to Seventeenth streets through town. It would pass under the huge banner—WELCOME HOME, BEVO—that was stretched across the street in front of a reviewing stand. Oliver and Francis, perched atop the backseat of a convertible, led the procession. Three thousand cheering people greeted them along the route. The other Redmen followed in open cars. "We were more interested in the girls we saw than anything else," Ripperger remembered. John Viscoglosi and Bob Mundy, both Wellsville natives now with the Redmen, enjoyed the hoopla. Mundy had been attending Maryland but had recently transferred to Rio Grande to join his former high school coach and teammate.

With a newsreel crew recording it all, marching units and floats rolled slowly by. One float, sponsored by the Red Cross, revealed that Bevo had endorsed the blood drive and sported a sign that read, "Bevo says roll up your sleeve." The footage shot by the newsreel cameras showed up on television sets throughout the East that week.

After the parade was over, the team had several hours to kill before game time. The players were busy signing autographs for the teenage girls who crowded around them. "We were more interested in phone numbers and names," McKenzie said. Clearly flattered by the unaccustomed attention, the players hung around until Oliver shooed them back to their rooms.

The crowd filled Beacom, scene of so many Bengal triumphs the previous season, to overflowing. Outside, Ed Satow, the local promoter, was under siege. "There simply is no more room," he shouted to the throng. "There isn't another place to sit or stand in the entire hall."

Inside, Rio Grande took to the floor to an enthusiastic welcome from more than two thousand spectators.

Pikeville, the opposition, was already on the floor warming up. The Pikeville coach, Clarence Manor, strolled over to Oliver and handed him some papers. "What's this?" Oliver asked.

"It's a contract for next season," Manor said. "I want you to sign the commitment now."

"No way!" replied Oliver, roughly thrusting the papers back at him. "We'll see about next season next season. Not tonight."

"Well, if you don't sign, I'm going to take my team off the floor and go home," Manor threatened.

Oliver was having none of the Pikeville blackmail. "Look, I'll take my squad and divide them up, and we'll play a scrimmage before I'll sign your damn papers," he snapped, whirling back toward his bench.

When he saw that Oliver was standing firm, Manor shouted at his back, "I've got me two boys who've transferred from Kentucky here, and we're gonna whip your butt right here in front of all your supporters."

"We'll see about that too," Oliver hurled back over his shoulder.

Bevo's response was typical. He sank his first free throw to open the scoring and then converted his first eight attempts from the floor before finally missing. He had 18 points in the first quarter and added 14 more in the second as the Redmen took a 53-27 lead to the dressing room.

In the third quarter, with Rio Grande comfortably in front, Bevo cooled down to a mere six points before adding 23 in the final period. He finished with 61 points but could easily have had more if Wiseman, Ripperger, and McKenzie had not opted to entertain the crowd with their patented ball-handling and dribbling show. Near the end of the contest Wiseman fired Bevo a behind-the-back bullet pass the length of the court, drawing a standing ovation from the appreciative crowd.

Even with their antics, the final score was 97-62, and the team left the court to immense applause from the loyal crowd. Bevo's father and half-brother Bob were both on hand, as were Jean and her parents. They all basked in the reflected glory of their famous relative.

As Oliver approached, Manor stood, hands on hips, staring disgustedly at his shoes. "Congratulations," drawled Newt.

"Congratulations for what?" he asked warily.

"Why, I thought your team did real fine," Oliver remarked snidely. "They managed to beat *Bevo* by a point!"

His face flushed scarlet with rage, Manor whirled away from the mocking grin and stomped through the milling crowd to the locker room. Oliver's laughter followed him all the way.

The warm Wellsville reception was a moving experience for Bevo and Oliver. But their reception back at Rio Grande was decidedly chillier.

8

Undefeated and Unappreciated

By now relations between Newt Oliver and J. Boyd Davis had deteriorated further because Newt had refused to inform the president of his plans and the team's schedule. Now the two maintained a frosty and aloof distance that they relaxed only for public conversations—and only when absolutely necessary.

"The school felt that there was too much emphasis placed on the basketball team," Jean Cooper explained. Diles had a somewhat different take on the problem: "The pious Baptists at that tiny school down in Appalachia simply couldn't deal with all that had happened to them in such a short period of time. They felt it had become a circus there. They said the tail was wagging the dog."

Oliver recalled that "someone said to me there, 'You've created a monster!' Well, I probably did. In later years, I was told I should have brought things along slower and that might have worked better. Hell, I didn't have time. The place was getting ready to close down when I got there. Time was one luxury among many that I didn't have in that situation. I had to move, and move quickly—or there might not have been any school to bring along."

Although the faculty was receiving regular paychecks for the first time in memory, most professors resented the attention that Oliver was getting. One can well imagine the reaction when Oliver emptied their classrooms to stage a shot for a newsreel crew in the middle of the teaching day. It happened more than once, and the professors were never given any advance warning. Newt was feeling their thinly disguised enmity.

All the players noticed the altered atmosphere, but they could do little about it.

Davis and the trustees were growing increasingly alarmed at the reams of publicity that the college was garnering because of the accomplishments of Francis and the team. They were simply over-whelmed—ill-prepared to handle it and at a loss for how to cope. The media circus would have swamped a university the size of Ohio State, and it had a full-time sports information staff and personnel to deal with press relations. Rio Grande had Newt—and that was it.

Davis inadvertently delivered a prime example of the inability of the administration to deal with national media attention. He confided to a reporter that, until the team became so successful, he'd feared that the school might have to close. While accurate and candid, his assessment triggered a firestorm of negative reaction from the trustees when it appeared in print because they felt it reflected poorly on them. Shocked at the backlash, Davis quickly backtracked and denied he'd ever said any such thing. "Things were never particularly good, financially, at Rio Grande," he hastened to explain. "Many of our alumni are teachers and ministers and cannot afford to contribute much to the school."

In their attempt to deal with the crush, the harried trustees were meeting nearly every other day. The once pious and unassuming atmosphere of the tiny school was now a garish carnival sideshow on the national stage. The trustees were not pleased that the rest of America was amused at the unflattering images drawn by the press about their countrified college of ninety-four students. The butt of jokes and the victims of cartoonists' ridicule, the trustees felt a growing need to circle the wagons.

Each day, it seemed, they would be asked to react to yet another outlandish Oliver proclamation and felt the need to apologize for his misstatements. On one such memorable occasion, Oliver announced to the press that he would name a new gymnasium after anyone who would donate ten thousand dollars to the building fund. "We need a new gym," he said. When the trustees learned of the offer, and the like-lihood that the donation would come from a brewery, they hastily issued a press release denying that any such "naming rights" existed. The situation, they felt, was becoming unbearable. They were clearly *not* in control of what they regarded as the runaway locomotive of Oliver's fabrication, fancy, and half-truths. They wanted to apply the brakes. But no one seemed to know how to do it.

At the same time the people of Gallia County, who felt a strong proprietary interest in the school, resented Newt's taking "their" team on the road. Initially, he'd raised the price of admission to Community Hall to fifty cents, which was met with howls of indignation. The local animosity increased as the escalating financial success of Oliver's planning made it apparent that local residents would have few, if any, opportunities to see the team in the Hog Pen at any price.

Oliver, who felt, with more than a little justification, that the team was saving the school, was at a loss to understand the animosity from town and gown. "I will never understand why we were never accepted, as such," he said. "We were shunned. Derogatory remarks were made. I resented it."

Spurious rumors were circulating about Oliver's handling of the growing gate receipts. His abrupt and abrasive dismissals of the criticism only exacerbated the rapidly deteriorating situation, placing the trustees in an untenable position between their coach and the town-gown community.

"I can't stand anybody that's jealous to begin with or has that type of contempt," Oliver said. "We would have liked to be treated with respect."

The beleaguered trustees soon came under pressure from yet another, more ominous, source. The Ohio College Conference, of which Rio Grande was an associate member, added its voice to the din of disapproval descending on the board.

As the season wore on, conference officials began complaining vigorously to Davis about the number of games that Oliver was scheduling and voiced their growing displeasure with the circus-like atmosphere that Oliver had intentionally created. They addressed the haphazard manner in which games were being shifted and rescheduled on the fly. They cited their concern about the commercialism that seemed to be replacing their scholar-athletes' normal pursuit of an education.

While the complaints undoubtedly were instigated by Ohio coaches and schools, both within and outside the conference, that resented the attention paid to Rio Grande, Davis and the trustees were sensitive to the conference's objections and feared the loss of their affiliation. So the trustees acted.

They announced the appointment of an athletic council that they vaguely empowered to oversee the athletic programs of the school. Because basketball was Rio Grande's only intercollegiate sport, their intent was clear: to rein in Oliver—who hadn't been consulted. He learned of the council's creation only after he returned from a road trip. He was not pleased.

"You know what seemed ironic to me?" he remarked. "I'd had enough sense to get this situation underway myself—without any help from anyone there—but once I had it going, [they thought] I wasn't smart enough to run it. Naturally, I resented that fact."

Meanwhile, Oliver decided to tolerate the council and its oversight as just another minor annoyance. "I couldn't even buy so much as a pair of sweat socks without their approval," he complained. But he wasn't going to let a little jealousy and oversight deter him. He was confident that the council represented only a short detour from the road to national recognition.

The Redmen enjoyed a five-day breather before they had to travel to Middleport to meet Mayo State in a return engagement on Saturday, February 7. The team had not had much rest since the end of the holiday break. The welcome respite allowed the players to catch up on their class work.

But Newt and Bevo enjoyed no such relief. "We were out nearly every night," Bevo remembered. "I'd get home after midnight and have to be up again early for class. It never seemed to stop." Oliver explained that "we were in such demand that we could have gone seven nights a week. I felt we were giving the college a lot of good, strong public relations."

The schedule included radio and television shows as well as appearances before civic and service clubs. At night Bevo would appear at a high school game and put on a shooting exhibition. "I tried to keep up with all the schoolwork as best I could. But it was hard because I was never home or on campus very long at all. I was always on the go. Even when I was home, there was always someone Newt wanted me to talk to or a photographer coming around."

In Middleport the Redmen encountered their first empty seats since Bevo scored his monumental 116 points. Tickets for the game against Mayo State were set at the unheard-of price of two dollars each. That was far too rich for Middleport-area fans, even though they had a rare chance to see Bevo. The crowd of about four hundred included native son Dave Diles, and Thad Gardner, there on assignment for his paper, the *Post-Herald* of Birmingham, Alabama.

Those there did get to see Bevo rack up 60 points as Rio Grande stomped Mayo State, 126-98. They also got to see and enjoy Wayne Wiseman as he executed perfect court-length alley-oop passes to Francis, who converted them, to the delight of the crowd.

The Redmen next headed north to meet Cedarville, the team that had put them in the "Deep Freeze" in their first meeting at Troy. Oliver had gotten the February 10 game shifted to Springfield High School's gym instead of Cedarville's tiny one. While Cedarville did not resort to the extreme slowdown tactics that had marred the first game and earned Cedarville the enmity of Hobart Arena fans, the Yellow Jackets proved to be less than competitive at full speed. Rio Grande crushed Cedarville, 104-48. With 51 points Bevo Francis outscored the entire Cedarville team as Oliver exacted revenge for Rio Grande.

Going into their game against Mountain State on February 13, the Redmen held a spotless 30-0 record, with Bevo averaging 50 points a game. The contest was set for Memorial Field House, across the river in Parkersburg, West Virginia. Oliver had chosen the site because the field-house could hold more than twenty-five hundred, and the demand for tickets far exceeded the capacity of Mountain State's home court.

Those fortunate enough to finally gain admittance numbered more than three thousand. They saw Rio Grande continue its winning ways with a crunching 116-65 win. Francis accounted for 37 points, while Ripperger, with 19, brought the crowd to its feet with a dazzling, spinning, underhanded lay-up that he made look easy. Barr added 19 points, and Wiseman and McKenzie performed their ball-handling tricks earlier than usual, to the amusement of the large crowd.

For more than an hour after the game ended, Bevo patiently signed autographs for the horde of fans that surrounded him. The press corps, growing larger with each game, peppered him with questions throughout the signing session. He politely and softly answered them all before making his weary way to the showers at last.

⊕ ⊕ ⊕

As the Redmen continued undefeated and Bevo rewrote the record book with each game, the criticism of their level of competition increased. "Who do they play?" the critics demanded.

Oliver's response was always the same. "Anyone who will play us," he'd snap.

In fact, most major colleges wanted nothing to do with Rio Grande. The consensus among them was that they had everything to lose and nothing to gain by playing Oliver's high-scoring squad. If they won, their reasoning went, fans would deem it a hollow victory against an overpowered foe with but ninety-four students. If they should—perish the thought—lose to Rio Grande, they would be subjected to universal ridicule. It was a no-brainer. The larger colleges and universities would ignore Oliver's entreaties while chafing at his utter audacity to challenge them.

The mounting criticism of Rio Grande's "weak" schedule stung Bevo, who had no control over its composition at all. The press badgered him about it at every turn and demanded to know whether he thought he could do as well against "major college" foes. Their probing insinuations—implied if not spoken—were that he could not, and they hurt his pride. (*Time* magazine noted that the win against Bliss College "gave Bevo . . . another college record, breaking the single-season mark of 1,051 set by Seattle's little [5 ft. 9 in.] Johnny O'Brien, who sets his records in basketball's major leagues.") To Bevo the persistent questions about the validity of his accomplishments somehow tainted what he'd done. "I just play them as they come," or, "The people saw me do it," he'd reply when pressed.

Oliver could do little about the schedule now. All his approaches to the larger schools met with universal rejection. The schedule he was playing, while longer, was similar to Rio Grande's schedule in the past. Of course, back then the Redmen were losing and no one questioned the level of competition.

Oliver was well aware of the mounting criticism and used the press to plead his case for better foes. To no avail. Left with no takers to his challenge, the Redmen would continue to play their scheduled games and accept the criticism as it came. They could do nothing else.

By the second week of February, Bevo and his teammates were sailing through the schedule with ease. More important, they had already beaten all their remaining opponents once. So they were understandably optimistic about their chances of remaining among the five undefeated squads in the country as they prepared to face Bliss Business College again on February 14 in a game sponsored by the Downtown Coaches Club at Wellston, Ohio.

Bliss offered little resistance, racking up only 69 points to Rio Grande's 105. Bevo, using his considerable height advantage, accounted for 49 points, only two less than in the initial meeting.

Now Rio Grande traveled to Portsmouth for a rematch against George Steinbrenner's Airmen from Lockbourne Air Force Base on Tuesday, February 17. Oliver explained in his 1995 memoir how that game came about:

A group of civic leaders from Louisville, Kentucky, visited Rio Grande. They wanted us to play a forthcoming game there. I agreed to move our next game there for a guarantee of $4,000. (The equivalent of $30,000 [in] 2005 dollars.) However, President Davis informed me that we were to play this game in

Portsmouth, Ohio. A college trustee had a friend there that belonged to the local Kiwanis Club and Davis wanted to accommodate them. There would be no guarantee. The Kiwanis Club set the ticket price at $3.00. In today's money this would be $18.00. Portsmouth was a basketball town but its working class residents could not afford to pay this kind of money for a game. A small crowd turned out to see us play! . . . Playing there to please the administration cost the college several thousand dollars it could have used to pay expenses.

Steinbrenner's recollection is somewhat different.

"I had called Oliver and then gone down to Rio Grande to talk to him about the game. I do not recall any discussion about playing in Kentucky but I do remember that the place was absolutely crawling with reporters and camera crews. You could not walk anywhere without bumping into someone from the press. When I left there with the signed contract I knew this was a major national story."

Although Steinbrenner had scouted Francis several times since their last meeting, his team simply could not execute his plan to stop Bevo. Jumping out to a 20-point lead after the first period, Rio Grande was never behind and left Portsmouth with a 95-80 win. With 47 points Bevo was only slightly below his average. His total did eclipse the old gymnasium record of 38 points, set a few years earlier by a fellow named Newt Oliver. Steinbrenner still remembers that February 17 game, saying Bevo was "just too good for us. No matter how we tried, we couldn't stop him. Rio Grande was a great college team. It wasn't just about Bevo. They had an outstanding guard, Wiseman, and Roy Moses played great against us. We were used to playing college teams and beating most of them and they stacked up with the best we saw."

The return game against Lees College on Thursday, February 19, was shifted on short notice from Community Hall to Chillicothe, but the result remained the same. The diminutive Generals, who had no starter taller than six feet, were blasted 128-57. Trying in desperation to avoid a repeat of their earlier humiliation, the Generals tried to slow the game down. When the crowd reacted, predictably and unmercifully, by showering the Generals with a loud chorus of boos, they abandoned the tactic—and along with it any chance for victory. Francis hit for 63 points on 22 field goals and 19 foul shots to outscore the hapless Generals by six points himself. Wiseman and McKenzie had 19 points apiece, and Oliver emptied his bench, putting every Rio Grande player on the scoreboard.

From Chillicothe the Redmen went to Cincinnati, where they were to be the showcase attraction in a triple-header slated for the spacious Cincinnati Gardens Auditorium on Friday, February 20.

"BEVO TO LURE LARGE GARDENS CROWD," predicted the banner headline that greeted the Redmen that afternoon. Their opponent would be Wilberforce College. Rio Grande originally had been slated to meet Cincinnati Bible Seminary in the Gardens, but the Seminarians withdrew after failing to convince incredulous Gardens officials not to sell beer at the game. "We will not play where beer is sold," declared the minister who headed Cincinnati Bible Seminary, as he passed up the biggest payday his school would ever see.

Before the game President J. Boyd Davis met with local businessmen and gave an impassioned plea for donations to Rio Grande.

For Bill Ripperger the Cincinnati appearance was a special homecoming. He was returning to the city he had left a few months earlier. Chase College, whose decision to drop basketball had forced Ripperger to accept Oliver's offer to come to Rio Grande, had played in this very arena. Sycamore High, where Ripperger had been an All-City star, greeted him as a returning hero. The school's principal and Bill's former coach were on hand to present him with a special trophy before the game. For Ripperger, who had clawed and fought his way through Oliver's taunting criticism to stay on the team and had become a valuable starter, the night was something special. "I thought to myself, 'How lucky I am to be here,'" he recalled.

He responded by scoring 19 points and performing brilliantly in Rio Grande's pasting of Wilberforce before a crowd of more than eighty-five hundred. The other players, aware of the importance that the game held for Ripperger, gave him every scoring opportunity they could. To Newt's consternation, even Bevo passed off repeatedly to his teammate.

Although he gave up numerous shots to Ripperger, Bevo accounted for his share. The Rio Grande-Wilberforce game was sandwiched between two others featuring the University of Cincinnati and nearby Kent State; their freshmen played each other in the first game on the bill, and the varsity performed in the final game. There was no doubt, however, that Bevo was the reason for the large crowd. In the final period, with the crowd urging "Score, Bevo, Score," he approached the Gardens' scoring record of 49, which Robin Freeman had set while at Hughes High School. The Rio Grande team, aware that the record was within reach and urged by an animated Oliver to "feed Bevo," did so. With thirty seconds remaining, Bevo scored on a turning, twisting jumper to break the record. He finished with 52 points, again outscoring the opposition single-handedly. He managed 25 rebounds in the 100–51 win.

The large and appreciative crowd gave Francis a standing ovation when the announcer proclaimed that they had seen a record perform-ance. The ovation lasted nearly five minutes. The fans filtered slowly out, still shaking their heads in wonder at the display that they had witnessed. Fewer than two thousand remained to see the two "major college" teams from the area, featuring Jack Twyman, a Bearcats star and future NBA standout. The *Cincinnati Post* summed up Bevo's performance the following day by saying, "He came. He was seen. And he conquered."

Following the game, Bevo and Oliver appeared on the *Waite Hoyt Hall of Fame* television show in Cincinnati, where the former baseball great presented Francis with a trophy. With Oliver "guarding" him, Bevo demonstrated his hook and jump shots for Hoyt's viewers. In response to a question about Rio Grande's precarious financial situa-tion, Francis told Bob Gilmore, the co-host, that "even if the school closes down, I'll stay in Rio Grande because I like the people there."

The Redmen returned to campus to prepare for their first appear-ance at Community Hall since the game against Ashland Junior College that had accounted for their "discovery" by the nation.

Their return coincided with the publication of several articles in various national periodicals. All recounted the impoverishment of the campus and noted that the trustees were not supportive of Oliver's efforts because they disliked seeing the sad condition of the school exposed in the national spotlight. Because Oliver was the principal source for the material published, the trustees put the blame for the unflattering aspects squarely on him.

When Davis and the trustees confronted Oliver about the disturbing publicity, he snapped, "How many times did this school get into *Life* and *Look* and every other paper and magazine in this country before I got here? Answer me that, huh? How many? I'll tell you!" he answered for the stunned group. "NONE. We need this kind of publicity, and we're getting it now. So leave me alone and let me do my job." The star-tled trustees drew back reflexively from the fiery coach's attack, no more satisfied than before with the way things were going.

Oliver's next move did little to help ease the tension locally. When he posted the ticket price for the February 23 game against Bluefield College at Community Hall, local fans let out a collective howl. He had set a price of $1.20 for the 250 seats around the court, and 75 cents for those seats on the stage and for standing room. The locals griped that they had been "supporting the school for years. Now he raises tickets out of our reach."

"Yeah," Oliver snarled, "you've supported us all right. You *supported* us with forty people in the Hog Pen. That's how you supported us. You'll be paying $2.50 next season to see us and be happy to do it. Now, I don't want to hear any more of this crap about how you *supported* us. If we had to depend on your support, this place would have closed down months ago!"

Despite the grumbling, more than four hundred shoehorned their way into Community Hall to see Rio Grande take on Bluefield.

Echoing the local critics, Homer Alley wrote that "the crowd paid more money to see Bevo and Company than any audience in Community Hall ever paid to see anything or anybody else before."

What they received for their money was a spectacular 53-point outburst from Francis and a razzle-dazzle ball-handling display in the waning moments that thoroughly entertained them while exasperating the Bluefield quintet.

McKenzie passed the ball around his body, over his shoulders, and down his arm immediately in front of a defender who proved powerless to stop him. With his back to McKenzie, Ripperger bounced the ball between his legs as he sent it to McKenzie, bringing the crowd to its feet. Community Hall had never seen such a display. The fans would have seen even more if Wiseman, the best ball handler among the Redmen, had not fouled out. He could only look on, laughing, as his teammates entertained the crowd.

Bevo, dueling with Bluefield's six-foot-eleven center, Tom Savage, again proved capable against a bigger man. Bevo held Savage to only 10 points, dominating the bigger player throughout.

In another fine effort Ripperger accounted for 25 points, while Moses chimed in with 21 and Wiseman added 19. Rio Grande earned its thirty-sixth straight win, 128-73, and moved on to its rematch later that week against Ashland Junior College, which was eager to redeem itself after falling victim to two national record-smashing performances, Bevo's personal best and the 150 points scored by the Redmen for the national team record.

McKenzie warned Oliver that Ashland was seeking vindication. "I had heard that they had recruited practically an entire new team just for this game," McKenzie recalled.

Coach Bill Carter of Ashland was pretty much free to do as he pleased in that regard, because he was under no restraints, from the

National Collegiate Athletic Association or the Ohio College Conference, regarding eligibility. Carter simply picked up players that he wanted and quietly "enrolled" them in a night school class. After the game the players would just as discreetly drop the course.

"Carter had called Newt to tell him they were going to get him," McKenzie recalled. "They went out and got big John Thomas, seven-foot-one, whom Rupp had run off at Kentucky for not attending classes. He was a railroad worker at the time we played them. They got Slater and Hobbs, both six-four, and some transfers from Marshall to suit up for the game. Then Carter got two local boys to be the referees.

"Thomas was out of shape, but he started. The first time Bevo went up with the ball, [Thomas] put Francis and the ball both down on the floor," McKenzie continued. "In all, [Carter] had six new players that hadn't played in the first game."

Carter's referees, apparently unaware that basketball was not a contact sport, helped his cause by ignoring the roughhouse tactics and flagrant fouls. The result was a brutal affair from start to finish. "They were just beating on Bevo, unmercifully," Ripperger remembered.

This revamped and much more talented edition of the Thoroughbreds gave the Redmen all they could handle. The first half ended with Rio Grande's holding a slim eight-point lead. In a game that resembled a war Rio Grande saw the lead shrink to but one point at the end of the third period. With Wiseman and Ripperger using all their skill to control the ball and harass the Ashland guards in the last stanza, the Redmen were able to eke out a 70-63 win. Francis accounted for only 25 points. He did manage to control Thomas offensively and limited his production to just four points.

Carter, intent on handing Oliver and Rio Grande their first loss, was incensed at the result. Oliver was simply happy to escape with his winning streak alive and headed back to Ohio as fast as possible. John Thomas went back to working on the railroad.

The Redmen continued to attract feature coverage in the major metropolitan papers. Milton Gross of the *New York Post* had seen Francis and the team in action. In a long column that was but one in a series that he would produce about the Redmen for his *Post* readers, Gross criticized the Madison Square Garden officials who seemed, to him, to be contriving some means to keep Rio Grande out of the National Invitation Tournament. Later, Gross retracted that accusation, saying only that "the committee was studying the matter."

Additionally, the *Boston Globe* and *San Francisco Chronicle* had run lengthy profiles of Bevo. In Seattle, Gene Russell of the *Times* wrote,

"Basketball never had a scorer in Bevo's class before." That was a high compliment, coming as it did from a scribe in the city where Johnny O'Brien attended college.

The penultimate contest on the schedule was to be played two nights later on the stage at Washington High School in Gallipolis. The opposition would be the Cincinnati Bible Seminarians, who had opted out of the scheduled date at the Gardens. Instead, they would face the Redmen on a court laid out across an elevated stage, before an SRO crowd of eleven hundred. Tickets for the February 27 match were sold at five local drug stores, with only one hundred reserved for sale at the gate.

As the Redmen took the court, they passed the Seminarians' dressing room. "We could hear them inside singing, 'Rock of Ages, cleft for me, let me hide myself in thee,'" Ripperger remembered.

They must have been praying feverishly, because the Seminarians took a brief lead after four minutes on a Royce Robey field goal. Bevo retaliated with a jump shot from the corner to regain the lead for Rio Grande.

The Seminarians' prayers went unanswered as Rio Grande rolled to a 112-86 victory, their thirty-eighth of the season. Francis added 59 points to his record-setting total.

His performance added yet another record to the flock he'd accumulated. He had eclipsed the Ohio collegiate three-year scoring mark held by Donald "Monk" Meineke of Dayton—and it had taken Bevo less than one full season to do so.

The Redmen now had a few days off as they were not scheduled to play again until Wednesday, March 4, when they would face Wilberforce in Cleveland for their final game of the regular season. As usual, however, there was no rest for Bevo: After the game against Cincinnati Bible Seminary, Bevo and Newt left for New York, where Oliver had arranged a grinding schedule of appearances and interviews for his star.

Readers opening their Sunday *New York Times* over bagels and lox learned—from the lead of Louis Effrat's coverage of the Saturday night NBA game that saw the Knicks beat the Ft. Wayne Pistons—that "Bevo Francis, the most-talked-about college basketball player in the land, was among the 4,500 spectators." Toward the end of his report, Effrat noted that "Bevo, in town for a television appearance tonight, turned out to be a pleasant, soft-spoken 20-year-old freshman. . . . [He] said he definitely is interested in playing pro basketball after his college days. [Knicks coach Joe] Lapchick, fully aware that Francis had amassed 116 points in a single game and close to 2,000 in a season, said he was interested in acquiring Bevo for the Knicks three years hence." Pictures of Francis and Oliver at the game, along with a shot of Bevo and Nate "Sweetwater" Clifton—the Knicks' star center—were sent out over the wire-photo system and appeared in papers nationwide that Sunday.

The next morning Francis and Oliver set off on a round of radio and television appearances across the city that culminated that evening when Bevo appeared on the popular *Ed Sullivan's Toast of the Town* television show, where he was given a rousing Gotham welcome before a coast-to-coast viewing audience. Sullivan, an inveterate sports nut and former writer, asked for "a really big hand for this really big star," in the patented style that spawned a whole generation of mimics. Bevo, attired in a suit and tie provided by Don Allen, rose slowly from his seat in the audience and shyly waved toward Sullivan on the stage, then toward the audience that was cheering lustily as the APPLAUSE lights prompted. When they flicked off and the QUIET PLEASE lights were illuminated, the crowd ignored them and the ovation continued to swell. Bevo Francis truly was the toast of the town that night.

Rising bright and early, Newt, with Bevo in tow, headed off to do still more taping sessions and appearances on local television shows, including those hosted by Jim McKay and Mel Allen. The pace was frenetic as Oliver attempted to cover every available outlet for publicity.

On Monday, March 2, the UP announced its All-America team for 1953. The first team was headed by the Seton Hall's Walter Dukes, Seattle's Johnny O'Brien (whose scoring records Francis erased), Bob Houbrugs of Washington, Tom Gola of LaSalle, and Ernie Beck of Penn.

The second five was comprised of Bevo Francis, Don Schlundt of Indiana, Bob Pettit of Louisiana State, Dick Knostman of Kansas State, and Frank Selvy of Furman. Bevo was the first and only freshman to be so honored. Floyd Stahl's star performer at Ohio State, Paul Ebert, could manage no better than a third-team selection.

The Redmen already held the national mark for most wins in a season, besting the 1935-36 season mark of twenty-six consecutive wins set by Long Island University and matched in 1950 by Holy Cross. In the current season Seton Hall had run up twenty-seven straight before losing to Dayton and Louisville.

While Bevo and Newt were in Manhattan, the lineup for the National Invitation Tournament was falling into place, and the

Redmen of Rio Grande were not even mentioned in *The New York Times* stories recounting which teams were accepting their invitations. At the time this was *the* national championship tourney. The NCAA tourney was second best, and the major powers all sought to play in the NIT first, a complete reversal of their roles today.

On Tuesday, March 3, the pair from Rio Grande were the featured speakers at the weekly luncheon of the Metropolitan Basketball Writers Association, where Asa Bushnell, chair of the NIT, announced the draw and schedule for the tournament. Rio Grande was out. Seton Hall was in. An NIT spokesman told reporters, who clamored to know why Rio Grande was omitted, that "there is no question they could fill the Garden in their first game but we were afraid they would absorb a fearful whacking."

Bushnell indulged in the sort of double talk that usually comes from politicians: "Only those teams invited were seriously considered while others were considered." Oliver, among many others, was incensed at the snub. "My team can stay within 10-15 points of anybody," he told the basketball writers during their luncheon.

"Sure, we are disappointed," Bevo told the writers, who pressed him for his reaction to the rebuff. "We would have liked a chance to prove that we have a good team." When pressed further, his only additional offering was to say quietly, "I'm sorry we weren't invited." After the luncheon Bevo and Newt spent the afternoon giving interviews to the print media.

Oscar Fraley, the UP's syndicated columnist, offered, "The big fellow from tiny Rio Grande College isn't a basketball goon or publicity hungry clown. He's a young man whose story is strictly American. I don't know whether Bevo is a great basketball player or not. I don't even care. I can tell you that he is a pleasant, keenly intelligent young man who hasn't lost his balance in all the uproar." Fraley characterized the treatment of Bevo Francis and Rio Grande by the NIT as a "hidden ball play."

As Bevo and Newt boarded the plane that would whisk them back to Ohio in time for the game against Wilberforce, they carried with them a check for $500 from the appearance on the Sullivan show; Newt turned it over to the college.

The Wilberforce game was half of yet another hastily arranged twin bill. Seton Hall, the eventual national champ, was to meet John Carroll in the nightcap of the double bill. Led by All-Americans Walter Dukes and ball-hawking Richie "the Cat" Regan, Seton Hall had been in the top ten all season long.

In a piece for the *Gallia Times* on game day, Homer Alley predicted no postseason games, adding, "This game is the last game. It will be Rio Grande's 39th win of the season. Bevo will finish with 50 points per game. The Redmen will average 100 points per game, and sports fans and writers will haggle for time immemorial over how really good Rio Grande is." His foresight would prove uncanny.

The Polio Foundation had asked Rio Grande to participate in a benefit at Madison Square Garden against St. Francis of Brooklyn. Rio Grande's Athletic Council swiftly vetoed the offer. Dan Ferris of the Amateur Athletic Union (AAU) extended an invitation to play in his prestigious AAU Basketball Carnival event, also at the Garden. The council turned down that offer as well. A former member explained, "The feeling was that the team had played enough games. We felt it was time they got back to their classes." No one consulted Oliver about either offer.

When Bevo arrived in Cleveland for the Wilberforce game, the usual horde of unruly reporters and camera crews greeted him. The magic of his name, coupled with the appearance of Seton Hall University and All-American Walter Dukes, was expected to draw ten thousand fans to the venerable arena. Before their two losses, the Pirates had been the nation's top-ranked team. At game time Seton Hall was ranked third behind Indiana and LaSalle and would go on to be crowned national champ after taking the National Invitation Tournament.

Photographers insisted on posing Francis and Dukes together. The country's most controversial star and its acknowledged top player stood awkwardly together and smiled as photographers begged for "just one more."

Bevo's fans were not disappointed in his swan song performance of the long campaign. The Redmen closed out their season the way they'd begun. With Francis pouring in 54 points, smashing the arena's scoring record along the way, they coasted to a 109-55 win against Wilberforce. Ten thousand fans stood and cheered as Bevo, hoisted on the shoulders of his teammates, was carried from the court.

"I watched from the courtside near our dressing room," said Richie Regan, who was Seton Hall's point guard and went on to serve the university as both coach and athletic director. "He [Bevo] was quick and agile and had a great touch. I was really surprised to see he was that good. We didn't know what to expect, and we were impressed with what we saw. Don't forget, this was in the era before televised games, and all we knew about him was what we read in the papers. We were as curious as the fans, and what we learned was, he could shoot as well as anyone I'd ever seen."

By the time Regan, Dukes, and the Pirates (later named one of the top twenty-five teams of the century by *Sports Illustrated*) took the court, most of the fans had left.

"Here we were, with arguably the nation's best player and a top-three team, and nobody cared," Regan recalled in amazement. "They had all come to see Bevo. When we took the court, the place was nearly empty."

After the game Honey Russell, the legendary Seton Hall coach who was one of the nation's most respected mentors, would speak of Bevo Francis to a Cincinnati reporter, saying, "The kid's terrific. I'll admit I just expected to see a big kid who can score. He can do everything. He's fast, strong defensively, great off the boards, and a fine team player. Bevo could make any team in the country today. He and Walt Dukes are the two greatest players in the country. Of course, I've seen other players look great the first season and then do a complete flop, but I'm convinced Bevo's the real thing. Furthermore, I figured Rio Grande would be just Bevo and four other guys. Let me tell you something: that Rio Grande has a fine team."

Not everyone shared Coach Russell's appraisal. Several days after Russell had placed Dukes and Francis in the same class, The Associated Press announced its All-America team. Dukes topped the list of first-team selections. Francis, in the "surprise of the balloting," was the top vote getter on the third team.

In Seattle diminutive Johnny O'Brien closed out his career with a three-year total of 2,701 points. "Now Bevo can have it," said the five-nine O'Brien, who had already seen Bevo erase his two-year total in one season.

In his final season of college play, O'Brien had scored 854 points in a 31-game campaign, averaging 28.5 points per game. Francis, in 39 games, had rolled up 1,954 points. His average of 50.2 points per contest was more than 18 points better than his nearest competitor's. In fact, Bevo's season point total was 1,026 more than the total rung up by runner-up Vernon Purnell of Alcorn A&M—and he played 50 games.

Bevo, the subject of so much controversy during the year, finished third in Player of the Year voting. In addition, he was one of only two basketball players to receive first-place votes in the balloting for Athlete of the Year. The other was Bob Cousy of the Boston Celtics.

9

Fouled by the NCAA

Postseason tournament play was underway in Kansas City, site of the NCAA Men's Basketball Championship Tournament.

At the same time the nation's basketball coaches converged on the city for their annual convention, at the Muhlbacher Hotel on March 17. Newt Oliver was not among them because Rio Grande had no money for such a trip—but he was not far from the minds of the conventioneers.

In an ordinary year the annual convention of the National Association of Basketball Coaches would have attracted little or no national attention, but 1952-53 had been anything but ordinary for college basketball. What transpired during that meeting reaped as many headlines as the tournament action on the hardwood across town. The coaches had accepted the recommendation of their rules committee to define what should be considered college competition.

During the convention, in an executive session that was closed to the media, the association president, Cappy Cappon of Princeton, appointed fellow Ivy Leaguer Howard Hobson of Yale to head the committee and to report its findings to the convention. Hobson was joined by Tony Hinkle of Butler and Joe Hutton of Hamline College.

According to the official minutes, Hobson met briefly with his committee, then reported to the convention that they had "some recommendations we thought would be to the welfare of the game and the Association."

The minutes continue:

First, on the matter of NCAA records, we recommend the NCAA records only consider and include games played between four-year accredited degree-granting institutions. This would eliminate from the records such a game as played in Los Angeles [Sax Elliots' staged scrimmage contest]. It would also eliminate from the records alumni games, games with service teams, and independent teams, and probably most of the games of an international nature. That seemed to us to be the only sound basis to consider records on, because these records are what go in the official guide, of course, and are the records our players shoot for year after year, and our teams too, of course. That was our recommendation.

Ben Carnevale, then the coach at the Naval Academy, told him, "Read it again."

"We recommend [that] the NCAA records and statistics include only games between four-year degree-granting institutions," Hobson repeated.

Thanking Hobson for his report, Cappon said, "First, of course we will have to find out whether this body wishes to go on record in recommending to the NCAA Statistical Bureau and the press associations [wire services] this idea of what is college competition. That will be open to the floor at this time before we have any motions."

He then recognized Dr. Henry Carlson of Pitt, who said, "Mister President, I think it is a grand report, except that the committee has taken in a little too much territory, because they have moved over into the academic side when you say accredited colleges. Unfortunately, there are colleges in this country that go on and off the accredited list every so often, and their credits are not accepted at any other institutions at this time. There is no use in mentioning any names but that is a fact.

"Therefore I think the committee ought to consider removing the word 'accredited.' Four-year degree-granting institutions is all right."

Don White of Rutgers asked, "Does that mean whether they are members of the NCAA or not?"

Hobson replied quickly, "Oh, yes. That wouldn't enter into it. There are a lot of schools that aren't members of the NCAA."

Following another brief discussion about the meaning of "accredited institution," Cappon recognized Floyd Stahl of Ohio State, who had risen to speak.

"Mister Chairman, I am sure that all our Ohio coaches represented here will agree with me on this statement. I think we, as a coaching body, should go on record as indicated here that trumped-up records made by a school against any kind of competition they can get and any number of games required in a season to break records is against our principles." A spattering of applause greeted his statement, and Stahl grinned before continuing.

"We have to be a little careful in Ohio about saying anything derogatory about Rio Grande or Bevo Francis, who may be a great ballplayer. I say this because he is a sort of common peoples' All-American." Snickers greeted this last remark, and Stahl moved on.

"We do feel that when many of the games that a college plays against competition that is so inferior to some of our high school competition in the states, that records such as that should not be kept, that when a coach makes a statement he has 30 ball games, and if that isn't enough for a boy to break an existing record, they will schedule six or eight more to do it. You see what I mean? We make ourselves look a little absurd if we accept records like that. I think that would meet the approval of all our Ohio coaches who have constantly seen this."

This last was a reference to Oliver's remark that "had I known Francis was going to score so many points so soon, I wouldn't have scheduled so many games." However, Alcorn A&M had played fifty-five games against questionable opposition, and nothing was said about that. Of course, Alcorn was in Alabama and didn't have Bevo Francis.

Stahl, who had waited impatiently all season to vent his spleen about Rio Grande and Francis, and especially Oliver, returned to his seat with a contented smile.

Cappon asked whether anyone else had anything to add. Carlson did: "His high school record is mixed up in there because he hadn't graduated from high school during the basketball season. How are you going to call that collegiate records?"

Stahl rose quickly to his feet and, without being recognized, said, "Doctor, his record will be a college record next year, because when his coach was asked what they are going to play next year, he said the same teams in bigger places with bigger guarantees. He will have a record next year."

Carlson sighed unhappily: "That is just a sign of the times."

Someone asked Hobson whether he planned to include "team and individual records" in his report, and Hobson replied, "I am sure it [sic] intended to be team and individual." The discussion returned to accreditation and court size. Ray Oosting of Trinity College, who had never seen Community Hall but had undoubtedly heard about it, opined, "I think if a team has a very tall player and played on an exceedingly small type of court, it would be ridiculous. It is just the type of thing we are trying to get away from."

Cappon chimed in from the podium, "If we are going to pass any recommendation, I think we ought to have a retroactive clause in there that any records in the past that do not conform to this thought should be expunged." Cappon informed the group that Paul Arizin of Villanova had run up "70 or 80 points" against a service team. "But a record such as that is not a fair one for anybody on a regular competition set-up to compete against. I think there should be something of that sort in the recommendation, if it is the wish of this body to make such a recommendation. Does that sound logical or not?" he asked.

Carlson replied, "I think you are logical."

Cappon then asked Hobson whether he would "care to rephrase [his] recommendation. I would judge it should be the [NCAA Service] bureau and all press associations as a recommendation. It is not a rule. It is just a recommendation." (The NCAA Service Bureau was the official record keeper and disseminated records to the public.)

Hobson readily agreed. "Yes, with the permission of Tony Hinkle and Joe Hutton, who were on the Committee, I would rephrase it to read: *That the NCAA official records, team and individual, include only games between four year degree granting institutions and that the policy be made retroactive*" (emphasis added). Hobson, turning to Cappon, then asked, "How far retroactive?"

"Any records that do not conform to that could be expunged is all," Cappon answered.

"Does that include everything?" Hobson wanted to know.

"I think it does."

The motion had been made and seconded when White suggested that perhaps "Hobby would feel better if he takes the suggestions and has a meeting with the members of his committee before this is voted on."

Hobson, the uncertainty of a moment before now absent from his voice, dismissed the notion, according to the minutes. "I don't think it makes any difference," he shrugged.

After Cappon had separated the question of the records from the committee's other suggestions, he said, "The question has been called for. All in favor, please make it known by saying 'Aye'; contrary, 'No.'"

The motion, Cappon declared immediately, was carried.

With an anonymous voice vote the National Association of Basketball Coaches conveyed to the NCAA its recommendation that Bevo Francis and Rio Grande College be stripped of all their records.

In Shawnee Mission, Kansas, the NCAA heeded the advice and

made it official the next day.

The "Bevo Rule," as it would forever be known, meant that all the records that Bevo Francis had set were wiped from the record book.

Public reaction to the most publicized defrocking since Jim Thorpe was immediate and intense.

If the basketball coaches, in attempting to appease Floyd Stahl, thought their action would wipe Bevo out of the public's mind as well as their record book, they couldn't have been more wrong. Sportswriters gave the action their full attention. In Columbus, Fritz Howell spoke for most Americans when he termed the action "the most flagrant injustice in the history of sports."

As the story dominated the national sports pages, the outcry grew. Every Lunch Pail Louie and average working stiff felt the sting as if he had been slapped down personally. A whole generation of fans and just plain folks, people who had survived the depression, World War II, and then Korea and now were struggling to make ends meet in their workaday world, felt betrayed and put upon. The "establishment" had struck down one of their own, and they felt the pain and humiliation. Bevo Francis certainly didn't need any additional fans. But the coaches' action galvanized a whole new base of supporters. Seeing the Ohio farm boy's hard-earned records snatched from him by the big guys enraged the public and steeled Americans in their support of him and tiny Rio Grande.

Oliver, who learned of the action in a telephone conversation with a reporter, said, "It is an insult to the team and the game of basketball." Then he threatened to sue the NCAA in retaliation.

When Oliver informed Bevo of the decision, the young star said simply, "The people saw me do it. They can pass all the rules they like, but they can never change that."

Turning to leave Oliver's office and the jangling phone, Bevo said, almost as an afterthought, "If you can, Coach, toughen the schedule up a bit next year."

Although seemingly unfazed by the whole affair publicly, it is unlikely that Bevo was so blasé inside. For a young man whose self-esteem was derived from basketball, the decision had to have exacted a terrible toll. In high school he'd been branded guilty of a never-specified sin and suffered two seasons of ignoble suspension from competition. Once he was able to play in college, another monolithic bureaucracy had come along and robbed him of his honestly won honors, forcing him to deal with yet another public humiliation—only now it was spread across the pages of every paper in the nation.

On March 23, five days after the NCAA made the "Bevo Rule" official, Oliver announced that Rio Grande had resigned from the NCAA in protest of its treatment of his star. "From now on," he stated, "we are members of the NAIA [National Association of Intercollegiate Athletics, the small colleges' ruling body] and they are accepting all our records. I want nothing to do with the NCAA."

Don Allen, whose initial funding of Rio Grande basketball scholarships had made the records possible, sued the NCAA to force the organization to restore the records. After much delay, a court ruled that it was without jurisdiction in the matter, and the case was dropped.

The East-West College All-Star game was played in Kansas City on March 28. The Ararat Shrine Temple, sponsor of the Charity Classic, tried to get Rio Grande to play a warm-up before the All-Star event. The fund-raising game was in only its second year, and the Shriners believed that an appearance by Bevo and Rio Grande would boost attendance, which had been disappointing in the inaugural year. But the Rio Grande Athletic Council declined the invitation to send the team, replying that "they've played too many games already, and the players had worn themselves out," the *Gallia Times* reported.

The council did, however, grant permission for Bevo Francis to attend so that he could put on a shooting exhibition at halftime. The Shriners were delighted to learn that they had landed him. They promoted his shooting exhibition more prominently than the All-Stars. In trumpeting the appearance of "Fabulous Bevo Francis of Rio Grande," the Shriners' newspaper ads and broadsides listed the records he had established:

Most points in a single game—116
Most field goals in a single game—47
Most points in a season—1,954
Most free throws in a season—538
Most field goals in a season—708
Highest average per game for a season—50.1

But what had happened at the coaches' convention two weeks earlier had an even greater effect. The All-Star game and the Shriners became the beneficiaries of the controversy that the coaches' decision had touched off. The crowd was twice the size it had been the previous year.

As the All-Stars completed their first half of play and headed toward their respective locker rooms, Bevo Francis walked slowly onto the court. The house lights were dimmed, and the announcer began to intone his long introduction. The emcee recited in dramatic fashion the long litany of records that the player had set that season and built slowly to "and here he is with us tonight. The fabulous BEEEEVOOOOOH FRANNNCCCISSS!"

The spotlight caught him in its white-hot glare, and the lights came slowly up while the crowd, which had greeted the introduction of the galaxy of All-Stars with polite applause, roared its welcome. Francis, with no time to warm up, dribbled in for an easy lay-up—and missed. "If there had been a hole in that floor to crawl into, I'd have gone there," he recalled. A smattering of boos and nervous laughter echoed through the arena. Looking for all the world like someone who did not want to be there, Francis moved out to the top of the key and turned to loft a softly arching jump shot.

Swish.

He continued to bomb from outside and eventually sank twenty-one of the thirty shots he tried, including eleven in a row. He left to a standing ovation from the crowd, which by then included a number of All-Stars who had come out to catch a glimpse of the man who had eclipsed them all in publicity.

Back at Rio Grande, Francis and the team were feted at a banquet in their honor on May 1. Dave Diles, who had first brought them to the attention of the world outside Appalachia, was the master of ceremonies. Fritz Howell and the Notre Dame gridiron coach Frank Leahy were the featured speakers. After a four-course meal the team members were each presented with a trophy. Wiseman received Oliver's MVP Trophy for most assists and Barr the runner-up award.

Leahy presented the school with the U.S. Rubber Company Pro Keds Award, designating Rio Grande College the most improved team in the United States. The award, given annually, was based on season-to-season improvement as measured by the Dunkel rating system for assessing the relative strength of various teams. Leahy noted that no team in the history of the award had ever made such a significant improvement.

In an obvious reference to the recent NCAA action, Leahy, coach of numerous Fighting Irish championship squads, told the team: "Champions are ever penalized. You must accept the fact and try all the harder because of it."

Part 3

Goodbye Mayo State, Hello Miami

Bevo Francis launches a shot against Villanova, December 4, 1953 in Philadelphia. The Rio Grande Redmen lost 93–92 in overtime. Francis had 39 points.

10

Getting Ready for Takeoff

It is not the critic who counts; not the man who points out how the strong man stumbled or where the doer of deeds could have done them better. The credit belongs to the man who is actually in the arena; whose face is marred by dust and sweat and blood; who strives valiantly; who errs and comes short again and again; who at best knows the triumph of high achievement; and who, at the worst if he fails, at least fails while daring greatly, so that his place shall never be with those cold and timid souls who knew neither victory nor defeat.

—President Theodore Roosevelt

When baseball season begins in April, fans and sportswriters usually abandon college basketball for the summer, and it is difficult to find anything at all written about the sport until late fall. This was not the case in the spring and summer of 1953.

Newt Oliver issued a spate of press releases that alluded to mysterious eastern trips for the coming season without mentioning specific teams, places, or dates. His releases always referred to his hope that he would be able to build a schedule against four-year schools with the guts to face Rio Grande.

Predictably, because of their leading roles in the enactment of the "Bevo Rule," his first choices for the coming season were Ohio State and Yale. In lengthy letters to both Floyd Stahl in Columbus and Howard Hobson in New Haven, Oliver offered to meet them anywhere, anytime, and to devote the proceeds to charity. "Since you obviously feel that we do not play a representative schedule," he wrote, "perhaps you would be willing to play us so we can settle the question, once and for all, where it should be settled. On the court."

Oliver had in fact challenged Yale right after the coaches' meeting that led to the stripping of Bevo's and Rio Grande's records. According to an AP report that ran in *The New York Times* on March 24, 1953, Oliver wrote to Hobson, the coach who had made the motion that Bevo's records be nullified, saying that Rio Grande would be "willing to over-look the size of your enrollment to give you the opportunity to back up your statements that Bevo's records are unworthy of consideration."

Bevo recalled that "the ones that were doing most of the bitching, we challenged. And they wouldn't play us. Ohio State was number one on our list, and they refused to play us. They said they had everything to lose and nothing to gain. Maybe so, but if you say something about someone and then they come back to you about it, and you refuse to back it up, then you've lost all respect. He [Stahl] refused to be man enough to play us."

Oliver persisted, hounding Hobson and Stahl throughout the spring. Bill Ripperger remembered one scene: "Oliver had been screaming at someone on the phone in his office as I came by. When he slammed the phone down in disgust, I asked him who it was. He told me it was 'that damn Hobson! He wants to pass rules about us, but he doesn't have the guts to play us.'"

Neither coach accepted Oliver's challenge.

Meanwhile, Bevo completed his freshman year with decent grades—Bs and Cs—and headed home to Wellsville for the summer. He found a job working at a nearby racetrack, where he attracted the notice of a photographer. The picture soon appeared in papers across the country: Bevo, in uniform and pith helmet, standing alongside a five-foot jockey perched on a soda crate. The player supplemented his income with carpentry work after the racing meet, staying busy and active throughout the summer. Regardless of how hard the young husband and father worked on construction sites during the hot, hazy days, Bevo devoted the twilight hours to basketball. Imbued with a quiet but fierce determination to prove the critics wrong, he shot basket after basket until darkness enveloped the hoop.

After the records had been stripped and the resulting furor died down, Bevo remained silent in public but acknowledged the sting privately. "I definitely felt personally persecuted. I was hurt. But you've gotta go on living," he said. "That summer I worked harder than anything to show them that I could do it. Even on Sundays I'd go and shoot and shoot. And with every shot I took, I thought, 'If I ever get the chance, I'll show them.' With every single shot, what they had done was on my mind."

Toward the end of the school year J. Boyd Davis had summoned

Oliver to a meeting. Davis and the trustees had received a letter from Bland Stradley of the Ohio College Conference outlining the rules by which Rio Grande was expected to abide in the coming season: no more than twenty-five games and no practice until November 1, the customary date for college teams to begin practice. Oliver read the letter from Stradley, who also happened to be athletic director at Ohio State, and told Davis that he would have little or no trouble conforming to the rules as presented. Then Davis told Oliver that the rules applied only to Rio Grande College.

Oliver was incensed. But Davis informed him that the trustees and the Athletic Council were most eager to comply with the rules and stay on good terms with the conference. In fact, the trustees, who had been overwhelmed by the mountains of publicity and the storm of controversy swirling around their little school, had welcomed the directive from Stradley.

Davis went on to inform Oliver that the trustees had decided to empower the Athletic Council, headed by Dr. Francis Shane of Gallipolis, to conduct the day-to-day affairs of the athletic program (read: basketball) at Rio Grande. At one of its many meetings, held without Oliver present, the Athletic Council had recommended these steps to the trustees, who went even further in reining in the obstinate Oliver. They appointed one of the area's most respected attorneys, John Halliday, to travel with the team and deal with the promoters and arenas on financial arrangements. "If we don't take this precautionary measure," one trustee remarked cryptically, "we might not have any money left."

The trustees eagerly accepted the council's recommendations, stripping Oliver of all responsibility save coaching the team and arranging the schedule. "The trustees felt that the tail was wagging the dog," recalled Jean Cooper, the retired secretary for the board of trustees. "It became a question of whether we'd be a basketball factory or an academic institution. The trustees opted for the latter."

Among the many factors that the trustees were ignoring was that Oliver had put together a basketball schedule for the 1953-54 season that was expected to bring in nearly $50,000 in gate guarantees, which represented more than a quarter of the school's $164,000 budget for that academic year.

Many others have confirmed Cooper's assertion about the trustees' position. What is not clear is whether the school would have survived without the success of the basketball program. The tail wagging had generated enough profit for 1952-53 to stave off the creditors and to keep the faculty's paychecks from bouncing. The team had brought in more than $15,000 for that academic year, even with all the travel expenses and the benefit games that produced little income. Additionally, enrollment would jump by 26 percent, to 125 students, for Bevo's sophomore year. No doubt, this was in some measure attributable to the publicity that the team generated.

No matter how the trustees phrased their dismay and discomfort at being in the national glare, they felt driven to do something. Oliver was the obvious target. He had ignored, insulted, and infuriated them for an entire year. They had had enough.

The question was, how long would Oliver stick around under such constraints? "When I was told of the conditions I would have to work under," Oliver said flatly, "I wanted to quit." The jealousy and suspicion of the administration, once behind closed doors, now was out in the open. "I felt like we were treated like criminals when we should have been treated as saviors," the coach said.

Exacerbating the situation was Oliver's request for a raise of $1,000 in recognition of the more than $15,000 he had turned over to the faltering school. He did receive a raise: $120 a year.

That summer Oliver headed back to Wyoming to finish his master's degree. Before he left, he talked to Don Allen about the treatment he'd received and about leaving the school. "I didn't use a lot of finesse with the situation," Oliver acknowledged. "I never felt that I got any help from the college. I felt that the team belonged to Don Allen—they [the Redmen] didn't belong to Rio Grande." Perhaps that reveals the root of Oliver's problems.

"Here was a chance to make some money and to keep the school alive," Oliver continued. "But there were a lot of jealous people around. Cutting on us and trying in every way in the world to downgrade us. Here we were, a little college with a hundred students, getting the kind of publicity around America these other major colleges couldn't get. We [the Redmen] were just too big a situation at the college. The people couldn't realize what I was trying to do. I got very little cooperation. They said I was belligerent. Possibly, I was. But you had to be a very dominant person to accomplish this. The average man couldn't walk in off the street and pull this off." Allen persuaded Oliver to swallow his pride and stay on as coach despite the humiliating restraints that the trustees had placed on him. But, if anything, he was even more embittered than before.

Putting together the schedule for the coming season was really not difficult. After all, Rio Grande College and Bevo Francis were the biggest attraction in college basketball. "We could almost pick where we wanted to play," Oliver remembered. "Promoters were coming to me all the time. Between the promoters' offers and my letters, we put this schedule together."

Oliver felt certain that his team's immense popularity and Bevo's scoring could take them where he'd predicted they could go from the start. He planned a swing through the Northeast, home of his staunchest critics, as well as southern and western trips. He would garner as much attention in as many places as possible within the constraints placed upon him. The aggressive schedule and travel requirements did little to ease the tension between him and the administration.

Years later Dick Barr, who had become a successful marketing and sales executive, remarked, "Newt had a plan. He devised it and he executed it to perfection, from his standpoint. From a marketing perspective it was a tremendous success."

Everybody did want to see Bevo and the Rio Grande Redmen, and Oliver was in a position to give fans what they wanted. He had told the players that they would be "getting out of here" and "moving up," and they certainly would be. He had ordered new uniforms: Patterned after those worn by the All-Stars at the East-West Classic, the crimson jerseys were emblazoned with stars circling the numbers front and back. If Rio Grande was truly America's Cinderella team, the coach reasoned, the new uniforms would reflect its transformation from rags to riches.

Arriving back on campus for the fall semester, Bevo and the rest of the returning Redmen eagerly awaited the start of the new season. If Notre Dame's Frank Leahy could have seen their determined faces, he would have known that the Redmen were united in their determination to acquit themselves well before fans eager (and prayerful) to learn whether they were for real.

Replacing the likes of Mayo State, Cincinnati Bible Seminary, and Sue Bennett College were the University of Miami, Providence College, Butler, Creighton, Villanova, Wake Forest, and North Carolina State.

"When I first saw the big-time schedule for the season," recalled Ernie Infield of the *Record* of Wooster, Ohio, "I couldn't help wondering if Bevo would become an American success story. Would he go on to greater things or become an American tragedy? Would it all come crashing down? I guess there are elements of both."

The team was not awed by the challenge. "I knew we were a good team," Ripperger said. "We had proven it time and again. Now we'd get a chance to show the country we could play with anybody." There was another reason that the Redmen were so sanguine. "We were disappointed when the records were stripped," Wayne Wiseman said. "We entered that season with a feeling that we would show them all it wasn't a fluke. I think we all felt a sense of mission."

That mission would place them in huge arenas in major cities where eager fans gobbled up tickets as fast as they became available. Americans wanted to see for themselves whether basketball's most controversial star was another George Mikan or just a Cardiff giant in shorts.

In a feature story for the International News Service, John Barrington managed to put into words the allure of Rio Grande and Bevo Francis: "Seldom has a sport so captured the public interest. It is the Praying Colonels of Centre College. . . . Jim Thorpe and the Carlisle Indians . . . the early Notre Dame teams all over again in a different guise. All the world loves an underdog, and Bevo Francis and Rio Grande fit perfectly into that mold."

※ ※ ※

The stage was set for Act Two of the drama that had gripped fans across the land. Before the curtain went up, Oliver teased the audience with another stunt that grabbed headlines yet again. Despite the reams of publicity that the team had received during the off-season, he still wasn't satisfied.

In late October, Oliver noticed that the ballot for Raccoon Township, where Rio Grande was located, had no candidate listed for the office of constable. The incumbent constable never had opposition, so he never bothered to formally file for office; a few write-in votes from friends usually were sufficient to ensure his reelection. But Oliver hatched a plan to write in Bevo's name on the ballot and enlisted the aid of several others. Scurrying around the village on Election Day, Oliver managed to convince enough people to write in Bevo Francis' name that the star center easily won election.

Immediately after the results were known, Oliver was on the phone to reporters. The next day photographers descended on the Wicklines' home to photograph the new constable in a coonskin cap and Rio Grande jersey. The pictures were reprinted widely. The Oliver hype was off and running again.

Francis was more than a little concerned about Oliver's stunt. The former constable of Raccoon Township was a kindly old gentleman who was retired and used the position to supplement his meager pension. He needed the money, and Oliver's stunt had hurt him deeply. When Bevo learned of the man's distress at losing for the sake of a cheap publicity stunt, he assured the constable that he wouldn't take his job. "I simply refused to be sworn in, and the old gentleman got his job back," Bevo said. The election did give rise to an unflattering piece by John Lardner for *Newsweek* entitled "Rio Grande Law." It did not escape the college administration's notice.

While waiting for the season to start, Oliver kept Francis busy with interviews and personal appearances. The press, relentless in its determination to chronicle Bevo's every move, was with him constantly. Only on the court could Bevo find peace, and he was more eager than ever to get on with the business at hand. The pressure off the court was more discomforting than any game situation that he could imagine. Oliver, who could have shielded Bevo just as UCLA's John Wooden would later do with Lew Alcindor and Bill Walton, instead was a publicity hound.

"I didn't like it at all," Bevo said. "But I felt like I had to go along with it. If it had been just me and Newt, I wouldn't have done it. But I felt I owed it to my teammates. They had done so much for me, I thought I should go along with it all for them. I never did get used to it, though. I really didn't have any kind of private life."

Before embarking on their ambitious schedule, the Redmen would have several tune-ups. The first would come in mid-November at the University of Dayton, where they scrimmaged Tom Blackburn's Flyers for two days. Dayton, featuring Bill Uhl, Dave Demko, and Arlen Bockhorn, was ranked fourth in the nation in preseason polls and was a legitimate major college power. Blackburn, unlike Stahl and most other Ohio college coaches, was a supporter of Francis and the Redmen. He had been a hill country boy himself, and he applauded their efforts to pull themselves up from obscurity.

The first day was devoted to a controlled scrimmage designed to help both coaches appraise their offensive and defensive patterns. The second day the two teams played a regulation game in uniform in the Dayton fieldhouse. Rio Grande held a one-point lead at the half before forcing Dayton to freeze the ball in the waning moments of the contest to preserve a six-point win. Don Donaher, a member of the Dayton team and later a coach, assessed the Rio Grande squad that day as the finest talent that any Dayton team had ever faced.

Blackburn, who would guide his squad to a twenty-five-win season and into the NIT, congratulated Francis and the downcast Redmen in their locker room after the contest. "Don't worry, boys," he told them. "You have nothing to be ashamed about—you played a great game. You guys are going to surprise a lot of people this season."

"Hearing him say that boosted us all up a bit," Francis remembered.

For their final scrimmage before play began in earnest, the Redmen visited George Steinbrenner's team at Lockbourne Air Force Base in early November. Steinbrenner was one who felt the NCAA was wrong in their punitive action against Bevo. "We were a good team and had played and beaten some outstanding college clubs. For the NCAA to say that those games (with non-degree granting four-year schools and service teams) shouldn't have counted was just not fair." he said. "I was not high on the NCAA at that time. It was run by Walt Byers and whatever he said, they did."

It was supposed to be a scrimmage and nothing more, but the stands were packed with spectators. Steinbrenner's Airmen executed his defensive strategy to perfection this time. "With Bill McCollum in front and Lloyd Sharer behind we effectively denied Bevo the ball." Playing Bevo tighter than a glove they held him to 25 points. "We got homered by the refs up there," Wiseman remembered. "The officiating stunk and they beat us by five points. Newt about went out of his mind."

Under Steinbrenner's guidance Lockbourne handed the Redmen a valuable lesson: Facing top-flight competition, they were not as invincible as their 39-0 record would indicate. They realized that this year would be a whole new season. And everyone would be gunning for them. Being the most famous underdogs in the country made them not just the opposition but a hated enemy. One bad night, the Redmen feared, and they would be back in the pumpkin patch, where they had started and where some critics maintained they still belonged.

"Those scrimmages were a good experience for us. We needed a wake-up call, and those two games provided one," Ripperger recalled. "Our attitude after the first year and then having all the records stripped was, 'We'll just go out and do it all over again.' After those two scrimmage games we began to realize just how difficult that task was going to be."

The obstacles that lay in front of the Redmen were but another challenge to a group that was used to being tested. Forged in the white-hot glare of national publicity, they had been transformed during the process. Tempered by countless blows from critics and bureaucrats they had become a solidly constructed team with an unbreakable will to win.

In arranging the schedule, Newt had made a special effort to get Rio Grande to Buffalo, where Don Allen had his headquarters. When Oliver had promised a year earlier to bring the Redmen to Buffalo to play a game, Allen had not taken the pledge seriously, yet here they were, ready to play in the arena that Allen could see from his office window. The opponent for the Allen showcase game was Erie County Technical Institute, a two-year school. "That was a mistake," Oliver acknowledged. "I should have scheduled a four-year school."

The game was scheduled for November 26 at Memorial Auditorium and at the time Oliver, intent on pleasing his benefactor, had given little thought to the opposition. It would be the only two-year school that the Redmen would meet that season, and the NCAA did not count the game for the record books.

What Oliver and his team did think about as they boarded their flight to Buffalo was how far they had come in a year. Their new crimson uniforms had replaced the bleach-stained relics of the previous season. They would be playing in a spacious auditorium that could hold more than five thousand fans. No longer would they have to contend with the failing lights and the rainwater leaking from the ceiling at cramped Community Hall.

Gone too were the rickety station wagons that had bounced them throughout the Ohio Valley the year before. The Redmen were headed for the big time and the date with destiny that Oliver had promised them only fourteen months earlier. And they were *flying*—on a scheduled airline—to get there. The players could scarcely believe the transformation, but they sure were enjoying their new status.

The Erie Tech game was as much a tune-up for the Redmen as it was a tribute to Allen. Afterward they would be embarking on a trip that would take them to New York City, Philadelphia, and Boston. Oliver wanted them to be ready.

And the Redmen appeared to be primed and ready to take on the world without fear of defeat. A crowd of 5,467 saw them turn back Erie County by 120-59. Francis smashed the Memorial Auditorium scoring record with a superb 64-point outburst that exceeded the total combined output of the opposition. The old mark of 42 points had been set the year before by Larry O'Connor of Canisius College. The Rio Grande team's total also set a new auditorium record.

After a slow first half in which he managed only 17 points, Francis had the crowd on its feet in the final two periods as he tallied 18 points in the third and capped the evening with 29 in the fourth quarter. Erie County had tried to contain him with a collapsing zone defense. Rio Grande's aggressive, hard-charging play rattled its opponents, and the Erie County strategy failed to thwart the Rio Grande attack. Ripperger with 16 points, and Barr with 14, hit consistently from the perimeter to draw the zone out and away from Francis.

Afterward, Oliver met the horde of reporters outside the dressing room. For the first time since his humiliating meeting with J. Boyd Davis, his pent-up anger and sense of betrayal surfaced publicly. When a reporter asked about the college, Oliver brusquely told the startled scribes, "I'm not too happy with the way things are going there. I'm open to offers."

"Was that for publication?" one asked.

"Hell, yes," snapped Newt. "I'm looking around for another job."

"Does the school know that?" the reporter asked.

"They know it," he replied emphatically.

Sensing a major story, the press swarmed around Bevo and asked him for his reaction to Oliver's statements about leaving Rio Grande. "I like it here and I'd like to stick it out," he offered. "But I came with Newt. If he leaves, I guess I'll go with him. In fact, I guess I'd go with him wherever he goes." Across the room Oliver allowed a smile to appear briefly on his dark countenance.

Oliver's remarks and Bevo's reaction made national headlines. The incident did not win Oliver any fans among those who saw his threat as an opportunistic move by a slick promoter willing to hawk his star to the highest bidder.

The student newspaper at the University of Kansas ran a banner headline in its next edition: "BEVO COMING TO K.U." In a tongue-in-cheek story the students reported that Phog Allen, the legendary Kansas coach and Naismith disciple, was stepping down and that Oliver was taking over. No doubt the Kansas campus found the biting, satirical piece humorous. But elsewhere Oliver's threats only added to the cloud of controversy that Francis and the team were trying to escape.

As they flew home from Buffalo to the airport in Charleston, West Virginia, strong winds buffeted the plane, only the second flight that most of those aboard had ever taken. Their roller-coaster flight and bumpy landing left the entire squad white-knuckled with fear. The plane swerved severely upon touching down, but the pilot brought it safely under control.

"The next time I get into one of these things," Carl Benner gasped, "I'm taking out insurance. That was too close."

After the Thanksgiving recess the team once more clambered aboard a Capitol Airlines flight, this time bound for New York and a game with Adelphi College at Madison Square Garden on December 3.

ALL-STAR ... Bevo Francis posed in his uniform for the 1952 North–South High School All-Star Classic played at Murray State College in Kentucky after he completed his eligibility at Wellsville High in Ohio.

IN THE GARDEN... Francis puts up a layup during a loss to Adelphi at New York City's Madison Square Garden on December 3, 1953, ending Rio Grande's remarkable 40-game winning streak.

ON THE CIRCUIT... Francis and coach Newt Oliver at a banquet in Akron, Ohio for Goodyear Tire in March 1953.

JACKSON, Ohio
FEB. 2, 1954
BEVO FRANCIS SCORES
113 POINTS AGAINST
HILLSDALE

BIG GAMES... A rare photo from Bevo Francis' 113-point game in Jackson, Ohio, and, below, the site of Francis' 116-point game, Community Hall, aka the Hog Pen, in Rio Grande, Ohio. It was later razed and all that remains is a plaque commemorating the achievement.

NEMESIS...
Bevo and Dr. J.
Boyd Davis, the
Rio Grande
president who
would eventually
expel Francis.

NATIONAL SENSATION... Bevo Francis became a national name, as evidenced from this editorial cartoon from the *Birmingham Post-Herald*.

UNDER PRESSURE...
Francis is interviewed
during a January 20, 1953
game against Cedarville,
Ohio. Known as "The Big
Freeze" game, Cedarville
refused to shoot and
surrender the ball. The other
players around Francis are
standing and waiting for
something to happen.

WALKING AWAY... Student manager Carl Benner leads Francis and the Redmen off
the court in Kansas City, Missouri, March 22, 1954, in protest of the refereeing during a
loss to Rockhurst. Student assistant coach Caroll Kent beckons as well.

SIDELINED... Bevo, wife Jean and their son, Frank Jeffrey, pose for photographers April 14, 1954, after Francis was expelled from Rio Grande.

BEVO TODAY... Francis poses at the Rio Grande student center in front of a mural depicting his playing days. Below, Bevo with his wife, Jean.

1952–53 REDMEN... From left, John Viscoglosi, Jim McKenzie, Wayne Wiseman, Jack Fossett, Bill Frasher, Bevo Francis, Zeke Zempter, Dick Barr, Roy Moses, Bill Ripperger and Bob Mundy. Kneeling are student coach Carroll Kent and coach Newt Oliver.

1952–53 REDMEN... At their 50th anniversary reunion in 2002. From left, Dick Myers, Roy Moses, Wayne Wiseman, Newt Oliver, Bevo Francis, Lee Weiher, Don Vyhnalek, Jim McKenize and Dick Barr.

11

An
Unforgettable
Night

For college basketball teams and players there was only one
Garden. That was where the game came of age on December 29,
1934, when more than sixteen thousand crammed in to see the
first in a long series of double-headers that pitted the city's local
college teams against out-of-town powerhouses. Basketball entered the
modern era that night by demonstrating that college teams could
attract crowds big enough to fill the Garden, which became the showcase venue for the sport. The Garden-sponsored National Invitation
Tournament outclassed the NCAA's tourney, and, until the unsavory
events of 1950 tainted the venerable venue with the stench of scandal,
the NIT was an easy first choice of coaches who were invited to both.

The Garden's basketball promoter, Ned Irish, had struggled valiantly
against the venue's despoiled image, which had convinced coaches at
many out-of-state schools not to make the trip east. Irish shrewdly
recognized that Bevo's magical name could go far in restoring the
Garden to its rightful role as the Mecca of the sport.

In town three days before Rio Grande's game against Adelphi,
Oliver and Francis met with an anxious Irish. He was facing a
promoter's worst nightmare: The New York newspapers, then the
prime source of pre-event publicity, were all on strike with no sign of
settlement. Irish, who had been confident that Francis and Rio Grande
would sell out the Garden's eighteen thousand seats, now admitted to
Oliver that selling ten thousand tickets would be a more realistic goal,
considering the newspaper blackout that they faced.

Not one to give up easily, Irish sent Francis and Oliver on a whirlwind tour of the city that had them appearing on every radio and television show that would have them. The duo went from dawn until

dark, dashing from studio to studio. Francis did interviews with Mel Allen, Bill Stern, Jimmy Powers, Jim McKay, Marty Glickman, and a score of others. The out-of-town press corps, nearly as large as that which used to assemble only for an NIT title game, followed the blitz with interest. One reporter logged eleven appearances by Francis and Oliver in a single day. They appeared on all the local television stations during the evening sports segment and hyped the contest. Constantly on the run to meet the demanding media schedule that Irish had prepared, they had but one afternoon free to practice at the Sixty-ninth Street Armory. The rest of the time was devoted to the media.

Meanwhile, the rest of the team was ensconced at the Paramount Hotel, staring wonderingly at the skyscrapers surrounding them. "We felt about like a hog in heaven," Wayne Wiseman said. Bill Ripperger recalled the trip to a famous New York tourist spot. "Don Allen had arranged for us all to eat at Mama Leone's Restaurant. He'd bought us all new blazers and slacks and took us out for a night on the town. We were all seated in the restaurant when one of the players, reserve Bob Zurcher, obviously confused by the vast array of plates and cutlery in front of him, sought the attention of the waiter. 'Excuse me sir,' he said, 'I think you gave me someone else's fork. I already have mine.' Don had to explain salad forks to him. We were in the big city, but we were still country," he laughed.

As for their opponents, all was quiet on the Adelphi campus in Garden City, Long Island. Adelphi approached the meeting with Rio Grande with more than a little trepidation. The Panthers had already played two games that season and had lost both. Badly. The most recent loss was by 49 points to Fordham. Like Rio Grande, Adelphi was making its virgin appearance at the Garden. Most observers gave Adelphi little or no chance to beat the ballyhooed Francis and Company (the savvy New York bookmakers thought Adelphi was so outgunned that they kept the game off the line, accepting no wagers). Adelphi was meant to be nothing more than an appetizer for the main attraction.

In fact, Adelphi had become Rio Grande's New York opponent for its Gotham showcase quite by chance. Irish had sought teams with larger followings and more credentials and tradition but had failed to convince those he approached to risk their prestige against the likes of Rio Grande. When John Condon, a young sportswriter and part-time sports flak at Adelphi, learned of Irish's difficulty in securing an opponent, he approached the promoter.

"Actually, Irish wanted Hofstra University to be the opponent," Condon recalled. "When that fell through, I convinced Ned to use

Adelphi instead. We received a $1,000 guarantee, an unheard-of amount for a school like ours. Of course, the main attraction was Bevo. Irish wanted to see his drawing card do well, and if he did, he planned to have him back several more times."

The game date, December 3, 1953, finally arrived. Outside the Garden the brightly illuminated three-sided marquee shimmered in the frosty night, announcing RIO GRANDE VS. ADELPHI to a city whose sports fans and writers fancied themselves among the most sophisticated in the nation. The hotly debated rebuff by the NIT and the decision by the Rio Grande administration not to play at the Garden at the end of previous season had served only to intensify the interest of New York fans. Add the highly publicized record stripping and the Irish-inspired drum beating that led up to the tip-off, and you have the ingredients for a big event—even by New York standards.

Despite Irish's fears about attendance, more than thirteen thousand passed through the spinning turnstiles for the inaugural double-header of the season. The second game was to feature St. John's University, runner-up in the previous year's NIT and the only city power that had escaped the scandals unscathed. St. John's would be playing Lafayette College of Easton, Pennsylvania.

But the crowd had come to see Bevo. Fans wanted to see for themselves the man about whom so much had been written and said. Ned Irish knew this better than anyone. In an unprecedented move he had inserted in the contract that he sent to Rio Grande a clause stipulating that the contract would be null and void "unless Bevo Francis be present and physically able to perform." Irish had further promised Oliver that the Redmen would be featured at least once each season for the remainder of Bevo's college career.

An AP story that newspapers ran the day before the game summed up the enormous impact that Francis had had on the sport: "Bevo Francis will attempt to prove he's more than a basketball freak and Ned Irish will seek to prove that the game isn't dead in New York when the 20th season of college basketball in Madison Square Garden opens tomorrow night. Francis, who set a series of unmatched and almost unbelievable marks for tiny Rio Grande College last year, will be the lure by which Irish, the Garden basketball boss, hopes to bring back the fans."

Lost on the writer was the irony in the proposition that a player from a school of 125 students hidden in the hills of southern Ohio could hold the key to resuscitating college basketball in the most hallowed venue in the country.

As the turnstiles clicked to a total of 13,832 ticket holders, little doubt remained. The only question was just how good Bevo Francis and Rio Grande were.

❋ ❋ ❋

As Rio Grande, the smallest school ever to field a team at Madison Square Garden, took the floor, a tremendous welcoming ovation greeted the Redmen. The hill country boys were the darlings of Manhattan. Nervous grins graced their faces. This wasn't a dream. Even the headline on the lead story in the 25-cent sage-colored Garden program reflected that reality: "BEVO, YOU'RE ON!"

The starters were Ripperger, #24; Wiseman, #25; Dick Barr, #30; Jim McKenzie, #21; and Francis, #32. A year earlier they had been playing to empty folding chairs in the Hog Pen. Tonight they were in the Garden!

"When I ran out onto that floor, I just stopped and looked around and thought, 'What am I doing here?'" Ripperger recalled.

"It was a massive place. It was awesome to kids like us. A dream come true," Barr said.

"I had never seen anything like it," Wiseman remarked. "I wanted to prove to the world we belonged. I wanted to do well there."

"I never saw a place that big," Bevo recalled. "But the fans all seemed to be for us. That would be that way everywhere we went. We never did play a home game after the first season, so it was nice to have some people there cheering for us."

Adelphi was not without supporters. The school, which until 1946 had been a women's college, had an enrollment of eighteen hundred. Yet the athletic office reported that it had sold more than four thousand tickets for the game.

Cast in the unflattering role of "the opponent" for the heralded visitors from Rio Grande, Adelphi nevertheless took its Garden appearance seriously. Despite the two thumpings that the Panthers had endured, their coach, George Faherty, was confident that they could stop the celebrated Francis. "A friend of mine, Taps Gallagher, coach at Niagara College, had seen the Erie Tech game, and he'd called me with a scouting report on Rio Grande," Faherty related. "He saw what he thought was a flaw in their offensive scheme that could be exploited. We discussed what he'd seen, and I drew up a game plan based on his report." Faherty mapped a plan that he felt could thwart the high-powered Rio Grande offense.

Based on Gallagher's observations, Faherty told his players what they could expect from Rio Grande: "They can run and execute the fast break as well as anyone. They are particularly good ball handlers and like to feed the pivot man from the front and sides. But they are weak defensively, particularly man-to-man, and their defensive principle seems to be to simply outscore their opponents."

Faherty outlined his plan on the blackboard in the Panther locker room. First, he listed seven points he wanted his team to emphasize and execute:

- Press as much as possible.
- Gamble all.
- Press and disrupt the feeder guards, especially Wiseman.
- Throw off their timing with aggressiveness.
- Steal the center taps.
- Rush the feeders and then drop back into the pivot.
- Hit the ball from Bevo's hands and knock the ball out of bounds after each Adelphi goal to allow time to regroup and slow Rio Grande down.

"Bevo seldom passes off, so we must stay on him like a magnet," Faherty told his players. Then he erased the list of keys he had written and outlined the strategy that they would use to try to stop Bevo. Even years later the coach exactly remembered the plan:

"I had Marty Funk, a skinny six-five freshman, play tightly between Francis and the basket as high in the pivot as he could take him. [Harvey] Pachter and [Bill] Moje, both around six feet, would cover the left and right flanks and collapse on Francis whenever the ball went in to him. Maher, a six-four senior, would move out in front of Bevo and use his height to harass Wiseman, dropping back to place himself in the lane between Bevo and his principal feeder. Only Don Payne, six-three, would be free to roam beneath the boards to grab rebounds we hoped the pressure would create."

Although opposing coaches had assigned as many as four men to Francis with little success, Faherty was convinced that his plan would work. Before the Panthers took the floor, he reminded them again: "Slap at all passes to Francis. Don't let the ball ever get to him, and we'll win this game." Their coach's confident instructions ringing in their ears, the Panthers sprinted onto the court to meet the Redmen.

The first quarter was a carbon copy of Rio Grande's forty earlier performances. The Redmen held a 24-19 lead when the buzzer sounded. Ripperger and McKenzie hit several long shots, while Francis was bottled up inside the smothering Adelphi zone. However, unlike other opponents, Adelphi refused to yield to the temptation to abandon the garrison surrounding Bevo and pick up the outside shooters. The Panthers stuck resolutely to Faherty's plan.

The pattern stayed the same throughout the second period. At Oliver's strident urging, Wiseman and Ripperger tried repeatedly, with little success, to force the ball through the forest of arms and hands to Bevo. Turnovers mounted. Play was rough and ragged, but the Redmen converted enough from the line and perimeter to build a 43–32 lead at the half. Bevo had managed to elude his convoy of defenders long enough to garner 18 points. In their respective locker rooms, both teams were confident.

Rio Grande, a notoriously good second half team, felt that it was only a matter of time before Adelphi, like all the others, would abandon its tight cocoon defense around Bevo and come out to play. Then, as always, the Redmen would race off to victory. Oliver was not concerned about anything he'd seen except their inability to get the ball to Bevo—and he told them so. "We'd won forty in a row, and I wasn't about to switch just because we were in the damn Garden," he recalled.

At the intermission Faherty encouraged his charges: "I told them to remain aggressive. I felt the plan was working and told them to remain aggressive in their coverage of Francis at all costs. 'You can win this,' I told them."

As the Redmen returned to the floor, their usual swagger was missing.

"We all knew what we had to do in New York. We had to win and Bevo had to score. Newt had made that crystal clear to all of us," Barr said.

"Possibly, we were a little tired and didn't realize it," Wiseman speculated. "But Newt made no attempt to adjust. I remember we just kept pumping the ball in to Bevo, and they would just slap it away. We still continued to force it in anyway. Newt may have been blinded by picking off the Garden's scoring record."

Some fans may have reinforced Oliver's natural inclination to stick with his tried-and-true strategy. "There was a particularly obnoxious and loud fan seated close to the Rio Grande bench that continued to scream and curse at Oliver throughout to 'Let Bevo score,'" Benner recalled. In fact, several particularly boisterous fans seated near the Rio Grande bench took up the cry—obviously, they had placed bets that Bevo would pass the 50-point mark.

Oliver confirmed that "I was worried about all the betting that was going on there. They were betting on whether Bevo would get fifty or not," a reference to the over/under play that the bookies had substituted for the game line.

"In those days, as soon as you entered the foyer at the Garden, there were bookies all over the place—you couldn't miss them," a former coach of the era recalled.

For whatever reason, Rio Grande, at Oliver's urging, continued to try to penetrate the picket line defense around Francis, with little success. Compounding the Redmen's problems was the failure of Barr, McKenzie, and Ripperger to convert open shots from the outside. "McKenzie missed a few in a row and his confidence sank," Wiseman said.

"I missed four shots in a row from the corner," Barr recalled. "Shots I was making all along wouldn't drop."

"It was," Ripperger remembered, "a disaster."

Even when things would seem to break in their favor, they turned out wrong. When Adelphi lost three starters to fouls because of their aggressive play, the substitutes that replaced them turned out to have shooting luck that they'd only ever dreamed about before. They couldn't miss. And Rio Grande couldn't hit. "We couldn't throw one in the ocean with two hands," Wiseman said flatly.

"When they came back to tie us in the last quarter, I couldn't understand what was going on," Ripperger said. "Newt probably put a lot of pressure on Bevo to break the Garden scoring mark. We never did stop trying to get him the ball until it was too late."

"None of us played above average. . . . We just plain stunk the place up," Wiseman said.

McKenzie recalled that "when we'd gotten about a ten-point lead, Newt called a time-out and told us to get the ball to Bevo. 'They want to see him score,' he told us. So we tried to do it. But it never did work."

As the clawing, scratching Panther defense swarmed around Francis, the Adelphi players batted aside pass after pass that the Redmen directed at Bevo. Shots that Barr and Ripperger usually hit with ease turned into frozen bricks instead. The usual bucket barrage that had foiled so many earlier opponents failed to materialize. Instead, the Panthers grabbed the lead five minutes into the final period. "It was the worse night we ever had," Oliver acknowledged. He might have added that it couldn't have come at a worse time or in a worse place. In the media capital of the world, in the most venerated arena in the world, Rio Grande stumbled to defeat.

As the final buzzer sounded, the Adelphi bench and fans erupted onto the floor, hoisting coach Faherty aloft and carrying him around the floor in triumph. "It was our day in the sun," Condon recalled.

"We were so much better than they were," Wiseman lamented. "But not on that night we weren't."

As the joyous Panthers paraded around the court, Wiseman "wanted to find a crack in the floor and disappear. I was in shock and depression." The huge scoreboard over center court told the tale: Adelphi 83, Rio Grande 76. The streak was over. The Redmen's bubble had burst. What was to have been a gala showcase for Bevo and Rio Grande had disintegrated into a dismally ineffectual parody. During the nightmarish evening the usually deadly Rio Grande free-throw shooters had missed twenty-four foul shots.

Francis, a 75 percent shooter from the stripe, made only twelve foul shots on twenty-one tries, or 57 percent. From the floor, under intense pressure, he finished with ten baskets in eighteen attempts. In the final minutes his teammates' inability to get the ball to Bevo sealed their fate. He would garner, as one writer put it uncharitably, "only" 32 points.

"It may have been Gardenitis that got them, as it did so many others on their first visit," Condon offered. "It was a shocker."

Adelphi had been led by the swift-footed Don Payne, who accounted for 18 points. When he'd been sidelined with fouls, little-used Larry McDonough added eight points to sustain the Panthers' rally. Despite the dismal showing by the Redmen, the crowd cheered the hoopsters from Rio Grande as they trooped slowly from the court. In a state of near shock, they barely heard the applause.

Hundreds crowded outside the Rio Grande dressing room seeking Francis' autograph. The dejected center masked his disappointment as he signed programs and scraps of paper thrust at him by admiring kids.

In the locker room the rest of the team was distraught. "We couldn't have beaten a high school team with that performance," Barr remarked to no one in particular.

"I apologized to Milton Gross [of the *New York Post*], who'd written some kind articles about us and then [I] just slipped out and back to the hotel," Wiseman recalled. "I didn't want to talk to anyone." Expressing a sentiment shared by all the Redmen, he said sadly, "I felt like we let a lot of people down that night."

"After that," Barr related, "a lot of people just wrote us off. We'd picked the wrong place to lose."

Once Bevo managed to extricate himself from the crowd of autograph seekers to get into the locker room, he faced another horde. The large press contingent, pads and pencils poised, pounced on him as he entered. "What is your excuse for your poor performance?" they asked, never mind that for any other player in the country, 32 points would have been a spectacular showing. But Bevo Francis had set the bar so high with his previous performances that such an effort by him could be deemed poor. However, before the 1953-54 season, only six players *in the history of the game* had managed to average more than 30 points a game.

"I just couldn't get any shots off in the second half," Bevo told the reporters matter-of-factly. "The Adelphi guys were all over me. I just had a bad night." He offered no apology.

The reporters seized the opportunity to instruct Francis on how to play better defense and gruffly and pointedly critiqued every facet of his game. He stared at them numbly as their battering continued. He listened stoically and answered their questions and criticisms as politely as he could. The majority of New York-area reporters had remained the most skeptical of Francis. They were now eager to crow about the validation of their reservations.

Not all, of course, were so eager to prove the Francis story a myth. Milton Gross of the *New York Post* was just as upset as the players were about their failure to fulfill the potential that he had told his readers about. "That loss did a tremendous amount of damage to their credibility," he recalled.

Bevo remained patient and polite through the intense grilling by reporters, even as it stretched to more than an hour and the crowd started to thin out. Eager to get his shower and escape to the sanctuary of his hotel room, he tried to extricate himself. Only a few reporters remained, and they, understanding that spent competitors need to relax, turned to Oliver for some final comments.

But one garrulous writer continued, in his thick Brooklyn accent, to pepper the retreating Francis with criticism. He wouldn't let Bevo get away. The youngster, who had been more than accommodating with a press corps that took obvious delight in his perceived failure to live up to expectations, was losing patience with the stalking reporter. The writer ignored Bevo's polite protestations as he followed the now towel-draped Francis to the showers. Finally, Bevo sought Oliver's assistance. Through tightly clenched teeth and jaw, he asked Oliver insistently to "get that man off of me before I lose my temper."

Oliver, sensing the rage that was building in his star, interceded before an even bigger public relations disaster could occur. When the gentle approach failed to deter the writer, Oliver grew more animated and angrily told him to leave. The writer finally got the message and undoubtedly ambled off to the nearest watering hole to tell his drinking buddies of Francis' shortcomings. His subsequent article, recounting the events of the Adelphi game, was one of the most scathing and cynical indictments of Francis and Oliver to appear.

Distributed by the Newspaper Enterprise Association, the article was preceded, in at least one Ohio paper, by an unusual editor's disclaimer that explained that "it represents the opinion of some kind of minority and is presented here for what it is worth." The editor continued, "It may be added, that no other reports of this kind have reached this office and we are at our wits' end to discover where the discrepancy lies."

With that introduction the article, bearing the byline of one Jimmy Breslin, followed. A brief introductory paragraph sneered at Francis' exploits of a year earlier. Then Breslin wrote:

> Francis' scoring and the selling job by his coach, John 'Newt' Oliver, soon attracted the attention of Madison Square Garden's Ned Irish and the little southern Ohio school was given a date in the New York basketball Mecca.
>
> The booking against Adelphi, a small local college, turned out to be one of the two mistakes Oliver has made, basketball people point out. It was a mistake because Adelphi, 50 point losers to Fordham two nights before, came on to expose Rio Grande and Bevo as something less than a good junior college team by beating the visitors, 83-76.
>
> The other mistake was in the handling of Francis. Although he scored 32 points against Adelphi's five-and-six-inch smaller kids, basketball-wise New Yorkers were sorely disappointed. They saw a nice, gangling country boy, who is, incidentally, a couple of inches less than the billed six-nine [and] who has a lot of basket-ball to learn. What bothered them more was the fact that Bevo has basic flaws that the fast-talking and cocky Oliver does not seem able to comprehend.
>
> Oliver sat and listened wide-eyed as a writer gave him advice. It wasn't supposed to be this way for Newt Oliver, you see. He has made no secret about the fine coach he is supposed to be.
>
> But he listened—and he was learning.

As Breslin recounted the unsolicited advice that he and the other locker-room second-guessers had offered Francis and Oliver the night before, he left out little in the list of shortcomings. He continued the diatribe with a backhanded compliment: "Francis still has to learn how to play basketball. The job could be done. Bevo has as fine a scoring touch with his one jump shot as can be found. He'll always score some with it—but against first-class opposition he won't score enough. Actually, Francis played a fine game for the equipment he has."

The concluding paragraph contained Breslin's cock-sure prediction of things to come: "Oliver, 29, should keep his kids in their class, the cage experts agreed. Newt has a date with North Carolina State in Raleigh, Dec. 22. That should take care of big time ideas."

While Breslin was less forgiving in his criticism of Francis than others who had seen the game, many shared his opinion of Oliver's future.

So what was the appraisal of Bevo by the much-respected Arthur Daley of the venerable New York Times? "He has as lovely and delicate a shot as you'd ever want to see. The adjective, lovely, is not incongruous. It's accurate. In pre-game practice, he stood near the foul line and flicked in ball after ball. Each throw was almost a caress, so gentle and tender was it. The ball never brushed the hoop. Kerplunk! It swished through."

The dean of New York sportswriters, who in covering Garden basketball had seen just about all the game's greats, added, "If ever a man screamed aloud for top flight coaching, that man was Bevo Francis. It might take a couple of years, but a Joe Lapchik, a Henry Iba or a Phog Allen could make another George Mikan out of him."

According to many who saw Bevo play that night, Daley's effusive praise in likening Francis to the sport's biggest star was in no way hyperbolic. Mel Allen said, "[Bevo] was a top-level performer with great crowd appeal." Marty Glickman, the radio voice of the Garden, said much the same: "He was a great story. I saw him play several times, and he displayed the ability to become a great star."

But while Bevo won plaudits, Oliver was panned mercilessly for his lack of coaching acumen and inflexible offensive strategy during the game. "I know what they said about me," he said years later. "But I won ninety percent of my games. None of those other coaches can say that. Let me say this. Maybe he was saying then that Bevo would have averaged 75 [points] a game. I haven't ever noticed any of their [other coaches'] players scoring those totals. The object of the game is to get the ball in the hoop and win. They said he had one shot. Well, Babe Ruth only had one swing. And Bevo was pure poetry. Sure, they were knocking us. We were the idols of America—and we'd done it in three months. I saw people here and around the country hammering us— hell, they couldn't get to the Garden in twenty years."

Meanwhile, the mood on Adelphi's Long Island campus was Mardi Gras, Christmas, and New Year's rolled into one. A special edition of the school paper featured articles on the contest and several unflattering cartoons of Francis while extolling the virtues of Faherty's gladiators. The marching band paraded impromptu through the hallways, playing the victory march at earsplitting decibels and disrupting classes. After several failed attempts to restore order, the dean of students prevailed and classes resumed. Its day in the sun savored, Adelphi College retreated into the long winter shadows of frosty Long Island.

⊕ ⊕ ⊕

While the Panther faithful partied, Rio Grande made a long, glum trip down the highway to Philadelphia, the next stop on the eastern swing that Oliver had fashioned to showcase his team. That evening, December 4, the Redmen were scheduled to take on the Wildcats of Villanova University in the Philadelphia Arena.

The Alex Severance-coached Wildcats were a huge step up in class from the Panthers of Adelphi. A perennial powerhouse, Villanova played a first-class major-college schedule that included Princeton, Louisville, Dayton, Duquesne, North Carolina State, Seton Hall, and Houston, as well as an appearance in the Kentucky Invitational. The Wildcats were coming off a 22-9 season and had debuted with a win against Mount St. Mary's that presaged what would turn out to be a 20-win campaign.

The promoter was Herb Goode of the Philadelphia Basketball Writers Association. He had secured the spacious Philadelphia Arena in expectation of a large crowd. If he was concerned that the derailment in New York would dampen the ticket buyers' enthusiasm for Francis and the Redmen, he shouldn't have been.

Both the *Philadelphia Inquirer* and the *Bulletin* had been running articles for two weeks heralding the arrival of the Redmen and Bevo. The Sunday supplement of the *Bulletin* carried a full-page article and picture of Francis. The headline asked, "HOW GOOD IS BEVO FRANCIS?" The subhead wanted to know, "Is basketball's most sensational scorer a genuine star or has he just been lucky against small-time opposition?" Ed Magill's lengthy article concluded with this observation: "This is the season that makes or breaks the legend."

The players were acutely aware of what their loss to Adelphi had done to their campaign for credibility and respect. As they checked in to the Penn-Sheraton Hotel on Chestnut Street, they were a silent and sullen group. There was none of the usual lighthearted banter and good-natured ribbing about being in the big city. Even Wiseman's usual pre-game teasing of the studious Benner, whom he had taken to calling "Stud" to embarrass the bookish manager, was missing. They filed quietly to their rooms to prepare mentally for their first "true test" against a major power, as one writer put it.

"We took the game at the request of Herb Goode," coach Severance explained. "It was to benefit [a worthy cause promoted by] the local writers, and we felt it would be a good idea to help them out. Of course, Bevo was a great draw, and we knew it would be a huge gate. I recall [that] we split the proceeds with the writers and Rio Grande, each getting one third. They used the arena because we couldn't hold more than thirty-five hundred here on campus. Bevo was getting an enormous amount of publicity at the time. He was . . . the forerunner of the great centers. The stories were that he was impossible to stop."

Severance, of course left nothing to chance: "We had them scouted. We got Charles 'Obey' O'Brien, a great coach at LaSalle High School here, to scout them for us at the Garden. He told me that if we could hold Bevo down, then he thought we could handle their supporting cast. But if we couldn't, then he was going to do us a great deal of damage. To stop him we were going to have to front him to keep him from getting the ball. We fronted him with Jack Devine, and then we sloughed off to collapse from the wings." Under Severance's game plan, Devine would have to handle the job of guarding Bevo, but he'd get plenty of support from the flanks.

At game time the arena, which had a capacity of about five thousand, was packed to overflowing. Fully seventy-five hundred fans, including Tom Gola, LaSalle College's All-American, were on hand to see the most publicized athlete of the day. "I was just as curious as the rest of them," the future NBA star recalled. "I wanted to see for myself what all the furor was about. I wasn't disappointed."

Fans spilled out into the aisles and filled the spaces around the wall. A large contingent of Korean War wounded was arrayed in wheelchairs and on stretchers behind the baskets up to the end lines. In many spots the feet of courtside spectators stretched out and over the sidelines.

In sports, at least, Philadelphia's nickname, the City of Brotherly Love, is a gross misnomer. Philly fans are notoriously brutal. In a town where local heroes are hissed at and even Santa Claus gets booed, fans are not timid about voicing their opinions. They were there en masse that night to see the fabled Francis. They would not be shy in delivering their verdict.

As the contest began, it was a different Rio Grande team than the one that had stumbled off the floor in shock the night before. The change in their body language was perceptible. They looked and played like the Rio Grande Redmen who had swept to forty wins in a row. Confident and quick, they executed to perfection with a devil-may-care attitude. They were back in stride.

"We all knew going down there what we had to do," Ripperger said. "No one had to tell us. We knew we couldn't fail again."

"I made one of the shortest pre-game speeches I ever made," Oliver recalled. Perhaps sensing his players' gritty resolve, he said simply, "You know what you have to do. Let's do it."

Wiseman led the familiar fast-breaking offense with crisp passing and adept ball handling. Their tried-and-true outside arsenal of fire-power, which had deserted them at the Garden, was back. McKenzie was transformed. He was as hot as he had been cold in Gotham. Francis, again up against the same kind of suffocating defensive crowd he'd faced in New York, was held in check in the early going. Jack Devine, aided by John Cirino, Tom Foley, and occasionally yet another floating teammate, shadowed Bevo's every move.

"I had gone down to the Garden to see them the night before," Devine said. "After seeing them [lose], we weren't that impressed. As a result, we probably took the game lightly." Bevo soon earned Devine's respect. "He was an excellent shooter from anywhere," the Villanova center recalled. "His range went out to the dead corners. He was dangerous out to twenty-five to twenty-eight feet. He was and is the best corner shooter I ever saw."

Rio Grande jumped out to a 27-17 first-quarter lead. Francis managed but seven points. As the Redmen huddled on the sidelines with Oliver, it was clear that the New York game had been a fluke. Their confidence brimming, the Redmen charged back out for the second stanza.

They built the lead steadily to 32-19. But this wasn't Bliss Business College. The well-schooled Wildcats didn't panic. They fought back gamely. The Rio Grande margin evaporated as Villanova, led by Bob Schafer, chipped away persistently. McKenzie kept Rio Grande alive as he hit from long range with his two-handed set shots. "I was in the zone," he said, referring to the elusive comfort level that athletes seek, when everything is effortless and they literally cannot miss. Jim went five for six from outside to keep the Redmen in the game. Francis, still shackled by Severance's defensive scheme, was held to just four points in the period and ended the half with eleven. Villanova took a one-point lead, 44–43, to the dressing room.

Severance was surprised that Rio Grande was fielding such a strong supporting cast. "They had some pretty heady ball players," he said. "They were far more talented than I'd been led to believe they would be. You had to respect their other players."

In the Rio Grande dressing room the Redmen's gloomy mood had lifted. "We were animated and determined that we wouldn't allow what had happened in New York to happen again," Ripperger said. They'd seen a seventeen-point lead evaporate in the Adelphi game, and on this night they'd failed so far to hold their lead against the Wildcats. But they were determined that history would not repeat itself.

With Wiseman and Ripperger leading the way, they charged back out onto the court amid wild applause, certain that they weren't going to let it happen again. They'd fought too hard, come too far, to see it all come crashing down around them. They were confident they would prevail.

Although Villanova was the hometown team, the opening moments of the third period saw the huge crowd begin, spontaneously and raggedly at first, to chant "Let's go Bevo," gradually blending their voices in unison and repeating their urging from the rafters down to courtside. With the chanting, sing-song chorus washing over them, the Redmen were invigorated and refused to fold. They fought back, regaining the lead. "It was a see-saw battle from then on. Neither side could gain an advantage," Severance recalled.

The battle was a classic. Momentum flowed and ebbed as the two squads traded basket for basket through the third quarter. The stanza ended with Villanova again clinging to its tenuous one-point lead, 61-60.

Perhaps encouraged by the chanting crowd, or perhaps benefiting from the fatigue of his opposition, Bevo finally got on track in the third period. He managed to shake free long enough to make several critical baskets. Ripperger also found his range and picked up where McKenzie had left off, nailing several rainbows from the perimeter. Wiseman was clearly back in control. After seeing so many of his passes swatted harmlessly away the night before, now he refused to force the issue. He waited patiently for small seams to develop in the Villanova defense then fired his sharp crisp passes to Bevo. Barr was a tiger on the boards, battling courageously for rebounds against the taller Wildcat players.

The Rio Grande effort was, as Severance had figured out, far from a one-man show. And as the Redmen fought Villanova point for point and basket for basket, their crowd support swelled. The din in the arena was tremendous. Sportswriters seated elbow to elbow in the press section could not hear each other over the deafening tumult.

As the Redmen began play in the final quarter, the crowd was on its feet cheering. With the outcome clearly in the balance, Francis responded to the challenge. He shook loose again and again, moving far outside the key to launch his deft trademark jump shots. When the defenders forced him to the corners, he launched them from there.

The lead changed hands seventeen times as the battle raged amid the ear-splitting noise. The tides of fortune shifted with the possession of the ball as both teams fought toward the final seconds of play.

"[Bob] Schafer had a great game. He was all over and we just couldn't contain him," Wiseman remembered. "When we switched off and Ripperger picked him up, he still ate us up. He was quick and he was good."

Less than a minute remained, and Villanova held a two-point lead and the ball. Relentless full-court pressure from Wiseman and Ripperger forced a Villanova turnover in the Wildcats' end. Rio Grande still had a chance. With twelve ticks remaining on the clock, Wiseman rocketed a pass through the Villanova screen around Bevo on the far left side of the court. Grabbing the high pass, Bevo turned in one fluid motion and launched an eighteen-footer. Swish. The score was knotted at 81.

The explosion of sound that erupted from the crowd shook the old arena with its intensity. A final desperate Villanova shot failed as time expired. They'd go to overtime.

Nearly all seventy-five hundred fans were on their feet, hoarse, emotionally spent, and cheering, as the two teams came on the court for the overtime period, their adrenaline flowing. Rio Grande, of course, needed the victory to silence the critics. For the Wildcats, losing to tiny Rio Grande, and at home no less, would be an embarrassment that they didn't want to contemplate. Both teams had played forty minutes of the most exciting basketball in memory. The Cinderella team from the hills had fought the big-city giants to a standoff. Now in overtime they'd have to do it again. Surely, the fans and writers thought, this would be a storybook ending.

Overtime was but more of the same. With the score tied at 83, Francis hit a jumper to put Rio Grande on top. Villanova quickly countered with yet another Schafer bucket, before Bevo came back to make it Rio Grande by two. The pace of play was torrid as the two squads, running on fumes, battled to break away. With only thirty-five seconds left, Rio Grande was trailing by two. Bevo went to the foul line for two shots that could tie it. He hit the first, but the second bounced away, and Villanova clung to a 1-point advantage, 91-90.

As the clock ticked relentlessly, Rio Grande stopped it with a foul. Villanova, however, failed to score. Ripperger yanked down the rebound and sped up court, drawing a foul as he was about to break clear. He would have two opportunities as he stepped to the line. Less than ten seconds remained.

Ignoring the wall of sound, Ripperger calmly took deliberate aim and fired. The ball dove home. The game was tied at 91. The crowd exploded yet again. "It was a madhouse—you couldn't hear anything above the crowd noise," Wiseman recalled. Ripperger stepped back from the foul line and took several deep breaths before attempting the shot that would give the Redmen the lead and perhaps the game. Retrieving the ball from the official stationed beneath the basket, Referee Jocko Collins, whistle clamped hard between his teeth, gave Ripperger the ball.

"I took my normal position off to the left of the foul shooter, about ten feet back," Collins said.

"As the ref moved away from me and to the left, I looked back over my shoulder to see that we had a man back there to protect our basket against a hanger," Ripperger remembered. "I saw McKenzie behind me, about midway back towards the center court line. I didn't see anyone else."

Trained since grade school to always determine that no threat was behind him to receive a long uncontested pass, Ripperger was satisfied that all was well as he stepped up to the line. "There was no one back there. I'm certain of it," he said.

"I had fouled out earlier trying to hold down Schafer and was on the bench," Wiseman explained. "After the first shot went in, I saw they had a player back there. He was crouched down behind the referee and almost up against the crowd on the sideline. I started to yell at Jim to get back and to point behind him. It was no use. In all that noise and confusion, he couldn't hear me."

"I was back behind Ripperger where I could guard our basket," McKenzie said. "There was no one behind me. I'm certain of it. I didn't see anyone back there."

"The reason he didn't see anything—and I remember this vividly," Severance said, "is because Marty Milligan was hiding behind the official. He was right directly behind him. That's why [Rip] didn't see anyone."

Devine recalled that after Ripperger sank his first free throw, "Marty

Milligan came up to me in the lane and said, 'If he makes it, get the ball and throw it down court. I'll be there.' I looked at Marty and thought, 'Sure.' From where I was in the foul lane, you could not see Marty at all. He was completely hidden behind the referee."

In the excitement of seeing Ripperger make the first shot to tie the game, McKenzie edged toward the foul line, yelling encouragement to Ripperger for the second shot. As the second shot from Ripperger went up and in, the crowd went berserk. Rio Grande had the lead with less than five seconds to play.

The crowd was screaming. The Rio Grande players on court were celebrating. No one saw Milligan.

Devine continued: "I grabbed the ball as it fell from the net and jumped out of bounds as quickly as I could. I looked up court and saw Marty streaking out from behind the referee. I threw a pass that hit him in full stride at the foul line as he angled towards the basket."

Said Milligan, "I darted out from behind the referee as soon as the ball went in. I took the pass and deposited it in the goal for the winning basket." It was a cheap high-school trick, but it worked.

The scoreboard flashed Villanova 93, Rio Grande 92. The crowd was shocked into a deflated hush.

The Redmen stood uncertainly on the court in shocked confusion, almost unable to comprehend what had just happened. Time and again they had fought back against mighty Villanova, and now, with the victory they thought they'd earned only moments earlier snatched cruelly from them, their hearts sank in despair. The emotional roller coaster had taken them from the heights of triumph to the valley of despair in nanoseconds.

With a much relieved and elated Villanova team celebrating around them, the Redmen started slowly, haltingly to leave the floor, unwilling or unable to accept the finality of the moment. Perhaps, they thought, they were never meant to wear the glass slipper after all. Maybe their critics were right. Maybe they were destined to remain a pumpkin in a patch back in the hill country.

As they stumbled off the court, the Philly fans, the toughest crowd in the country, gave them a standing ovation. But it did little to salve the wound. "That was one of the times when I felt Newt was simply outcoached," Barr said. "That should never have happened."

"You talk about falling down a hole and coming up with a diamond ring, that's what we did that night," Severance acknowledged. "We stole that game from them. Francis was a great player in his own right. He proved that. He was the Mikan of his time. He would have been a great player at any time. Remember, they were playing a dynamite schedule, and this kid had to go into the lion's den on the road every time they played. In those days, the minute you stepped onto foreign soil you were ten points back, travel weary, and I hate to say this, but sometimes the officials can be intimidated by thousands of screaming fans. With all those factors, week after week on the road, he played—and I think he did a great job. I heard the criticism against him, but I never bought it. Put Rupp, Claire Bee and Everett Case in the position of having to play all their games on the road and see how well they'd do."

As for the "Bevo Rule," Severance said, "I think it was a little unfair in that it discriminated against him personally. He had gone out and demonstrated his ability time and again. It wasn't just a one-shot deal." After the devastating college basketball scandal, "Bevo brought back some dignity to the sport," Severance said. "He took the sting out of it. He restored it to its place, the way Ruth and Gehrig had done for baseball after the White Sox scandal. He had a unique ability to stimulate the crowds. He mesmerized the country."

There wasn't a dry eye in the Rio Grande dressing room. It was one thing to blow a game with a school like Adelphi, but to have a cherished, hard-fought victory snatched from their grasp by a schoolyard trick was more than the proud players could bear. Behind closed doors they wept openly and unashamedly.

Ironically, the bitter loss earned Rio Grande the respect of the sportswriters. In the United Press account of the game, Fred Down of the New York bureau wrote, "Bevo Francis and his Rio Grande teammates emerged from their second straight defeat today with a respect they failed to achieve with 40 consecutive victories over setups. The myth of invincibility was gone but it was replaced in the wake of a 93-92 overtime loss to Villanova by the firm conviction that Bevo and Rio Grande are capable of competing against 'big League opposition.'"

Herb Goode, the writer for the *Philadelphia Inquirer* who had promoted the game, agreed: "Lanky Clarence (Bevo) Francis and tiny Rio Grande College, Ohio, proved to the satisfaction of one and all last night that they could hold their own in big-time basketball competition. Villanova University (enrollment 2,300) found that out as it was extended to the limit by the scrappy visitors before eking out a 93-92 overtime decision at the Arena."

In the *Bulletin* Bob Vetrone concluded, "Bevo Francis is far from the greatest—but he'll do. Anyone who can score 39 points against Villanova and generate crowd excitement the way Bevo and his mates did last night must be all right. Even in the aftermath of a 93-92 victory, in what must rate as the most thrilling basketball show put on here in years, the people who squeezed into the Arena are still talking about Bevo and Rio Grande."

Recounting the many highlights and the "sleeper play" that "quelled whatever hopes Rio Grande had of knocking off the Cats and proving their record of last year was no fluke," Vetrone termed Bevo "amazing." He added, "It is difficult to explain the way Bevo took over the packed house, but all during the game there was almost a constant chant: 'Let's go Bevo,' and this from the supposedly tough Philly fans.

"Bevo and Co. didn't disappoint.

"The Redmen were beaten—but far from disgraced."

Vetrone went on to quote Devine and Schafer. Devine asked, "If he's not an All-American, who is?" And Schafer, who had contributed 25 points to the Wildcat victory, asked rhetorically, "He's something, isn't he?"

The three-game eastern swing continued the following night against Providence College in the Boston Garden. It would be the Redmen's final chance to redeem themselves after two heartbreaking losses. The Providence game was part of a tripleheader that featured Bob Cousy and the Boston Celtics versus the Milwaukee Hawks, and Boston College against St. Anselm's. Rio Grande's game against Providence was sandwiched between the two local attractions.

The Beantown appearance by Bevo on December 5 was heralded by extensive press coverage, including a full-page cartoon by Phil Bissell in the *Boston Globe* that depicted Francis and recounted his exploits.

The Friars of Providence College, coached by Vincent "Vinny" Cuddy, were on the threshold of a program that would take them to national prominence. The Boston Garden date would be their first step toward that goal. "Normally, we played our home games in a high school gym that held about fifteen hundred fans. But we seldom attracted more than four hundred," Cuddy recalled.

Tonight's contest would be played before a crowd of 12,018, drawn by the magical magnet of Bevo's name. Not even the hometown Celtics, in this the fifth season of NBA play, could ever hope to attract such a large crowd. Undoubtedly, as Cuddy observed, "They came to see Bevo."

For Rio Grande the game had become crucial, the players' lone remaining opportunity to salvage what, to their thinking, had been a disastrous eastern showcase. Although Bevo had scored 71 points in two nights, the team had absorbed two straight losses. Now, for the third time in as many evenings, they would try for an elusive victory.

After play began, they snapped quickly out of their post-Villanova funk. "I just remember thinking to myself, 'Wow, this is where Bob Cousy plays,'" Ripperger said.

Providence, led by its captain, Bob Moran, was equal to the task of maintaining contact with the Redmen. The two teams exchanged buckets and the lead throughout the first period, which concluded with Rio Grande on top, 20-18. The tempo picked up in the second quarter as Rio Grande, led by Bevo, poured in 23 points. Providence, however, was even hotter, accounting for twenty-nine. As the teams trotted off at the half, Rio Grande trailed, 47-43.

In the locker room between the halves, Oliver said little. The players, adrenaline pumping now with the pace of the battle, knew what they needed to do. Their mood and attitude had taken a dramatic turn. The sullen blackness that had enveloped them before the game slowly released its grip. Each offered the other encouragement. With backslapping, hand-clapping enthusiasm they charged out, energized for the final half.

"We were behind, but we still felt like we were in the game," McKenzie said.

"I wasn't too concerned," Barr said. "Everything seemed to be going well."

At one point early in the third quarter, it appeared that their confidence was misplaced as they fell behind, 58-50. Francis and Wiseman led the charge back from that point, and the Redmen clung to a slim 67-65 lead as the period ended.

The final ten minutes were a repeat of the first thirty as the two teams fought evenly to the wire. Providence regained the lead at 83-82, with eight unanswered points. McKenzie, who had enjoyed a great game against Villanova, came through with two quick baskets to put the Redmen back on top, 86-83.

With little time remaining, Bevo scored on two free throws, followed by a Providence basket, to make it 88-85. After Rio Grande converted still another free throw, a final Providence basket closed the gap to two points, but Wiseman, even under intense pressure, was able to maintain control of the ball. With five seconds remaining, he fired a pass to Bevo high in the pivot. The lanky center turned and launched a hook shot that went up and around the rim—and spun back out as the buzzer sounded. When the clock stopped, the score stood at 89-87. Rio Grande had won.

The crowd, which had been kept apprised of Bevo's scoring progress by the announcer all evening, let out a collective moan as his final shot failed to drop. They knew if it had, it would have established a Boston Garden record. As it was, Bevo had tied the old mark with his 41-point performance. He had scored on thirteen field goals and had sunk fifteen of eighteen attempts from the line.

For Friars' coach Vinny Cuddy the game was a real eye-opener. "I've been in basketball all my life, and I can tell you that Francis was a hell of a player. He had a great jump shot. He played like an earlier version of the present great NBA forwards," said Cuddy. "I'd compare him to the great Joe Faulks [who is generally conceded to have been the first great player to use the jump shot] of that era, who played for years with the NBA Warriors. Bevo had a great, soft touch with the basketball that I've seldom seen in anyone else."

As many others would, Cuddy also said "that Rio Grande team was no PR mirage. They were a real good team. It wasn't all Bevo, either. They had a kid, Wayne Wiseman, who was a hell of a guard. They may not have been a powerhouse like Rupp assembled at Kentucky, but they were far from the joke that many in the press made them out to be." That profound praise from the highly regarded Providence coach was echoed by others.

In the crowd was Bob Cousy, who saw the game with his Celtics teammates. They were every bit as curious as everyone else about the highly touted Francis. The normally blasé Cousy found himself "clapping my hands and whooping like a cheerleader," as Francis led his team to victory. "What a beautiful touch that fellow has," Cousy exclaimed to the *Boston Globe*.

The other Celtics agreed and were as much impressed with Bevo's speed as his shooting ability, the *Globe* reported. Coach Red Auerbach's appraisal was that "Francis would definitely make it as a pro." Fuzzy Levane, the Hawks' coach, agreed, telling the paper: "Bevo can put the ball in the basket. And you can't tell how much better he'll be in two years from now when he's eligible for the pro circuit." According to the paper, the NBA's finest free-throw artist, Bill Sharman, was another admirer. "I like the way [Bevo] handles himself physically," he said. "Smooth and fast."

After the game ended, Francis was mobbed by the usual crowd of autograph seekers and well-wishers that followed him everywhere he played.

That night Wiseman, ordinarily ignored along with the other Redmen, became an object of attention as well. Cousy had intercepted Wiseman as he left the court, offering his hand in congratulations. The NBA's premier point guard then offered Wiseman a position at his summer basketball camp. Wiseman nodded his head self-consciously as the game's pro performer nonpareil praised Wiseman's ball-handling skills in his clipped Boston accent, which was hard for Wiseman to decipher. With a final pat on the shoulder, Cousy departed. Wiseman, proud keeper of the Waterloo Wonders' flame, floated dreamily across the Garden's famous parquet floor toward the locker room. Winning sure was wonderful. "I couldn't believe it. It was the biggest thrill I ever had," he said. "I'll never forget it."

The Redmen had finally notched a win in the East and prepared to head back to Rio Grande, their heads held high. They had battled vaunted Villanova to the wire and defeated Providence. Not too bad, they thought, for a bunch of hill country farmers denigrated by the eastern press after the Adelphi debacle.

The return flight was uneventful, although Carl Benner anxiously clutched his receipt for his flight insurance policy. A small contingent of students was waiting to greet them as they arrived at Charleston's Kanawha Airport, perched high atop a mountain shaved flat to allow for a landing strip.

A spattering of applause greeted them as they deplaned. Among the welcoming committee was President Davis. Making his way through a group of squealing coeds, he approached Oliver. "How did you do back East?" he asked.

"I knew immediately he wasn't asking about wins and losses," Oliver said.

"Oh, we did pretty good, I think," Oliver replied. "We brought back about $10,000."

"Good," sighed an obviously relieved Davis, "now we can pay the faculty on Monday."

"Glad we could help," said Oliver, his voice as icy as the temperature on the windswept landing strip.

Both *Newsweek* and *Time* chronicled the eastern trip for their readers in their next issue. *Newsweek*, which had run a tongue-in-cheek article by John Lardner in its November 23 edition, followed with an account of the trip entitled "In from the Country." The tone of the stories in both newsweeklies remained somewhat skeptical, cautioning readers to wait and see what Francis' true ability would prove to be.

12

Fun in the Sun

E ven with the team on the road, reporters had not abandoned their stakeout of the Francis home in Rio Grande. One enter-prising photographer, finding himself on the desolate winter campus with no Bevo nor Newt Oliver around, invented his own story. After he found Bevo's wife Jean at home with their son, young Frank Jeffrey, the photographer managed to persuade the reluctant young wife and mother to don a police officer's cap and jacket and to strike a pose alongside her infant. The resulting photo, depicting a pretty young mother in a constable's uniform, complete with a holstered pistol and wielding a billy club, ran in papers everywhere. The caption read, "Pistol Packin' Momma." Though smiling at the insistent photographer's urging, Jean was cringing inside in embarrassment.

The team returned to the court against Bluffton College in Bluffton, Ohio, on December 11. Kenny Mast, the Bluffton coach, had been buoyed by the Redmen's less-than-spectacular start. "I felt pretty confident of our chances after reading about the Adelphi game," he recalled. Mast, however, had failed to factor in the level of competition that Rio Grande had faced since that game. Minutes into the game, "I realized we were in a lot of trouble."

The game was played in Founders Hall, which had been open only about a year and had a legal capacity of two thousand. According to Paul Jackson, then a starting guard for Bluffton and now assistant director of administrative computing at the college, the actual crowd was estimated at closer to three thousand and remains the largest crowd ever to assemble in that building. "The place was mobbed. The court was no longer squared off at the corners. It resembled an oval with people crowded into every available space," he recalled. "They

152

erected portable bleachers on the stage, and when they filled up, the people stood in front of the stage behind the basket. There was no out-of-bounds area left. There were people everywhere you looked."

The Redmen, playing for the first time in Ohio, albeit still on the road—"We were orphans," Oliver would say of the team—found the homecoming to their liking as they trounced Mast's Bluffton squad 116-71. Bevo returned to the form of the previous season, hitting on sixty-three percent of his shots from the floor.

"Nothing we did could stop him," Mast declared. "He was the best player I ever saw. He had a great jump shot. And he had a great ball club along with him. They knew where their bread was buttered and they acted accordingly," a reference to Rio Grande's tendency to feed Bevo. "After it was finally over, I thought I'd just seen the greatest player then alive—college or pro." The performance that had so impressed Mast saw Bevo tally 82 points from 36 baskets and 10 free throws in 40 minutes of action.

Jackson, at six-foot-two, was assigned the unenviable task of trying to guard Bevo Francis:' He was at least seven inches taller than me, and I had no chance of containing him. He was a great shooter and a genuinely nice guy. I tell everyone my claim to fame is that I blocked one of his jump shots. I don't tell as many people that I 'held' him to 82 points. Bevo was the best shooter I ever faced, but he also had some great players with him."

Because Bluffton College met the newly established NCAA criteria of a four-year degree-granting institution, the organization would have no choice but to list Bevo's 82 points as the new individual scoring record for a single game. Cruelly erased from the NCAA record books a year earlier, now he reentered it by meeting the criteria that the NCAA had used to obliterate his earlier achievements. There could be no arguments this time. Swallowing hard, the NCAA duly acknowledged his record.

"That was one of those nights when he just couldn't miss," Carl Benner recalled.

The Redmen traveled to neighboring Michigan the following night to meet Hillsdale College. The game would mark their final tune-up before their next important road trip, this time into the South. Florida and North Carolina fans were waiting for Rio Grande.

Against Hillsdale, though, the Redmen would waltz to an easy 82-45 win, with Francis accounting for 43 points. The drawing power of the team was as great as ever: More than five thousand people had watched them play in the two games that weekend.

⊛ ⊛ ⊛

While the rest of the Rio Grande student body was dispersing for the Christmas break, the Redmen were thinking only of basketball. The three-game southern trip that Oliver had arranged would take them from their frigid, wind-whipped Appalachian campus to warm and sunny Miami Beach, then on to Raleigh, North Carolina.

Before they left in mid-December, the players learned that they would be without the full-time services of forward Roy Moses. Roy had lost much of his hard-driving spunk and had been largely ineffectual in limited playing time that season. "Poor Roy had just worn himself right out," Wiseman remarked. The player they all called "Bull" had indeed. "I was diagnosed with anemia," Moses explained. "I was really weak. My blood count was way down, and the doctor said I needed to get some rest."

With the travel schedule that Oliver had put together, that was the one thing Roy wouldn't get. As the team made its way south, he knew he'd be playing only as a substitute and then only in short bursts.

The loss of Moses wasn't as severe a blow as it might have been. Oliver had taken the precaution of beefing up his bench during the off-season. He'd landed a former All-State performer, LeRoy Thompson of Canton. Thompson, who'd been Class B Player of the Year and a three-time All-Ohio selection, had had neither the inclination nor the money to attend college.

"My dad worked in the brick yards and he believed college and playing basketball was just a waste of time," Thompson said. "He thought I should just get a job and start making a living. In all the time I played basketball, he never did see me play." And Thompson really could play.

"A group of us from the neighborhood began playing ball together as youngsters and we continued through elementary school and junior high. We always played unless it was raining or snowing and we got to know each other so well that our moves were effortless. We were beating the high school players when we were only in seventh grade. They didn't like it much and would try to beat us up but we usually outran them too," he recalled.

When he did get to high school, Thompson and that same group of neighborhood kids would lead Waynesburg to the State Tournament Finals as a sophomore and junior. Both years they were beaten by a single point in the championship, and as seniors lost in the Regional Finals. In all, that tight knit group of kids from a school of less than

300 lost only five games in four seasons together.

"We were good and everyone knew about us. Oliver had come up to see us play several times when he was at Wellsville and he knew about me from that," Thompson remembered. Oliver had learned, quite by chance, that Thompson was still available, and he leaped at the opportunity to land the former star. "It took a lot of persuasion to convince him to come on down and join us," Oliver recalled.

"Oliver talked me into coming down there," Thompson related. "He told me and my parents about the big-time schedule and the cities I would get to see all over the country. I knew about Bevo and so I thought the whole thing sounded like a good opportunity. Even though my dad thought it was just a waste of time I decided to go on down there and give it a try."

Upon his arrival Thompson immediately thought he had made a huge mistake.

"There just wasn't anything there. I was so disappointed with the place I was really down in the dumps and ready to go back home and get a job. But Bevo and Barr and the others talked me out of leaving. They told me we'd be playing games soon and traveling and that everything would be all right then. They took me over to Bob Evans' place in Gallipolis and we talked some more there and I decided to give it a chance. Once I got into the gym and saw Bevo hitting those jumpers and the other guys around him I felt a lot better. I never thought about leaving again after that."

Oliver arranged to have Thompson enrolled, and the swift and agile player quickly became a valued sixth man off the bench. His fine shooting and rebounding skills were a welcome addition. But Thompson presented one other problem. Rio Grande would be playing in the deep south, and Thompson was black.

John Halliday, the attorney assigned by the Athletic Council to accompany the team and receive the gate receipts, urged Oliver to leave Thompson at home. "I warned Newt there might be trouble if we took him along with us," Halliday said. "I knew we would face trouble finding him a place to stay there." Oliver, to his credit, steadfastly refused Halliday's counsel. "He goes or we all stay home," Newt told him.

But they were making their swing through the south less than five months before the U.S. Supreme Court decision to desegregate schools in *Brown v. Board of Education*. Halliday's fears were not without justification. Nevertheless, Newt, facing a tough trip and already short-handed with the loss of Moses, stuck to his guns. He needed Thompson and he would make the trip, come what may.

Before leaving, the team was feted at the annual Christmas banquet held at the school. With the warm wishes of other students ringing in their ears, the Redmen flew south to Miami and its sunshine. The frozen Ohio hills were soon a distant memory far below the silver wings of their plane.

⊕ ⊕ ⊕

The Redmen were greeted on the tarmac in Miami by a gleaming fleet of brand new Chevrolet convertibles shimmering in the bright afternoon sun. They'd been provided by Don Allen, who made his winter home on Millionaire's Row in Miami Beach. Led by Oliver and Francis, who perched atop the rear seat of the lead car, the team made its way to its downtown hotel behind a police escort, sirens wailing and lights flashing.

Wiseman, gazing up into an azure sky with a dazzling sun that warmed his face, smiled. Turning to Ripperger, he drawled, "Rip, this is about as good as it can get."

"Only a season ago we had spent one night on cots in a basement of some college in West Virginia with no heat or blankets. We had practically frozen to death, and now this. It was hard to believe it was all true," Ripperger recalled.

In Miami Beach the team was driven to city hall, where the mayor and police chief greeted the players on the front steps. All were made honorary members of the Miami Beach Police Department, while photographers snapped photos. The ceremonies concluded, the procession proceeded through the streets of startled snowbirds to a beachfront hotel.

As quickly as they could, the boys threw off their winter clothes, donned swim trunks, and headed out to the beach. They spent the rest of the day frolicking in the surf and ogling tanned young women. Thompson kept a much lower profile, of course, staying behind when the Redmen went out to a nightclub later that night, Wiseman recalled. The Venetian Hotel management had told Halliday that Thompson would not be allowed to take his meals in the dining room and attempted to have him eat in the kitchen. Oliver and the team found out and told Halliday to tell the management that Thompson was going to eat with them even if it meant they would all be eating in the kitchen. Management grudgingly relented and placed the team in the rear, out of the traffic pattern—but Thompson ate with the team.

"I had never experienced segregation before and it was all new to me," Thompson said. "But the team stood by me and that made it easier. With them sticking with me I managed to get through it all."

He did follow Halliday's advice to avoid the beach and avert any incidents that his appearance might create.

Nor could Bevo hit the sand. Sweltering in his winter-weight blazer and tie, he was tugged along by Oliver to interview after interview designed to stir interest in the game.

Ordinarily, the University of Miami's team had a difficult time attracting spectators. With horse and dog tracks, jai lai, and numerous hotel floor shows vying for the tourist dollar, competition for sports fans in the area was intense. Invariably, the Hurricanes came out last in terms of spectators. This game, however, would be an exception.

"We booked Rio Grande to try to get the Miami area interested in college basketball," coach Dave Wike related. "This game was the beginning of our effort, and it was held at the Miami Beach Auditorium, where basketball flourished from then on through the Rick Barry years. We had a portable floor constructed for five thousand dollars. The seating capacity was enlarged to hold just short of three thousand fans." As game time neared, it became evident that even that number was too few. Additional seating was hastily installed.

On December 18, the evening before the game, a proud Don Allen hosted a lavish party at his mansion for the large press contingent and his many area friends. Caviar and champagne provided by the Redmen's financial patriarch flowed freely amid twinkling lanterns and the tropical setting. Bevo recalled that "we were all supposed to go to the party, but only Newt went."

Earlier, Allen had feted the local politicians and dignitaries at the hotel with the team present. That was when they had learned that he'd provided the Chevrolets at the airport. And, more important, that they'd have the use of the new cars for the few days that they were in town. "It was hard to believe, but true—the hill country hicks from Rio Grande were riding in style," Benner said, laughing at the memory.

While the revelry was underway at Don Allen's opulent estate, Bevo Francis was doubled up in pain in his hotel room. Wiseman found him there, next to the extra long bed that Oliver had installed for him. Wiseman quickly summoned Oliver. When he arrived, Bevo lay ashen faced as nauseating waves of pain knifed through his abdomen.

"I got us a cab and assisted him downstairs and into the car," the coach recalled. Bevo slumped there, clutching his stomach, head facing the window as they sped to the nearest hospital. The emergency room was alerted that the star player was on his way. "When we got there, I was still in terrible pain," Bevo recalled. "The doctors examined me there in the emergency room." What they found was not good. "They said he had appendicitis," Oliver related. "They wanted to operate."

"I didn't want any part of that," Bevo said, "no matter how much it hurt." No doubt, he was recalling the death of his mother during "routine" gall bladder surgery.

"Operate? You have to be out of your minds," Oliver yelled. "Why, we've got a game to play here in less than twenty-four hours. He's my star."

"The doctors warned us [my appendix] might burst," Bevo remembered. But Bevo was emphatic in his refusal to even consider a surgical procedure, so they accepted a prescription for painkillers from the startled physicians and left. "I spent the whole night just lying there in pain and the next day too," Bevo remembered. "When it was time to leave for the game, I finally got up. I was as pale as the sheet on the bed. I was weaving all over the room. And that's the way I played the game."

Swallowing the last of the prescription medicine, he left with the team for the game. Although the ordeal had drained and weakened him, he began to feel better as game time neared. He was determined to play.

The largest crowd in the history of University of Miami basketball jammed the spanking-new Convention Hall for a glimpse of the Redmen and their celebrated center. Outside, scalpers were offering tickets for an astounding twenty-five dollars a piece. Fully 3,521 paid admission, lured, no doubt, by the *Miami Herald* story that morning that revealed that Francis was leading the nation in scoring with a forty-seven-point average.

Dave Wike, the Miami coach, was no Blackburn, Faherty, or Cuddy. In fact, he was not even supposed to be the basketball coach. "I was pressed into duty to serve as the coach by the athletic director when the basketball coach had a heart attack and never considered myself a coach," Wike said. "In preparation, I did have the usual scouting reports and prepared the defense to play man-to-man when the court was out of balance to one side to try to force the imbalance to the left of Bevo. This would turn their off-side shooter loose, but we decided we'd rather take a chance with him [McKenzie] than with Bevo. Of course, he got hot and hit when it counted. I put our six-foot-seven Doug Howell on Bevo and instructed him not to overplay him on either side. The tactics worked fine for the first half."

Howell recalled that "I was supposed to take Francis on and try to foul him out if I could." Howell had taken a circuitous route to Miami.

"I had originally gone to Kentucky to play for Rupp and then the scandals hit," Howell said. "Rupp sent us off to a junior college to ride out the suspension time, and Harold Arterburn and I were there when we decided to go to Miami."

As play began, Francis was still below par physically. After only a few minutes he motioned to Oliver to take him out. Oliver sent Thompson onto the floor as Francis slumped on the bench in discomfort. On the court Thompson was going through his own battle. "We had never played against a black player," Howell said. "I was surprised to see him come out there."

The officials, all of whom were from the deep south, ignored the elbows and knees thrown at Thompson on the court. "He was absorbing a terrible beating," Ripperger said.

During their stay in Miami, Thompson had been ferried back and forth to his room in the freight elevator at the rear of the building, out of sight of the all-white patrons. Hotel management had insisted on it. Understandably, his stay had been an uncomfortable one. Now he was being manhandled on the court as well. Oliver screamed at the officials for some relief from the pounding.

"I was used to being tested by others and found that if you held your own they gave up pretty quick and went back to playing," Thompson, who never voiced a complaint, said.

On the bench Bevo saw immediately what was happening to his teammate. "I pulled myself back together and told Newt to put me back in." Thompson, battered and bloodied but unbowed, came out.

Miami had opened its season with a ten-point win over the University of Florida and was a strong, competitive team. In addition to the bulky Howell, the Hurricanes had two fine guards in Arterburn and Dick Miani. Willie Shayowitz, at six-foot-three, and Bob Klima, six-foot-four, were both skilled forwards with height.

McKenzie kept breaking free to foil Wike's plan to stop the Redmen. Rio Grande took a 28-17 lead at the end of the first period. McKenzie, Barr, and Ripperger continued their hot shooting in the second quarter, and the Redmen left the court at the intermission with a 45-38 lead. Bevo had managed just 16 points.

"They were a good, well-disciplined team," Howell said of the Redmen. "They had good-caliber players, which surprised us."

"Howell did a fine job in the first half on Francis," Wike said. "Unfortunately, it took its toll in fouls, and he fouled out early in the third period. I put Klima on him, but we couldn't hold him down."

The second half saw a different Francis as his strength returned, and his nemesis Howell was forced to the bench on fouls. Now Bevo came alive. Shaking off the effects of the illness, he put on the display that the crowd had come to see.

Sensing an opening with Howell's departure, Wiseman exploited the shorter Klima and fired pass after pass over him to the waiting Francis. In the second half of the game Francis burned the Convention Hall nets for 32 points. He finished with a new arena scoring record of forty-eight, as Rio Grande swept to a 98-88 win in front of a beaming Don Allen, among others. It was their fourth win in a row.

"What beat [Miami] was in the second half, we just ran them to death, as we did to most teams. They'd made some derogatory, smart-aleck remarks about us being country boys and such in the pre-game warm-ups, and we wanted to teach them a lesson," Ripperger said.

McKenzie, with 13 points, and Barr and Ripperger with twelve each, had kept Rio Grande in the game until Bevo turned on the fire-works in the second half. The first University of Miami sell-out crowd had gotten its money's worth. (In fact, well more than the thirty-five hundred ticket holders got to see that game. The disappointed hundreds who were turned away peered through the barred windows to see the fabled Francis.)

Wike, who contracted polio shortly afterward and left coaching, declared after the game, "That fellow is all they say he is."

The *Miami Herald's* Luther Evans told his readers the next day, "All Paderewski could do was play the piano, and maybe all the storied Bevo Francis can do is shoot—but Lawdy, how the big guy can hit the hoop." Writing in the *Miami Daily News*, Ralph Warner was now a believer as well: "Clarence 'Bevo' Francis, playing despite an attack of appendicitis, bolstered his bid for All-American by scoring 48 points as his team dumped the University of Miami Hurricanes 98-88 last night."

The team had a day off to rest and lie on the sunny Florida beach before heading north for a date with the Wolf Pack of North Carolina State University on December 22.

During the day Thompson had a visitor in his room. "Steve Bond from Ohio State (there for a game as well) came up to see me. He said, 'It's worse than you think, isn't it?' meaning the racism in the south. I don't think he had the same kind of support from his Buckeye team-mates that I had and he was having a tough time of it."

The extra day of rest and relaxation was especially beneficial for Bevo, although Oliver insisted that the still-ailing center pose for photographers while visiting the hotel gift shop and that he talk with the large press contingent traveling with the team.

The only loss that the team suffered in Miami was the disappearance of the red, white, and blue painted basketball that the Redmen used in their pre-game ball-handling and dribbling exhibition, which they had patterned after that performed by the Harlem Globetrotters. The display of ball-handling wizardry performed by the team in a loose circle around the key never failed to excite and entertain the crowds, while it seldom failed to infuriate the opposition, who felt it was an arrogant display designed to show them up.

The ball was stolen by a youngster who offered to help team manager Carl Benner with the bulky equipment bag. Benner, ever trusting, had fallen victim to a big-city ruse. "For days afterwards I was ribbed about 'the hidden ball trick,'" he said.

While the team enjoyed a hearty laugh at Benner's expense, what awaited the Redmen in Raleigh was no laughing matter. The Wolf Pack, coached by the legendary Everett Case, had won twenty-six games and lost only seven the year before. Ranked number seven in one poll and number eight in another, the North Carolina players were by far the most formidable opponents that the Redmen had met to date. Rio Grande's performance against North Carolina State would go far in determining just how good the Redmen really were.

Back in Gallipolis, Homer Alley asked the question directly in the *Gallia Times*. "How good is Rio Grande and scoring sensation Bevo Francis? This, the most perplexing question in sports today, will be answered Tuesday evening."

Alley gave his readers some perspective on the Redmen's problem:

"N.C. State is favored to win the Atlantic Coast Conference Championship, and has whipped the famed AAU Phillips Oilers—the first defeat of the team of former All-Americans since 1949. Rio Grande has picked quite a formidable opponent. If Rio Grande can give N.C. State a good game, they will have proved their ability with the best of the 'big league.' Should Rio Grande lose by 20 points or less, many fans will consider the Southeastern Ohio team as one of the nation's foremost."

But not even the usually optimistic Alley, the Redmen's strongest supporter, could bring himself to predict a Rio Grande victory. Alley concluded with this: "Tuesday's game could be the one—the big one—that decides if Rio stays in the big leagues or comes back to the bush."

Basking in the warm afterglow of the Miami Beach sun and their triumph over the Hurricanes, the Redmen arrived in Raleigh the day of the game, December 22, 1953. The game was to be played at fabled Reynolds Coliseum as part of a two-day holiday doubleheader that featured the Peoria Caterpillars of the National Industrial Basketball League (then considered to be on par with the NBA) against Wake Forest University. The following night, December 23, Rio Grande would face Wake Forest's Demon Deacons, and N.C. State would play the Caterpillars.

As usual, Bevo and Oliver were met by a crush of reporters eager to interview the game's most celebrated player. The inevitable round of nonstop interviews and taping sessions followed before Francis could escape to his hotel to meet Wiseman and the others, who were just about to leave for the Coliseum after resting all day.

"There was never any let-up. It was constant. Everywhere we went. I had a schedule Newt gave me of where to go and what to do," Bevo said. "There was no time for a break of any kind until it came time to go to the game. Even on those rare occasions when I would get to the room for a little rest, they'd call me and ask me to come up to cut a tape."

Benner remembered that Bevo was "constantly hounded in every city we entered. They wouldn't let him alone. He had no peace of any kind. It was a continual whirlwind that just engulfed him from the time he scored the one-sixteen on. Of course, Newt loved it and fed off it. Bevo just hated it, and that is what led to all the later problems."

North Carolina State and Rio Grande began the action in the first contest, with tip-off scheduled for 7:30. More than seventy-five hundred were in attendance.

Rio Grande was facing another team that, man for man, was much taller and possessed far greater depth. The Wolf Pack was led by its captain, senior Mel Thompson, who stood six-foot-three (and who, more than fifty years later, would be featured in the author Pat Conroy's best-selling tale of life under the intractable and irascible Coach Thompson at The Citadel, *My Losing Season*). Thompson was joined at forward by Dick Tyler, also six-foot-three. A sophomore, the six-foot-eight Ronnie Shavlik (who would become an All-American center and whose grandson, Shavlik Randolph, would go on to star for Mike Krzyzewski at Duke), was spelled by Cliff Dwyer, who towered at six-foot-nine and was a recent transfer who had just become eligible. The guard spots were manned by Dave Gotkin and speedy Vic Molodet.

"Coach Case was very concerned going into that game," Shavlik said. "He was scared we'd lose it, and he psyched us up by telling us they were going to go after us and embarrass us in front of all our fans.

'They're gunning for you. You'd better be ready for them,' Case told us."

Earlier, Oliver had caught the usually unflappable future Hall of Fame coach completely off stride. Ever irrepressible, the cocky Oliver had strutted onto the floor at Reynolds and looked around at the arena before asking of no one in particular, "What's the scoring record in this place?"

Stunned, Case didn't immediately reply. One of his assistants, standing nearby, replied for him. "Forty-eight," he said.

"Huh," snorted Oliver. "We'll break it." Wheeling abruptly, he strode quickly, leaving in his wake a startled Case, who stood slack-jawed in disbelief.

The contest began slowly, with both teams probing for openings. Francis was packed in tighter than the proverbial last sardine as three North Carolina defenders surrounded him. Finding the middle denied, Rio Grande went outside and grabbed an early lead on a Ripperger foul shot. But N.C. State scratched back to claim a 16-15 margin on a Shavlik hook at the end of the first period.

The second quarter was more of the same, only the pace quickened as the two squads gained a comfort level. Rio Grande was not hitting with its usual consistency when Francis put them back in the lead at 17-16. Mel Thompson answered quickly, but then McKenzie broke loose for a lay-up to push the Redmen in front, 19-18.

But the slick and swift Molodet was giving the Redmen trouble. "The first three times down court, he threw up three set shots that were good," Wiseman recalled. "He was also very quick, and he ran me to death chasing after him. I finally told Jim (McKenzie) to take him because I couldn't keep up with him. He ran Jim into the floor too. He just plain beat us up."

Under the boards the going was getting rough. "Size-wise, they had it all over us," Barr said, "and they just kept running new guys in all the time who were just as big as the starters. It didn't help us any when I missed about five in a row, either." The taller N.C. State players were keeping Barr boxed in, and Francis, hemmed in by the picket-line defense crowded around him, could offer little help. The Wolf Pack dominated the boards at both ends, out-rebounding the smaller Redmen by nearly two to one.

Still, tiny Rio Grande held gamely on. As the half ended with a Francis jumper, the Redmen went to the locker room, down by only three points against the number eight team in the country, 39-36.

At the intermission Everett Case, brow furrowed in worry, reminded his team of his warnings about Rio Grande. "'You had better start taking them serious,' he told us," Shavlik said. "'They are a good team. If you don't get going, they're going to beat you,' Case told us.

"They were a good ball club. They played you straight up and didn't back down. They knew how to get the ball to Bevo, and he had a great touch. As good as anybody we ever saw," Shavlik continued. "I had him when he was inside, and Mel would take him when he moved outside. The others took up the scoring slack when we had him [Bevo] tied up inside. But they didn't have enough height. And Vic just tore them up outside."

The Wolf Pack had not expected a close game at all. The North Carolina players knew, based on the first half, that they were in a shooting match with a good club—not the romp they'd anticipated. They would need some breaks, they thought, to pull away from the pesky visitors.

Their break came at the beginning of the third period. Inexplicably, Rio Grande had left its shooting touch in the locker room. The Redmen were stone cold. Nothing they threw up went in. "I missed about three in a row from the corner. Shots I usually made just wouldn't drop," Barr recalled.

North Carolina State took advantage and quickly ran off nine unanswered points before Wiseman canned a free throw nearly three minutes into the quarter to put the Redmen on the board.

Molodet continued his furious pace, and McKenzie and Wiseman continued their futile attempts to chase him down. Using a three-man weave and setting picks, the Pack stymied Rio Grande's attempts to stop them.

In the third period Case had inserted Cliff Dwyer to spell Shavlik in guarding Francis. The beefy center soon drew a foul while trying to contain the quicker Francis. Dwyer returned to the pine quickly, having earned five personal fouls in rough-and-tumble action in little more than nine minutes of play.

The final period saw the Redmen fight gamely back, but the deficit was too much to overcome. Barr, battling the lofty Carolina players for rebounds, left with five fouls and 18 points. Wiseman and McKenzie ran out of steam and were gasping for air in their attempts to contain Molodet. They couldn't.

Bevo began to hit with more ease in the final period as Shavlik, like Dwyer, was saddled with foul trouble. But it was too little too late. "They just kept running new and bigger fresh guys in all night," Wiseman recalled. In all, Case used twelve men to batter the Redmen into submission, 92-77.

In Bevo's personal battle with the future All-American and NBA performer Ron Shavlik, Bevo was the decided victor. He tallied 34 points on what was an otherwise-frigid shooting night for the Redmen. He hit eleven of twenty-six attempts from the floor under constant double-team pressure that earned him twenty free-throw attempts (of the twenty-five fouls that the Wolf Pack committed, twenty were incurred by those guarding Bevo). Bevo converted twelve free throws to tie the Coliseum record. Shavlik, held to 16 points, later said of the encounter, 'Bevo has the finest touch I've ever seen."

"[Mel] Thompson was a real good player and he hurt us bad. That guard, Molodet, killed us from outside. We just couldn't handle them," Bevo remembered.

Overall, Rio Grande made only thirty-five percent of its shots from the floor, while North Carolina State was making forty-three percent. The rebounds, though, tell the story: The Wolf Pack grabbed fifty-three caroms to Rio Grande's thirty-three.

Mel Thompson, who tallied 28 points, paced the Wolf Pack, with Molodet adding 19 points as he bedeviled the Rio Grande guards all evening.

Writing of the game for the Raleigh News and Observer, Dick Herbert acknowledged, "Bevo was much better than I anticipated. He could do more than just shoot and he proved it. Rio Grande was a much better team than I anticipated as well."

A fifteen-point loss on the road to a team ranked in the top ten is no disgrace. According to Homer Alley's formula, at least, the Redmen had earned the right to stay in the big leagues. And, of course, that is exactly where they would find themselves the next night—back at the Coliseum to meet the Demon Deacons of Wake Forest, no slouches themselves. After North Carolina State turned back the Redmen, the Deacons had followed with an upset of the powerful Peoria Caterpillars, 58-57. Earlier in the season the Deacons had defeated N.C. State.

Spearheaded by their six-foot-six All-America candidate, Ned "Dickie" Hemric, the Deacons—under Coach Murray Greeson—had won twenty-two games the previous season. In this, the inaugural season of the Atlantic Coast Conference (ACC), they were preseason favorites to win the conference crown.

Hemric was surrounded by a fine supporting cast: guards Billy Lyles and Maurice George and forwards Al DePorter and Lowell Davis. Although the Deacons were not as tall as the Wolf Pack, they nonetheless were an experienced team playing as a unit for the third season.

Rio Grande was certainly not an unknown quantity to them. The Deacons had seen most of the previous night's game from the stands and had been impressed with Rio Grande's spunky effort. "We had all read about Francis before the game. And we had seen most of the game the night before, so we knew pretty much what to expect," Hemric said.

More than eight thousand fans were on hand as the Redmen and the Deacons squared off. Buoyed by their more-than-credible effort against N.C. State, Rio Grande was up for the game. It didn't hurt that the vast throng in the Reynolds Coliseum was cheering the Redmen from the start. "It was the same everywhere we went," Bevo said. "The people just seemed to take to us. We never did play at home [that second season], so it was nice to have fan support when we were on the road."

Years before the Dallas Cowboys, and decades before baseball's Atlanta Braves would claim the title, the Redmen from tiny Rio Grande College had truly become "America's team." They enjoyed unprecedented support from fans, who saw a team of Horatio Algers who were acquitting themselves amazingly well against the slicker, better funded teams fielded by entrenched basketball powers. Rio Grande's cross-country odyssey to joust with the basketball giants capti-vated the nation and the affection of the fans wherever the Redmen went. "Even though it happened in every single arena, it never ceased to amaze me," Benner said. "It was something you could feel as well as hear. It was almost as though they were trying to will us to win."

In North Carolina, against Wake Forest, the Redmen would need all the support the crowd could muster. Rio Grande grabbed an early lead on key buckets from Wiseman and McKenzie. Francis and Hemric dueled for position in the pivot. Matched up well, neither would give an inch.

As the first quarter came to an end, Rio Grande held a 19-12 lead. In the second, Wake Forest fought back, scoring 25 points while holding the Redmen to eleven. Then Hemric scored six points in a row as the half concluded, giving Wake Forest a 35-30 edge. "We'd read about Hemric and were more scared of him than we were about North Carolina State," McKenzie said. Wiseman recalled that "it was close all game. They had a lefty [Lowell Davis] who was deadly from the corners, and he killed us out there."

In the dressing room beneath Reynolds Coliseum, the team remained upbeat. Both Wiseman and Barr were vocal in their belief that they could and would overtake the Deacons. "I felt we were in it all the way," Wiseman said. "We just needed to catch a break somewhere."

"[Coach] Greeson had us in a box-and-one defense, with a man fronting Bevo at all times. Usually, that would stop most big men, but Bevo could shoot from 'most anywhere on the court and that hurt us," Hemric said. "In our dressing room, Greeson and [assistant coach] Bones McKinney were urging us to stay with him. They reminded us we were in a fight. Not that we needed the reminder."

The third quarter was an ebb-and-flow affair. Rio Grande was playing a smoother, more controlled game. With Wiseman's pinpoint passes setting up easy shots, the Redmen managed to erase all but a single point of the deficit.

As the final quarter started, the score was Wake Forest 50, Rio Grande 49. The huge Coliseum crowd greeted the Redmen with a standing ovation as they took the court, urging them on with applause. The noise never subsided.

Momentum switched back and forth between the two teams with neither managing to pull away. With 4:45 to play, the score stood knotted at fifty-nine. Hemric pushed the Deacons back in front with a short jumper and followed it with a free throw to make it 62-59.

Francis answered with a jumper of his own, and the Redmen pulled to within one point. Hemric responded with three more points, giving Wake Forest a more comfortable margin of 65-61 with less than one minute to play. Hoping to protect the slim lead and preserve the victory, Greeson ordered the Deacons to slow down play. The stall, he felt, would ice the game for the Deacons.

Rio Grande was having none of it. With Wiseman and Ripperger leading the way Rio Grande picked up coverage of the Wake Forest guards beneath their own basket and applied full-court pressure. With but twenty-nine seconds remaining, the Coliseum crowd in an uproar, and the fate of the Redmen apparently sealed, lightning struck.

It came in the guise of wily guard Wayne Wiseman. With the blood of the fabled Waterloo Wonders coursing through his veins, and drawing on the considerable skills he had acquired on the primitive dirt courts of his hometown, Wiseman single-handedly turned the game around. "We were in a full-court press," Wiseman recalled. "Rip and I picked [the Deacons] up as soon as they in-bounded the ball. Rip turned his man, George, and I reached in from behind and stole the ball and converted an easy lay-up. Then, the next time they threw it in against the sideline, Rip and I trapped their guard there, and I stole it again and fired it to Ripperger, who streaked in uncontested for a lay-up. It was sixty-five-sixty-five."

Again, the Deacons put the ball in play under their basket. Forced out of their stall by the harassing Wiseman, they threw a long pass up court along the sideline. It sailed out of bounds. Rio Grande called a timeout.

On the sideline Oliver was as excited as anyone had ever seen him. His instructions, however, were as predictable as ever. "He told me to get the ball to Bevo," Wiseman remembered. "He said 'If we win this game, I'll buy you a new pair of shoes.' I told him, 'If we win this game, you ought to buy me a suit.' He said he would too."

Five seconds remained on the scoreboard clock when the referee's whistle ended the timeout.

Ripperger inbounded the ball to Wiseman from the near sideline at about midcourt. Wake Forest had forced Bevo far out of the pivot and had him tightly covered. "I was supposed to get the ball to Bevo down low, but I couldn't get it to him there," Wiseman recalled. "I looked quickly around and found Bevo had managed to get a slight separation from his defenders and [I] hit him with a pass at about eighteen feet out."

"I took the pass and just had time enough to turn and shoot," Bevo said.

The ball was in the air.

Swish.

The buzzer sounded.

It was over: Rio Grande 67, Wake Forest 65.

On the sidelines Oliver turned a cartwheel in gleeful celebration. The Redmen had scored three baskets in the final twenty-nine seconds of play, and the crowd was on its feet in homage to the battling band that had refused to die.

"The place was absolutely chaotic," Wiseman recalled. "With that win I felt we had vindicated ourselves. We had played two of the top teams in the country two nights in a row and beaten one of them. I felt we had nothing left to prove."

With the roar of the crowd washing over them, they hoisted Bevo on their shoulders and carried him from the floor.

"I reminded Newt he owed me a suit," Wiseman said. "But I never did see it."

"It was a whale of a game and the best game Bevo ever played under that type of competition," Barr declared.

Bevo had scored 32 points, including the buzzer beater. The Redmen held Hemric—who would be named ACC Player of the Year that season and who would close out his career at Wake Forest a year later with 2,587 college points and All-America honors—to twenty-four points because he made only nine of thirty-three shots from the floor.

"Bevo was a real fine ball player," Hemric said. "He was a pure shooter."

Oliver recalled that "Bones McKinney said to me after the game, 'We played Santa Claus tonight.' I told him, 'You didn't give us any present. We stole it off you like any good thief would do!'"

The Deacons, who enjoyed a twenty-two-win season that year, would later go on to two thrilling overtime wins in the ACC tournament before losing to North Carolina State in the finals, again in overtime.

The southern swing had proved a success. Sun, surf, and two wins out of three. With sunburned and peeling noses, the Redmen headed back to Rio Grande and scattered for the holidays. It was Christmas Eve. Nothing they would find under their Christmas trees could match the feelings of pride and satisfaction they took with them.

Bevo joined Jean in Wellsville at her parents' home. He hoped that the brief holiday break would afford him an opportunity to escape the clamoring press. But, he said, "they even found us there. There was no escape. Wherever I'd go, they'd track me down. It was really getting to me by then."

13

At Odds with
the Coach

S till savoring the taste of their Wake Forest win, the Redmen arrived
back on campus from their brief holiday and hit the road again to
meet Salem College of West Virginia in early January. The trip to
Carmichael Auditorium in Clarksburg found them in a lighthearted,
breezy mood. The stress and strain of the early-season litmus test behind
them, they entered Carmichael as a confident and cocky crew.

Experienced coaches know only too well that a mental letdown
often follows a big win, and they take great pains to overcome it in
their team preparations. Newt Oliver made no such effort.

Lying in wait at Carmichael was a 4-3 Salem College team with
nothing to lose. Blessed with an unusually hot hand on their home
court and a crew of very forgiving officials, Salem sped out to a lead
in the first half, sometimes by as many as 10 points over Rio Grande.

"They couldn't miss," Bevo recalled.

At halftime Oliver lashed out at the lethargic performance of the
team, hoping to wake his players up. But it was too late. Rio Grande
did fight back to tie the game three times before Salem rushed away
again, racking up another ten-point lead. The Redmen rallied, but
Salem took the contest, 100-96, an ego-deflating defeat for the boys
from Rio Grande.

The Redmen had had an off night—way off. Bevo managed 38
points in making 11 of 26 shots from the floor and 16 charity tosses.
The local referees had been blatant in their one-sided application of
the rules at Carmichael. But the Redmen had survived "homer" crews
before. This time they had not.

Oddly, in drawing up the contracts for the games that they were to
play that season, Oliver had neglected to insert a clause requiring the

use of neutral or outside officials for the games, even though all the games that the team would be playing in their vastly upgraded schedule were away games. Rio Grande would make its foray into the world of basketball giants at a decided disadvantage. Whether it was Oliver's arrogance or simply oversight didn't matter. It was, he conceded years later, a mistake. And it would cost them more than the game against Salem.

Rudely returned to terra firma with the loss to lightly regarded Salem College, the Redmen were quickly off to Indianapolis where they would face another big test.

Tony Hinkle's Butler University Bulldogs were a perennial midwestern power. They were currently the defending Indiana College Conference champions. In his twenty-fifth season as head coach, and with 324 victories behind him, Hinkle stood twenty-second on the list of all active coaches.

Butler faced a number of Big Ten schools each season, as well as major independents, including Notre Dame. "We had a fieldhouse that was huge. But normally we attracted only about a thousand [fans], except for the Big Ten and Notre Dame games, when we'd get five to seven thousand," Lodie Labda of Butler recalled.

"In those days, particularly in the midwest, traveling trinket shows were an important part of our lives. There was no TV to speak of, and each season would bring a new form of entertainment and amusement along in the guise of a sporting event. In the winter we would have the traveling basketball teams like the House of David, and in the summer we'd all watch the King and His Court with softball legend Eddie Feigner. To many, Bevo was a show like that. His appearance after all the publicity was as much entertainment as a sporting event, and we viewed Oliver as an original snake oil salesman," recalled Norm Ellenberger, who played for Butler and later served as a head coach at New Mexico and then as a top assistant to Bob Knight at Indiana.

"[Oliver] had coupled that Barnum and Bailey promotion with basketball and it fit right in with the way of life in our society at that time," he continued. "Besides, we all thought it was great that he would be putting ten thousand fans into that gym."

Hinkle, it should be noted, was a member of the rules committee of the National Association of Basketball Coaches, the very body that recommended the "Bevo Rule" the year before that resulted in the expunging of most of Francis' records. So why did he put a game against Rio Grande on Butler's schedule? Had he had second thoughts about the "Bevo Rule" and was he now trying to give the Redmen a chance against major college foes? Perhaps. But Ellenberger had another, not so altruistic, explanation for Rio Grande's appearance at the spacious Butler University Fieldhouse.

"As part of my scholarship I was responsible for sweeping out the gym and restocking the concession stands after each game," Ellenberger said. "Hinkle held the concession stand franchise. After each game was over, I climbed the stairs to those stands to restock them. After the game with Rio Grande, I climbed the stairs ten times as much as usual. Everything was sold."

Whatever Hinkle's motivation, he told the Bulldogs that they would be able to stop Francis. They were a veteran club coming off a 14-9 campaign and would go on to score thirteen wins against top-flight competition. "We believed Hinkle when he told us we would stop him," Ellenberger added.

As the Redmen arrived in Indiana, they were greeted by a big black headline in the sports section of the *Indianapolis News* on January 6: "WILL HINKLE LET BEVO TWINKLE OR SHACKLE RIO ACE?" Throughout the basketball-crazed Hoosier State, fans hotly debated the question as game time approached.

Hinkle, later enshrined in the Basketball Hall of Fame for his phenomenal coaching record, had not scouted Rio Grande. "I knew very little about them, so made no specific plans beforehand," he admitted. "We played them man-to-man with a two-one-two zone at times to spell some of the players. I assigned Norm Ellenberger, our best defensive player, to guard Francis. But Norm was only six-one and was no match for Francis."

"Ellenberger was to get help from six-five John Mustain, a sopho-more center who had been an All-State performer in Kentucky," Labda said. "With Norm in front and Johnny behind him, we hoped to hold [Bevo] down."

The rest of the team would play a basic man-to-man defense.

The spacious Butler Field House filled rapidly. At game time 11,593 fans had crossed through the turnstiles, a new national attendance record for a single college game. All were there to see in person what they had read and heard so much about. What they got for their money was a classic.

Opening up quickly, the Redmen responded to a crowd that was obviously pulling for them and built an early lead. The ice-cold shooting that had plagued them at Salem was replaced by a red-hot hand for Bevo, and his fire sparked the rest of the team.

The first period ended at 24-13.

"It was obvious as the second quarter started that Bevo was going to have one of those special nights," Ripperger said.

Ellenberger recalled that "Bevo had the nicest touch in a fall-away jumper I'd ever seen. It made him play like he was seven-six. There was no way to stop him."

"Bevo was fast moving and took a lot of shots from the top of the key when we rode him out there," Labda said. "But we had no one who could block his jump shots."

Wiseman's passes easily found Bevo over the top, and Bevo seldom missed.

"Their efforts to stop Francis resulted in Ellenberger and Mustain fouling him whenever he touched the ball. Soon they were both in foul trouble and forced to play off him more," Labda recounted.

"Francis shot phenomenally," Hinkle said.

With practiced efficiency, Wiseman and McKenzie exploited the resulting looser coverage and they fed Bevo, who matched the combined Butler output in the first two periods. As they headed to the locker room at the half, Rio Grande held a 43-27 lead.

"Hinkle's instructions to us at the half were to try to sag in more on the off-side on Bevo to try to help out Mustain and Ellenberger," forward Bob Reed explained. "It didn't help."

Indiana, which believes emphatically that it is the center of the basketball universe, is a state where the high school basketball championship tournament draws more attention than the World Series. Here, Bevo and Rio Grande were greeted with more skepticism than in most parts of the country because Hoosiers hold basketball teams and players to a higher standard. You could leave your press clippings and "b.s." at the door. All that mattered was what you did on the court—nothing else.

It did not take Bevo and the Redmen long to win the support of the crowd, which was quickly convinced that they were the real deal. The fans were on their feet, cheering the Redmen in appreciation of their talent and pluck. The once skeptical Hoosiers would root the Redmen on against the giants of the midwest and hope against hope that they'd prevail. The unmistakable outpouring of spontaneous adulation lifted the Redmen even higher as the second half began.

"It was very strange," Wiseman said. "We were accustomed, by now, to winning over fans, but there they just all seemed to be with us from early on." Each successive Rio Grande basket was greeted with a roar louder than the last one as they pulled steadily away from the Bulldogs.

Despite a game effort, Mustain was forced to the bench with five fouls in the third period. Ellenberger, Jack Mackenzie, and one other player would continue the battle to stop Bevo before they too would exit with fouls. Bevo was not going to be stopped.

"We'd lost two centers, and rather than use our third-stringer, coach Hinkle moved me over from the forward spot to guard Bevo," Reed recounted. "I thumped him as hard as I could get away with. He scored anyway."

As the last period got underway, Rio Grande held a 58-44 lead and Bevo had already scored 36 points, successfully smashing the Field House record that Paul Ebert of Ohio State had set a month earlier— and Bevo still had ten minutes to play.

The crowd was standing throughout as Rio Grande, led by Francis' assault on the record, held off the Bulldogs. Bevo added 12 points in the period to establish a new Field House standard of 48 points. The final score was 81-68. A crescendo of noise swept down on the Redmen. Carrying Bevo aloft on their shoulders, they were mobbed as they left the floor.

His Field House scoring record had eclipsed even the best professional mark, which had been held by Alex Groza since 1949. In a vain effort to get Bevo back out on the floor, the basketball-savvy Hoosier fans continued their demonstration for a full five minutes after the Redmen had disappeared into the locker room.

"At that time, a standing ovation for a competitor was a pretty rare occurrence," Labda said. "I had never seen one before. But Bevo deserved it."

According to Oliver, "the most amazing thing about it was that they'd booed and catcalled us for ten minutes while we were warming up with our ball-handling exhibition. Then after the game, they gave us a standing ovation."

Although it was many years later, Oliver still could not resist a sneering jab at the opposing coach: "Hinkle was supposed to be a great defensive coach. Hell, Bevo scored 48 points against him."

The next morning Jep Cadou Jr., sports editor of the *Indianapolis Star*, would recount the stirring events:

Cheering Butler avidly at the outset, the throng gave evidence that it had come to see the hometown boys prove that this hulking, nationally ballyhooed idol had feet of clay. But his feet looked more like the smoothly pirouetting extremities of a ballet dancer as he deftly maneuvered Bulldog after Bulldog out of position and floated gracefully into the air to arch another two points through the hoop. A skeptical Hoosier crowd in the tradition-shrouded Field House who had come to see a legend debunked remained to see history made. It was a thing you could feel—that gradual change of emotion which spread through the crowd and culminated in the greatest standing ovation in the arena's history.

The Butler game convinced the remaining doubters that Francis and Rio Grande were capable of meeting and beating major college foes. Their drawing power had never been in doubt, but they underlined it and added an exclamation point when they attracted twelve thousand to an arena that usually housed crowds of only one thousand. Even appearances by Butler's Big Ten opponents would fail to attract the numbers that Bevo drew.

That season Butler would go on to turn back three Big Ten foes, more proof that Rio Grande was no mirage. Hinkle later declared, "Francis convinced me. He was a great player. He was an excellent shooter from the floor and big enough to control the boards. And don't overlook his playing companions. They were an excellent college team." Then the Hall of Famer drew a modern comparison: "Bevo was to Rio Grande what Larry Bird was to Indiana State later." Hinkle's Bulldogs agreed. "The Butler players all were very respectful of Bevo's play," Labda recalled. And Reed said, "They were a very solid ball club backing up a very fine player."

Ellenberger, who became one of the best coaches of his day, was even more effusive in his recollection: "There wasn't a stiff in the bunch. They could all pass and handle the ball. The chatter was constant among them. They played a completely different brand of ball than anything we'd ever seen. Bevo could shoot with anyone in the game—even today. It's a shame that once Oliver got his fangs into him, he was a captive. He was never allowed to develop as a player because of it."

The Butler players, like nearly all the teams that Rio Grande would meet, also took note of the attitude and play of Wayne Wiseman. "He was a quick and crafty ball player and very cocky," Labda said.

Decades before the steaming asphalt courts of the inner city would spawn a generation of trash-talking players, Wayne Wiseman was in the face of his opponents. "Wayne would intimidate them," Benner recalled. "He would get on them and tell them, 'If you stick around after the game, I'll show you how to play.' And then he'd back it up by picking their pocket. It drove them all nuts. Of course, that only encouraged Wayne to do it more."

Leaving in their wake a large band of newly won adherents to their cause, the Redmen went home. They would have a brief two-day hiatus before meeting the Golden Eagles of Morris Harvey College in Charleston, West Virginia, on January 9.

✤ ✤ ✤

While at home, the players drove the thirteen miles to a restaurant where they were always welcome, the Bob Evans Drive-In in Gallipolis. It had only fourteen stools and was the first of what would become more than five hundred restaurants in the chain.

"Bob [Evans] was a great friend of the college," Wiseman recounted. "His father, Stanley, had helped them through hard times, and he continued to do it as well. He was always giving us a free meal when we showed up there. With times being what they were and money so tight, we all enjoyed his hospitality as often as we could."

Evans was born in 1918 on the family farmstead that practically abuts the campus at Rio Grande, and he became one of the Redmen's staunchest supporters. "I felt they were doing a great deal for the school and the area in general. I tried to help in every way I could," he said. "They were all good kids, and they deserved some support from the community."

Years later Evans' chain of family-oriented restaurants chose the slogan "Where memories are made." He would later display a pair of Bevo's sneakers, which he had purchased at a charity auction to benefit the school and had bronzed, in his Rio Grande store, which is located on the site of the Evans family homestead.

But the faculty and administration of Rio Grande still did not share the restaurateur's enthusiasm for their team. "When we came back in off the road, we would hear the faculty grumbling about all the work we'd missed and the make-up tests that were required," Wiseman said. "It was obvious that most, if not all of them, were not happy with what we were doing and made little attempt to mask their feelings. Of course, Bevo felt the brunt of it because, with Newt running him all over, he missed more than any of us."

"I defy anyone that had to face the schedule I had, to keep up with their schoolwork," Bevo said. "I would get home from some shooting exhibition or banquet Newt had arranged for me to go to and it would be one or two in the morning. Then the next day I had to get to a class at eight. Of course, with all the travel we did, we were hardly ever there, anyway. But I made up what I missed as well as I could."

Carl Benner, who went on to earn a doctoral degree in mathematics, remembered, "There was a lot of faculty jealousy at the time. I wouldn't say Bevo had the same degree of motivation academically as some of us. But I had several classes with him and can tell you he was no dummy. I resented it when they later tried to insinuate that he was. I found it ironic that some of the faculty were badmouthing him and the team at the same time that their salaries were being paid by their efforts."

Exacerbating the strained relations was what the team found upon their return from Indiana: a crew from NBC's *Today Show,* then hosted by Dave Garroway, which had come to film a story on Bevo and the school. While the rest of the team enjoyed two blessed days of rest, largely ignored by the cameras, Bevo was not so fortunate. Also on hand was the cadre of reporters that had been awaiting his return. "They were everywhere I went," the star player complained. "I couldn't get away from them."

The *Today Show* footage was telecast coast to coast. If anyone in the United States was still unaware of Bevo Francis, the telecast filled in the gap.

The press coverage of Bevo only intensified as the season took the Redmen through major media markets. The first season had seen them stay in the small markets of the tri-state area, and they traveled so much that reporters had a tough time catching up with them. Now they were arriving on the very doorsteps of the nation's largest dailies. In that era most cities had a news smorgasbord, thanks to their established radio stations, several competing newspapers, and local television stations. All clamored for Bevo—and Oliver made certain none was denied face time with his star.

"When we'd get to a place for a game, he'd hand me a schedule all printed up. One o'clock, Rotary luncheon speech; two o'clock, radio show; three o'clock, press conference; four o'clock TV show; four-thirty, radio spot; five o'clock TV appearance; five-thirty, tape an interview—and it would be like that everywhere we went," Bevo said. "I barely had time to get to the hotel before we would leave again for the game. There was no peace. And Newt was with me all the time."

Although Bevo was a better-than-average student during his first year at Rio Grande, the pace of his life and the enormous demands that Oliver placed on his time for publicity were taking their toll on his schoolwork—and his relationship with his coach.

"We were able to keep pace with our studies because we had time to ourselves on the road," Wiseman said of the team. "But Bevo never had a moment's rest. It got to the point where he didn't want to talk to reporters at all. Newt would badger him constantly to do it, and he'd ask me to help convince Bevo to cooperate. I would and he'd finally give in and do it—but he hated it."

"They were at odds a lot over it," Ripperger recalled. The relationship between Newt and Bevo was deteriorating before their eyes. "They were both stubborn, and it made things very tense and difficult. They were constantly butting heads like two ornery bulls," Wiseman said. Dave Diles said, "You couldn't find two people more different. Newt wanted the spotlight of publicity and craved it more than anything. Bevo just wanted to play and to be left alone."

For Bevo the situation was fast becoming intolerable. The team was always on the road, and the schedule—which Newt had designed to gain them maximum publicity—was a killer. In January alone they would play ten games in Ohio, West Virginia and Indiana and conclude with a trip to Buffalo. They were seldom, if ever, on campus for two days at a stretch before packing up and heading off again.

Whether he was on campus or not, Francis had virtually no free time. He was a prisoner of his celebrity, and his jailer offered no respite from the sentence he'd imposed. Even when they had a rare break in the schedule, Oliver used it to arrange personal appearances and speaking engagements to keep his publicity mill rolling.

"If I got after him to go and do some appearance or something, he'd get mad at me," Oliver said of Bevo. "He thought I was hard on him. Of course, I am a very domineering-type person."

"Newt would have been a good general and a hell of a dictator," Benner declared.

Through it all, Francis tried to drag himself to class. But as he fell still further behind in work assigned by professors with little sympathy for his plight, his efforts would flag.

President Davis and the trustees were more than happy with the financial benefits that the Redmen's foray into the big time had brought the school. But, covertly, school officials were still hostile toward Oliver, who made no attempt to fix the relationship. Davis and others wondered openly what might be the adverse effects of the schedule on their student-athletes. Referring to the recent scandals, Davis told a *Gallia Times* reporter that he was "acutely aware of the dangers involved" and that while Rio Grande was "enjoying their day in the sun," he didn't think "it should last forever."

"College," Davis reminded the reporter, "is for education."

Dr. Francis Shane, chair of the Athletic Council, acknowledged,

"Financially, things were getting better. The money we earned from basketball was going into the general fund of the school, and it was no secret we were using it to pay salaries and the cost of operations. But they were difficult times. Newt's statements in the press were becoming increasingly bolder and more preposterous by then. I tried to counsel him on abiding by all the rules and regulations of the conference and the college. But his head was swelled by then and he threatened to take me on, right then and there in his office. We were supposed to be running a school. Instead we were running a rumor-crushing mill. It was an impossible situation."

Oliver's pugnacious attitude toward college officials only exacerbated the situation. "I could see that it was never going to work out," he said.

Thoughts of leaving had been on Oliver's mind ever since the trustees had tied his hands by creating the Athletic Council. He had been bristling with indignation ever since.

"I had been told that I couldn't even buy a pair of sweat socks. Who'd they think was paying the faculty? Who brought this thing into scope and into being? What would have happened if we wouldn't have been there? The only thing I wanted was to be treated fairly and properly. I never felt I was. The first year they brought me in there and said you can do anything you want. Schedule anyone you want. Play anywhere you want. You're the best promoter I've ever known. Run the show. Then, I was told I no longer had any intelligence. I couldn't schedule anything, do anything. They were going to bring a guy in here to do this and do that. They told me to make three carbons of any correspondence I had, even if it were personal, et cetera. There was no way I could condone that. I still can't."

The chains shackling the fiery coach were starting to chafe. He was looking to break free. "We [Oliver and Francis] were always thinking of leaving," the coach remembered. "The jealousy was rank."

It was still early in the season, Oliver recalled, but "I had lost control of the team, and I wasn't able to control Bevo." Oliver's frustration with the situation that he had created was evident to the players. They just weren't certain how it would resolve itself.

"There was an uneasy feeling that crept in about that time," Ripperger recalled. "We all sensed that things were starting to come undone but that we could do little about it. We just concentrated as best we could on playing the games. But it wasn't the same as before."

⊕ ⊕ ⊕

Next on the Redmen's schedule was the game against Morris Harvey College of West Virginia, on January 9. The Golden Eagles, the defending West Virginia Intercollegiate Conference Champions, had been 21-9 the year before and were enjoying early success this season as well. They were coached by Eddie King and were on their way to a 16-13 season.

The Redmen added the Golden Eagles' tail feathers to their war bonnets as they rolled to an easy 83-63 win before a capacity crowd in Charleston. Francis accounted for 41 points, thanks to more fine passing from Wiseman and McKenzie throughout.

"We played them man-to-man with six-five Mario Palumbo and six-six Denny Garrett attempting to hold down Bevo," Dave Rosen remembered. "Once they [the Redmen] had the game in hand, they fed him a lot and he ended up with forty-one. I remembered him from when I was up at Tiffin College before going on to Morris Harvey. Bevo was going to a lot of independent tournaments at that time, and everyone knew he was a great shooter even then."

Back on campus the Redmen prepared for an odd two-game series with Alliance College of Pennsylvania set to begin on January 15. They would meet in Erie for the first game and then move down to Wellsville for a second contest the next night.

Before the Morris Harvey game Oliver, ever the optimist if not a realist, had tried to get the NCAA to restore Bevo's records from 1952-53. Citing Bevo's performances against major colleges thus far this season, he urged the NCAA to reverse course. The NCAA dismissed his appeal out of hand.

Bevo was averaging 44 points per game, which forced the red-faced NCAA to place him atop the list of the nation's leading scorers. Oliver's argument, which he had continued to press through the media when rebuffed by the NCAA, was that Bevo had never scored fewer than 32 points against the "major colleges" and had in fact accounted for as many as 48. That proved, at least to Newt, that Bevo's records should be returned to him.

Indeed, the caliber of competition seemed to matter little to Francis, who had answered the criticism of the previous year's schedule with factual understatement: "I don't make up the schedule. I just play them as they come."

Despite the decidedly upgraded class of opposition arrayed against him, he was just about keeping pace with his freshman performance. But now his records would count. Unless, of course, the NCAA figured out some new way to erase them.

Alliance College, located in Cambridge Springs, Pennsylvania, had fewer than three hundred students and was supported by the Polish National Alliance, a fraternal organization. The game provided a much-needed breather for the Redmen as they romped to an easy 107-77 victory over their hapless foes, evoking the previous season. Outmanned, Alliance was never in the game. Francis, firing at will, scored 61 points. The Redmen, with a 100-58 lead, went into their Globetrotter routine and spent the final four minutes entertaining the crowd without attempting to score.

Bevo broke the Gannon Auditorium record, and the crowd of three thousand provided Erie reporter Wes Driscoll with a unique moment in sports: "As Newt Oliver removed Wayne Wiseman near the end of the game, the crowd gave him a sustained ovation. It was the first time I had ever seen a player receive a standing ovation without having scored a single point." But then, of course, these fans had never before seen the likes of Wiseman's passing and dribbling.

Wiseman "had gotten a rebound near the end of the game and had turned and fired a pass the entire distance of the court to Francis, who had broken away," Ripperger remembered. "And he had thrown it the full length of the court, hitting Bevo in full stride, *behind his back!*"

"What Wayne Wiseman couldn't do with a basketball just wasn't worth doing," Benner declared. "He was simply amazing."

Wellsville, which had spared little in welcoming its prodigal son and his playmates a year earlier, greeted them with a sold-out Beacom Gymnasium for the rematch against Alliance. The Alliance players, no doubt still mesmerized by the awesome offensive show of the Redmen the night before, played their roles as sacrificial lambs to perfection.

Bevo and Rio Grande exploded for 131 points. Francis, hitting from all over the floor with ease, was unstoppable. He scored 84 points to top Alliance College's combined total of 70. In the process he broke his own NCAA record.

"I wanted to do well in my hometown. And I had a good night," he said modestly.

Next on Rio Grande's card was Ashland College of Ohio, in a polio benefit contest in Gallipolis on January 19. It was the team's fifteenth game that season but its first appearance in Gallia County. The local fans were eager to see "our team."

The Washington School Gymnasium was a far cry from the Butler Field House in seating capacity. According to press accounts, the building was jammed with as many as two thousand fans, far in excess of its legal occupancy of 750.

The Redmen, coming off their two laughingly easy wins over Alliance, were in peak midseason form. Ashland College was never in the contest, and the outcome was never in doubt. Rio Grande rolled over the visitors, 117-78. For the third game in a row the Redmen had topped the century mark. Bevo rang up 55 points, including eleven out of twelve free throws. He had, in the last three games, scored 200 points—and had done so while barely playing at all in the final quarter of any of them.

Si Burick, the Dayton sportswriter, still headed the Dayton Polio Foundation and had prevailed upon Oliver to bring his team back to the Dayton Field House for a benefit against Findlay College. The game had originally been on Oliver's schedule for February, but Burick convinced Newt to move it up to January 21—but not before Oliver put the squeeze on Burick to up the ante.

Burick was eager to see the Redmen play in his hometown again. He had used his *Dayton Daily News* column to defend Francis against the NCAA's punitive action, arguing that the records "had been gained against the same type competition the College had always faced and not setups."

Burick recalled his negotiations with Oliver: "I was the head of the local March of Dimes campaign and wanted the drawing power I knew Rio Grande, with Bevo, could bring. I went down to the college and met with Oliver in his office to discuss the terms. I was told by Newt that I had better speak to Don Allen about this before I decided. So I called Allen from Oliver's office, and we talked about the size of the guarantee. Allen told me to up the ante. I agreed to do so. The game turned out to be a very profitable one for the March of Dimes."

Oliver's version is more colorful: "I took him out into the Hog Pen and said, 'Look around at this place. This is just as bad as polio.'"

In any event, the game was on, and Burick lined up an impressive array of talent for the fund-raiser. The vivacious Hollywood starlet Terry Moore performed two musical numbers during the pre-game ceremonies. Also on the entertainment bill were the Maguire Sisters and the Shepherd Sisters. All three Dayton television stations were on hand and carried the entertainment live in a telethon format. In a radio appearance before the game, Bevo had pledged, "I'll do my best to help the cause."

It would be long past 2 a.m. before the test patterns appeared on tiny screens, signaling the end of the television day. The movie actors Wendy Barrie and Peggy King were still answering telephones, accepting pledges from viewers. At Burick's shrewd suggestion they encouraged callers to match Bevo's points with their dollars.

More than four thousand were on hand for the tip-off.

Findlay, which had extended the Redmen the previous year in an overtime loss, proved just as tenacious this season. Led by the bespectacled Ron Marquette, who stood barely five-foot-nine, Findlay never backed down. Marquette, averaging 16 points a game, was enjoying a career night. He threw long bombs from all angles and scored inside on slashing lay-ups. Usually a steady, if unspectacular, complement to the high-scoring Herk Wolfe, that night Marquette was the Findlay star.

"They just came out there and it was like all hell broke loose," Bevo recalled. "The two Marquette twins were throwing them in from all over, and big Herk Wolfe was getting baskets inside. We called a timeout to try and figure out what the heck was going on."

Wiseman has similar memories: "The two Marquette boys were just as hot as pistols. We chased them all night." The two guards ran Ripperger, Wiseman, and McKenzie ragged with their antics.

"We just couldn't stop them," McKenzie recalled. "They were hitting everything they threw up."

Although the Oilers trailed 37-31 at the half, they seemed to be playing better than what the score indicated. The Redmen knew this was not going to be another romp.

Findlay stayed in contact through the third period, with the Redmen unable to shake them. As the fourth period began, Findlay kept surging to whittle away at the margin. Although the Redmen were shooting well from the floor—making 16 of 33 tries in the first half and 16 of 32 in the second—they couldn't seem to ditch the pesky Oilers, who were nearly as accurate.

With 1:17 remaining, Wiseman missed a pair of free throws. On Findlay's next possession Ron Marquette sank both free throws to draw the Oilers to within a basket, at 72-70.

With twenty seconds to play, McKenzie sank a long set shot from far outside. Then Ron Marquette made the first of two foul shots. Seconds later Rio Grande, with the ball, saw the clock expire. It was over. Rio Grande had escaped with a 74-71 win.

Francis, with 32 points, was well below his average of 49.5, but he had gotten the help he needed from McKenzie, who had accounted for 15 points, and from Ripperger, who had 13.

Ron Marquette, with 36 points, paced the Oilers and in so doing could forever boast of having outscored Bevo Francis in a head-to-head competition—a claim few others could make. Bevo had held Wolfe, Findlay's big center, to 16 points with a strong defensive effort.

The next day Eurick observed in his column that "Francis was a team player. He rebounded off the enemy basket, he intercepted several passes, did considerably more on defense without ever fouling the enemy. Bevo was by no means a throwback to the old days as a 'stationary player.' He was on the move constantly up and down the floor from side to side. He is definitely more basketball player than some think, and his teammates, lacking height, are tremendous shots from the outside. They're not duds."

The Polio Foundation reaped $44,000 in pledges during the long evening. The Redmen, escaping Dayton with a hard-earned victory, headed back home with a life-sustaining check for $3,500.

With but a single day off to regroup from the tough Findlay contest, the Redmen were back on the road, this time to Troy, Ohio, and Hobart Arena, where they were to take on the Blue Jays of Creighton University on January 23.

Coached by Subby Salerno, Creighton was always a tough opponent. The Blue Jays regularly played many of the midwest's basketball powers and were a battle-tested team that was no stranger to big-time basketball pressure. The dapper, handsome Salerno had led his Omaha, Nebraska, quintet to an 11-14 record the year before, including upset wins over nationally-ranked Drake and Lawrence Tech. Leading his squad was Elton Tuttle, who had averaged nearly 19 points per game the previous year. The well-balanced, capably coached Blue Jays were eager to add the Redmen to their list of victims.

"My center, Elton Tuttle, was six-six and the tallest man on the squad. He had a fine fall-away jump shot and was an excellent rebounder, possessed good speed, and could drive extremely well from either the right or left," Salerno recalled. "Ray Yost, at six-four, was big and strong and possessed a fine right-handed hook shot at one forward, and Bob Kaminski, also six-four, was at the other forward. Eddie Cole, five-eleven, was one of the finest small players in the game. He was quick, could dribble with either hand, and was competitive beyond words. The other guard, Bob Meyer, five-ten, had fine speed as well. My bench, though, was limited, and we had little else to rely on past our starters. But Tuttle, Yost, and Cole could have played with any team in the country."

Creighton brought a 10-9 record into the game. With a schedule that included Michigan State, Wichita, and Seattle, the Blue Jays would provide yet another opportunity for the Redmen to convert naysayers into believers.

Salerno's teams characteristically used a half-court press and would try to destroy their opponent's offensive tempo by applying constant pressure on the ball. The tried-and-true Creighton strategy worked well as the Blue Jays matched Rio Grande evenly in the early going.

Francis kept the crowd of more than seventy-five hundred on their feet with an amazing shooting display. He finished the first half with 32 points. Rio Grande and Creighton left the court tied at 41. Rio Grande had played a more deliberate, paced game in the first half as a result of the Creighton pressure.

It remained a closely fought contest in the third period. "I had instructed the team at the intermission to sag in more from each side and attempt to intercept the passes that were directed towards Francis," Salerno remembered. This defensive switch resulted in Bevo's being jostled and fouled nearly every time he went down court. His usual accuracy from the line, where he spent most of the quarter, kept the Redmen in the game. As the third period concluded, it was 71-71.

Creighton, in its effort to stop Bevo, landed in serious foul trouble. Crippled by penalties, the Blue Jays were unable to stop the Redmen, who resorted to their familiar up-tempo game in the final stanza. Salerno eventually lost four starters to fouls. His charges couldn't keep pace, and their attack suffered considerably. "Once we lost any of our starters we were in trouble," Salerno declared.

With the free-wheeling Rio Grande offense in high gear, the Redmen were able to put some distance between themselves and the visitors. Oliver then used a semi-slowdown as Rio Grande attempted to nurse its six-point lead. The Redmen, uncomfortable with the tempo, executed poorly, allowing Creighton to fight back to tie the game again at 81. With time running down, Wiseman sealed the win. He converted two lay-ups off steals and added two free throws for good measure. Rio Grande had earned a 96-90 win. After his torrid start, Bevo finished with a total of 49 points. Once again the Redmen had proved they could play with—and beat—the big boys.

"Bevo lived up to all expectations," Salerno noted. "He would have been a welcome addition to any team in the country. He had an excellent jump shot and could hit from anywhere around the key. Despite the fact that Bevo *was* the offense, he did pass off well and set up many shots for his teammates. . . . His well-deserved publicity at a critical time for the sport proved a welcome boon to the game of college basketball."

❀ ❀ ❀

Sport magazine featured a long profile on Bevo in its January issue, and *Saga* followed with another. Francis and Rio Grande College were riding a wave of publicity that most people and schools only dream about. "We gave that little school twenty-five million dollars worth of free publicity. And they didn't appreciate any of it," Oliver declared.

The publicity continued to be a nightmare for Bevo. He was worn to a frazzle, and his patience with the domineering and demanding young coach was wearing dangerously thin. "I'd gone along with it all along. Mostly for the team. For their benefit. They'd given up so much for me that I thought I'd go along with it for them," Bevo said. "I owed them that for what they'd done for me. Actually, I owed them more. There just wasn't any more I could give them."

But Oliver's plan required relentless beating of the publicity drum. Bevo, increasingly reluctant to serve as the drum that attracted the crowds, wanted only to escape them. Sometimes he'd flee to Wellsville and the Chrislips' home. But reporters found him there as well. No haven was safe. "We were living our lives in a fish bowl. And I couldn't see any end in sight," Bevo recalled.

It might have been a bit more tolerable if he had felt that the faculty and administration were appreciative and supportive of his efforts. Instead, whenever he was on campus, he felt the cold shoulder of disdain and barely concealed contempt. "The president of the college wouldn't even speak to me. He just walked on by me like I wasn't even there," Bevo remembered vividly.

Indeed, the article in *Sport* characterized the school as "stamp-sized" and went on to note that "Rio Grande is real gone on Bevo the shot-maker, who is not only responsible for bringing his school more publicity than it ever had before but who may be the reason Rio Grande will stay in business despite its financial distress. Barely beneath the surface is a potential collision between what Newt Oliver thinks is fitting recognition of Bevo's talent and what school authorities think is fitting for a Rio Grande sophomore."

Oliver's failure to protect his star player from the press and campus politics was a precipitating factor in their now almost-daily clashes. Bevo had no one to turn to for support and guidance. There was only Newt, and he was always there during the day and literally next door to him at night. Indeed, Oliver had isolated his star player from anyone who could have offered him some solace and guidance in dealing with his problems. "He never did let anyone get close to me," Bevo said. "Wherever we went, he kept me with him all the time. I never was able to discuss my situation with anyone. He cut me off."

"Newt had the key," Diles remarked dryly. "He opened the doors."

Where Wiseman recalled that "Bevo felt he was being exploited,"

Diles said flatly, "There is absolutely no question he was exploited." Shane, the head of the Athletic Council, explained that "without Francis, Newt was nothing. Except a promoter."

"We all noticed the change in their relationship," Dick Barr said of Francis and Oliver. "It just got worse. They fought over everything. They were childish in their stubbornness." Eventually, Bevo reluctantly acquiesced to the entreaties of Wiseman and others to cooperate with Newt's demands. But he found it increasingly distasteful, and his disdain for the source of his discomfort—mainly Oliver—grew exponentially as the season dragged on.

Jean Cooper, who was a friend of Francis' landlady Edna Wickline, said that she noticed that Edna had grown quite attached to the young Francis family; indeed, Bevo often referred to Edna as his "second mother." Edna, Cooper reported, "was afraid that Jean was going to take the baby and flee back home with all the intrusions and commotion that Newt created around her. [Edna] would try to intercede on their behalf with Newt, asking him to leave them alone for a while. She even threatened to evict him from her home if he didn't. But it didn't help much in the long run."

14

113 Points of Vindication

With the Creighton win behind them, the Redmen traveled next to Cincinnati, where they were scheduled to meet Morris Harvey in a rematch slated for the Cincinnati Gardens on January 26.

The *Cincinnati Times-Star* heralded the appearance of Bevo and the Redmen with a twenty-eight-page "Basketball Special Edition" trumpeting their appearance. A full-page caricature of Francis graced the sports front under a headline that blared, "VIVA BEVO." The lineups appeared to the right of Bevo's caricature, and a story by Joe Minster, headlined "FABULOUS CAGER HERE," occupied the bottom right-hand portion of the page.

Minster's lead was simple: "Bevo is back. The fabulous scoring machine from little Rio Grande College will be the center of attention as a crowd of upwards of 5,000 is expected to watch Rio Grande tackle Morris Harvey."

After recounting the season highlights of Francis and Rio Grande to date, Minster offered, "Francis has shown beyond a shadow of a doubt he is no flash in the pan, but instead a sound player who would probably score more than his share of points against any type of opposition." Minster went on to present the enticing news that Francis, who held the Gardens' scoring record of 50 points, usually totaled more the second time he faced an opponent. That would mean, Minster concluded, "the record could be eclipsed tonight."

In Cincinnati the Redmen were lounging in their hotel lobby and reading the pre-game publicity while waiting to leave for the Gardens. But Francis was in his room and in no mood to break records.

"I had the flu. I had seen a doctor in Gallipolis before we left, and he'd given me a shot. I was still sick when we got to Cincinnati, and I saw another doctor there. I had diarrhea so bad I was afraid I was going to have to play with a pad in my shorts," Bevo recalled.

Because the contract with the Gardens—like all the others Newt had signed—required that Francis play to qualify Rio Grande for its gate guarantee, everyone involved in the promotion shared the player's discomfort.

In the lobby coffee shop an elderly gentleman overheard Wiseman describing his roommate's problems in graphic detail. He offered some advice: "Order some toast. Tell them to burn it black as coal. Crumble the toast in some warm water and tell him to drink it down without stopping. It will cure him for sure."

Wiseman did as he was told and took the foul-smelling and unappealing concoction up to Bevo. "I put it up to my lips and drank it all down. It tasted about as bad as it looked," Bevo recalled. Shortly afterward, he began to feel better. "I noticed I was spending less time in the bathroom than before, and I had Wiseman get me some more of the tea-like drink. I kept right on drinking it until it was time to leave for the game. It tasted awful, but somehow it worked."

Although he certainly was not 100 percent physically, Francis was able to play against Morris Harvey. In what the Morris Harvey players recall as the most physical contest they ever played, Rio Grande was able to eke out a 74-62 victory. Francis, weakened by the virus and brutalized inside by the defense, was held to 26 points. The record that Joe Minster had predicted might fall was never even threatened. In fact, Rio Grande struggled with the Golden Eagles throughout the contest. The Redmen had trailed by two at the end of the first period and were still down by a basket at the half.

The Redmen spurted in the third period, then gained some slack after the Eagles' Dave Rosen, who'd been guarding Bevo, fouled out. "I held his pants and grabbed anything I could to stop him. I was a pretty dirty player," Rosen candidly recalled many years later. He later described Bevo as "a country boy his coach led around."

Wiseman and Barr, making up for Bevo's less-than-normal production, tallied 31 points between them, sealing the fate of the Golden Eagles. "It was their outside shooters that beat us that night," Mario Palumbo recounted. "They were a much better team than I had expected."

The pre-game hoopla had drawn more than five thousand fans to the Gardens. In just five days, from January 21, when they met Findlay, until now, the Redmen had earned $11,500 for the college as their share of the gate receipts—not a bad week's work.

With another win neatly tucked away, the Redmen were off again to Buffalo to meet Buffalo State. The Orange, which owned a 6-2 record coming in, had seen the Redmen massacre Erie Tech. The Buffalo players knew they were in for a battle. Extra seats were hastily added to increase the arena's seating capacity to four thousand. The crowd that jammed into the Connecticut Street Armory easily exceeded that number.

Facing Bevo upon his arrival was yet another dreaded round of interviews with reporters and personal appearances with Newt. With a reluctance that was more readily apparent to his teammates than the press, he grudgingly complied with their requests and demands for access.

The game, for Bevo, was another sub-par performance. He accounted for 31 points as the Redmen rolled to an easy 81-65 win. But it was a far cry from his December appearance in the city when he'd blitzed Erie Tech for 64 points.

Buffalo State had provided far more resistance than Oliver and Rio Grande anticipated. The Orange double-, triple- and, at times, even quadruple-teamed Francis. At least Oliver had had the foresight to supply Bevo with a special cup to protect him from the flying elbows and pointed knees of his opponents.

"He was so roughed up that season that not even that cup, the type baseball catchers wore then, was enough," Benner said. "It was split in two more than a half-dozen times, and we were constantly replacing it. Yet he never complained."

Barr and Wiseman again came through to take advantage of the openings that Buffalo's one-sided defensive scheme presented. Al Schreiber, freshly transferred from Long Island University, provided a timely 10 points. A crafty five-foot-ten forward, Schreiber had honed his skills in the highly competitive Catskill Mountains Summer League in his native New York. When the point-shaving scandals hit Long Island University, the school administration responded by shutting down the Claire Bee-coached basketball program of the once fearsome Blackbirds, leaving Al with no place to play. Oliver, who had met the youngster when Milton Gross introduced them to each other before the Adelphi game, offered Al a chance to play at Rio Grande. In early January, Schreiber had eagerly joined the team. The unlikely presence of a big-city, street-smart kid good enough to have played for Bee offered the Redmen much-needed depth. Al could fill in at both guard and forward with equal ease and could provide the starters with a breather without slowing the momentum.

With their victory over Buffalo State, Rio Grande was 15-4 for the season. Through nineteen games Francis had accounted for 914 points. His average stood at 48.1 per outing. He had the highest personal point total as well as the highest average in the country.

Rio Grande had met some of the toughest major college teams in the country and had done more than simply hold their own. Despite the top-flight level of competition, Francis was virtually replicating the spectacular results of his freshman year. Yet even with all they'd accomplished thus far, the players felt that one task remained undone. On February 2, 1954, they had the opportunity to tackle that job in Jackson, Ohio.

That was where Rio Grande was to meet Hillsdale College of Michigan in a game that Oliver had shifted from Community Hall to accommodate a larger crowd. This was to be the last scheduled local appearance of the Redmen. Their Gallia County fans, who had been relying on radio and newspaper accounts for reports of their fortunes, would turn out in record numbers. They would see a show worthy of Broadway itself.

The court at Jackson High School had an unusual location—it was laid out on the stage of the auditorium. The first six feet of each wall of the stage was covered with dark-stained bead board designed to offer more cushion than the masonry. At one end of the stage, behind the basket, a long row of metal radiators hung about eight feet off the floor against the wall. Above them were clerestory windows that reached nearly to the ceiling. The back wall of the stage was cream colored and bisected by a large open entranceway. The official scorer and clock operator were seated directly in front of it, facing the audience, with the team benches flanking the scorer's table. To its right, the scoreboard and clock hung about eight feet up the wall. Donated by the class of 1949, they would provide a visual record of an incredible event.

Every available seat in the auditorium was occupied as the Redmen took to the floor to meet Hillsdale. "They were wall to wall in the place. You couldn't have gotten any more in there," Bevo recalled.

Having already dispatched Hillsdale earlier in the season, the Redmen were anticipating little trouble. In their first meeting the visitors had managed only 45 points. The Redmen and Oliver were prepared to face an offense that hinged on stalling and practiced ways to counter it if it happened. Their preparation would pay huge dividends, though not in the way that the players had anticipated.

Before the tip-off Bevo, who had struggled through two atypical performances, told the team he thought that he "might have a good night."

Rio Grande romped out to a commanding lead, meeting little opposition from the Dales. Bevo's intuition had been right. He was hitting with remarkable accuracy from all over the court. "He just couldn't miss," Ripperger recalled. And Wiseman remembered that "Hillsdale was hanging all over [Bevo] and he still scored."

The points rolled up and up. At the half, Rio Grande held an insurmountable lead, 58-33. Francis had scored 43 points.

In the dressing room Carl Benner cut the tape that Oliver had applied to Francis' ankle before the game. "It was applied too tightly and had cut through the skin of his arch. He was bleeding and his sock was filled with blood stains," Benner said.

Oliver grabbed the scorebook from Carroll Kent, the student who served as assistant coach, and quickly scanned the numbers. Turning to the team in the locker room, he said, "We've got to feed Bevo. He has forty-three now, and this might be our chance to get him a hundred again. Let's go out there and do it."

The team needed no encouragement. The players wanted the record back as badly as any of them had ever wanted anything. It was the last of the marks that the NCAA had stripped from Bevo—and them, by extension. Yes, Bevo was the athlete affected personally, but his teammates felt the sting of the rebuke as if it had been visited on them as well. They figured they could right last season's wrong by reclaiming Bevo's record under the very guidelines that the NCAA had devised to deny it. They had done it once and were determined to do it again. As they took to the court for the final half, their determined faces reflected their firm resolve. They would get the ball to Bevo as often as possible, any way they could, from here on out.

The final half was an awesome display of shot making. The players, who had seen Bevo do some incredible things over the course of a season and a half, were amazed at what was happening. "I had played forty to fifty times with him, and had seen him do some pretty amazing things, but I never saw anything like it before," Wiseman said. "It simply didn't matter what they did, defensively, he just couldn't miss. Hillsdale drove him deep into the corners with three men hanging on him, and he just poured them in."

"He had the hottest hand I ever saw that night," Ripperger recalled. According to Dick Barr, "From fifteen to eighteen feet out, he just never missed." His teammates unselfishly fed him the ball, and "it seemed like everything I threw up that night just went in," Bevo said. Shot after shot found nothing but net. When he was fouled (and he was, repeatedly and roughly), he made those shots as well.

The tactics that the Redmen had devised and practiced to stymie any effort to stall worked to their advantage now. Each time Hillsdale gained possession after a Francis basket, Rio Grande immediately fouled the first Hillsdale player to touch the ball when it was thrown inbounds. This killed the clock while Hillsdale went to the foul line, and it prolonged the game. The period was taking so long that the Hillsdale coach and his players were sure that Rio Grande was manipulating the clock. They weren't. But the clock was not running while Hillsdale was shooting from the foul line, and it was frozen while Bevo took his foul shots, stretching the period far longer than normal.

"I thought our coach was going to have a heart attack," Hillsdale's Jack Lowry recalled. "He was screaming at the officials that the clock was being manipulated. He even threatened to take us off the floor in protest but didn't. In the back of his mind was the return date the next season in either Battle Creek or Detroit, and the big payday it promised for Hillsdale."

"It was the longest damn game I'd ever been in," Barr said.

Wiseman said it best: "With all the fouls, it probably seemed like an eternity to them."

As Bevo's point total kept soaring higher and higher, the Gallia County fans were roaring their approval and encouragement. The din in the auditorium was deafening as each bucket drew another thunderous round of applause. Pouring in points at an incredible pace, Francis raced on toward the stratospheric 100-point summit that only he, in the long history of the game, had ever scaled.

When the third period ended, Bevo needed only 26 more points to re-emerge as the greatest scorer in the history of the game. His team wouldn't allow him to fail. "I told them that this was the night he would get the hundred points and that no one else should take any shots in the last period," Oliver recalled. "I also told them to keep on fouling Hillsdale to kill the clock and give Bevo every opportunity to get the record back."

"That was the only time that I recall where we did pass up open shots to feed Bevo," Wiseman said.

The final ten minutes of play were frenetic and seemed to take even longer than the third period. Hillsdale was all over Bevo because it was apparent that he was the only player shooting for Rio Grande. The Dales jostled and bumped and shoved him each time the ball came his way. Meanwhile, the Redmen continued their clock-killing tactics of fouling the Hillsdale players as soon as the ball was put into play. The starters were soon all lost to fouls, and reserves Don Vyhnalek, Al Schreiber, Lee Weiher and Dick Myers were on the floor to continue the record onslaught. Ed Clark of the *Jackson (Ohio) Sun-Journal* reported, "As the men guarding him, one by one, began accumulating five personal fouls, Bevo made it a point to shake their hands or pat them on the shoulder as they left the game."

Bevo added 39 points in the chaotic, foul-dominated, seemingly interminable stanza.

In the final twenty minutes of play, he amassed 70 points. His game total stood at *113 points*. It was a new NCAA single-game scoring record. What's more, he had done it under the conditions that the NCAA itself had dictated and was now forced to accept.

Bevo Francis became the only man ever to score more than 100 points in a college basketball game. And he did it twice.

The phenomenal performance sent shockwaves across the sports pages. Writers searched frantically for new superlatives to describe the feat. The media's preoccupation with Bevo and Rio Grande, which had died down some in the past week, began anew.

Francis had shot a stunning 54 percent from the floor, scoring on 38 of 70 attempts. From the free-throw line he was simply uncanny. He dropped in 37 of 45 for an average of 82 percent. His 37 successful free throws also were a new NCAA record.

In due course the NCAA announced, with a marked lack of enthusiasm, that the records established by Bevo would indeed grace its record books. The Basketball Hall of Fame in Springfield, Massachusetts, asked for the game ball and the official score sheet.

Howard Rolph, the veteran official who worked the game and attested to its legitimate length, termed Bevo's performance the "most sensational I've ever witnessed in a lifetime in the sport." Characteristically, Francis gave the credit to his teammates. "Most of the credit belongs to them," he said. "Without them, I couldn't have done it."

Howard Null, the Hillside coach victimized by the 134-91 shellacking and Oliver's tactics, which had driven him to near apoplexy, nevertheless said, "Without a doubt Francis is the greatest shot I've ever seen."

Oliver, also in character, said, "I believe, eventually, Bevo will be recognized as the greatest collegiate player of all time."

But in 1954, at least, most observers felt that honor belonged to others. Among the naysayers' nominees was Frank Selvy of Furman, the *Gallia Times* reported. When a reporter told Selvy of Francis' explosive performance, the stunned player replied, "Good gosh, it's almost unbelievable—113 points. I could never make that many in a game."

According to the news report, Selvy, who then led the major colleges in scoring, added, "I've only seen Bevo once—a few years ago in Murray, Kentucky, when he played in an All-Star game; and he only scored 13 points that night. He must be some shot today."

Less than two weeks later, on February 13, Selvy, in an obvious attempt to restore the credibility of the major colleges (and to dilute the effect of Bevo's achievement), would score 100 points against tiny Newberry College of South Carolina. Years later Wilt Chamberlain, of the NBA's Philadelphia Warriors, would match that mark in a professional game at Hershey, Pennsylvania.

To date, however, the only player—college or pro—ever to score more than 100 points is Bevo Francis.

With the unusually long respite of a week to savor what they had just achieved, the Redmen, vindicated at last (in their minds, at least), prepared to face Anderson College. The Indiana school's most famous alumnus was a baseball player: the Brooklyn Dodgers' ace Carl Erskine.

The week off for the team was not so leisurely for Bevo. While the players were enjoying some much-needed rest and a few trips down to Gallipolis to the Bob Evans Drive-In, Bevo was once more under siege. The apartment phone never stopped ringing after the Hillsdale game. The press, which had shadowed him constantly since the Ashland Junior College game a year earlier, now redoubled its efforts to reach him. They sought new angles and reworked old stories to appease their readers' insatiable appetite for any morsel about Bevo. As he recaptured his records, he rewarded the faith of his loyal supporters, who had hoped against hope that he would succeed. They simply couldn't get enough of Bevo.

For Bevo and Jean the week after the Hillsdale game was a nightmare of phones that jangled day and night, countless requests for photographs, and endless interviews. They realized grimly that no place was safe from the prying press and that their lives were no longer their own. Without rancor they wondered how and when it would ever come to an end. When, they wondered, would their marriage no longer include the Fourth Estate as a partner? And when, could someone please tell them, could they enjoy life and love together, away from the glare of the flashbulbs and blinding newsreel cameras?

Though neither dared voice their suspicions aloud, both realized instinctively that as long as Bevo remained at Rio Grande with Oliver, they would be subjected to more of the same. That would mean two more years. Could they stand it? The future that they faced was not a happy one.

Through nearly two seasons that seemed like a lifetime, with constant travel during the season and even afterward, they'd somehow managed to survive. Their infrequent time alone was special and according to Jean, despite Bevo's status as a national celebrity, he had remained, through it all, a simple country boy at heart—the unknown and uncomplicated guy that she had fallen for and married.

All the attention never did swell Bevo's head. Although, given a choice, he would have preferred a solitary evening of coon hunting, he remained largely accessible to the media. He voiced his intense dislike of and discomfort with the press only to Oliver, who, for his own obvious reasons, ignored it, and to Jean, who was powerless to help him. Their discussions, which they whispered in the apartment because only paper-thin walls separated them from Newt, inevitably concluded with a sigh and one saying, "At least in two more years it will be over." But for the besieged, confused, and confounded young couple, two years seemed like an awfully long time to wait.

But for now the task at hand was the game against the Anderson College Ravens in the Anderson (Indiana) High School Wigwam (gym).

For the NCAA's purposes, Bevo was credited with 929 points thus far, because it refused to count the Erie Tech game. Approaching the February 9 game with the Anderson College Ravens, Bevo was within reach of Johnny O'Brien's single-season mark, set the year before, of 970 points, which was the former Seattle star's total after the NCAA applied the "Bevo Rule" and subtracted numerous points from O'Brien's season effort too.

The wire services ran a picture of Bevo and Dodger ace Erskine posing together on game day.

The Redmen arrived in Anderson early on February 9, and Bevo and his teammates were walking toward the gym when a young man drove by in a Model-T Ford. Bevo flagged him down and went for a short ride with him, enjoying the experience while delighting onlookers.

His brief moment of frivolity over, Francis and the Redmen squared off against the Ravens before five thousand fans. The Anderson College band, clad in brand new uniforms and led by Professor Malcolm Gressman, played marches to inspire the Ravens as they warmed up. It was nice, loud, and ultimately ineffective.

From the early moments it was apparent that Rio Grande would have little trouble with the Ravens. Despite Anderson's efforts to contain him, Bevo was hitting with ease. The Redmen sailed out to a 32-10 first-quarter lead. Bevo had not lost the incredible shooting touch of the Hillsdale game and was pacing the club as usual.

Coach Ernie Rangazas, whose squad was fifteenth in the country in offense, had a potent scorer himself in Richie Brown, sixth on the scoring list at game time with a 26-point average. Rangazas had devised a defense that he was certain would contain Bevo.

"We used a collapsing man-to-man defense so that when he was under the basket, he had two or three men on him," forward Duke Ellis recalled. "He was the best shooter that I'd ever seen. He was versatile and could shoot about any shot from anyplace on the floor. He hit jump shots from deep in the corner with his back to the basket. He had a very soft hook shot from close in as well as deep. His jumper facing the basket was awesome."

Led by Francis, Rio Grande continued to roll in the third period. As the final quarter began, it was clear that Bevo would get the 42 points he needed to break O'Brien's mark and have his name reinserted in the NCAA record book.

He broke the record with a foul shot early in the period and went on to tally 59 points in the 101-85 victory, fulfilling O'Brien's year-old prophecy that his record would fall to Bevo. Bevo Francis had added the single-season scoring record to his mantelpiece, and the season was far from over.

As Bevo was leaving the court after the game, Newt caught him by the elbow and said, "The war is over." Francis knew that his coach was referring to his running battle with the NCAA for vindication and recognition. Shrugging his shoulders, he replied, "Yes, I guess it is."

Anderson's Duke Ellis said he remembers "feeling at the time that not only did they have the greatest individual ball player in the country, but they had a great team as well. Especially at the guards. Bevo was a phenomenal player."

Encircled by a crowd of eager autograph seekers, the weary Francis stayed near the edge of the court, signing the orange and black programs that were thrust at him while answering questions fired by reporters who had elbowed their way through. He was still there after the rest of the team had showered and dressed. He finally excused himself politely. "I've got to get some rest. Newt and I have to be in Lima, Ohio, tomorrow for another press conference," he said apologetically.

Oliver crowed that he and Bevo had scored a decisive victory in their war with the NCAA. "We showed them!" he announced. "I no longer have an argument with them. When I win an argument, I quit yelling."

Riding the crest of an eleven-game winning streak and secure in the knowledge that they had achieved their common goal of restoring Bevo's name to its rightful place in the record book, the Redmen moved on to Huntington, West Virginia. There the Redmen would meet Salem College, the last team to have defeated them. The boys from Rio Grande had revenge on their minds.

Salem proved to be mortal this time around, dispatched by the Redmen with a 115-76 romp. Francis accounted for 58 of those points.

The players had a rare and much-needed ten-day break ahead. They were happy to be back in the Animal Dorm over the cafeteria. Jim McKenzie strummed his guitar while the others accompanied him, badly but enthusiastically, with their Hank Williams impressions. For the first time in what seemed like ages to them, they were able to attend classes with the other students and resume some semblance of normal college life.

Bevo sought to use the break for a short trip to spend time with Jean in Wellsville. Newt saw it as an ideal opportunity for more personal appearances and shooting exhibitions by his star. With Bevo headed in one direction and Newt tugging him in another, they were at loggerheads again. Both were growing more stubborn and intractable with each flare-up. And those flare-ups were growing increasingly hotter with each passing week.

In their dorm rooms the players spoke openly of the growing rebellion by their high-scoring teammate. "We'd sit around and laugh about their latest incident. They were so childish about things that it became comical to us," Dick Barr said. "At the same time, I knew I only had a one-year scholarship deal, so I began to start looking around in case things unraveled."

The break also brought into focus just how bad relations were between Oliver and the administration. There was no mistaking the hostility, voiced and otherwise. "It was apparent that the jealousy and bitterness were worse than ever," Barr said. "Newt's unwillingness to compromise even one inch didn't help the situation any," Wiseman added.

The players all sensed that a showdown was coming soon. While continuing his public threats to leave the school and take Bevo with him, Oliver had begun to quietly feel the other players out about the future. "He was thinking about a barnstorming tour with the team," Ripperger recalled. "It was to come right after the season ended."

If the school didn't appreciate what Oliver and the team had done for it, why should they feel any loyalty to the school?, the coach asked them. Where their coach was headed was clear to the players, just as it was clear to them that the Rio Grande administration never would countenance barnstorming by the Redmen.

The tense and icy hostility beamed at the players and their coach certainly was not eased by the ongoing battle of wills between the coach and the star player. Eventually, as always, Newt and Bevo attained an uneasy truce that was as shaky as the one recently achieved in Korea.

When the Redmen left Rio Grande again, they were bound for Ashland, Ohio, where they were to play their rematch with Ashland College in a new high school gym. Predictably, it was a sellout crowd.

Although never close, the game was a particularly rough one, marred by 69 fouls. Ashland used every trick—not just to stop Francis but to put him out of action. The Ashland team used its knees and elbows as weapons and aimed them at the lanky center with abandon. One blow, aimed at his groin, was so violent that it split his protective cup in half.

Near the end of the game, with the outcome long since decided, an Ashland player jumped on Francis' ankle. Bevo crashed to the floor in obvious pain. After Newt and Carl Benner tended to him, he rose slowly, and they helped him from the floor, to a huge ovation from the crowd.

After the game Bevo was taken to nearby Mansfield General Hospital where x-rays revealed that nothing was broken. But his ligaments and tendons were severely strained, and the doctors informed him that, even with the ankle heavily taped, his mobility would be severely restricted.

The badly damaged ankle would transform the once fleet-footed Francis into a hobbling remnant of his former self. With 195 pounds distributed over his six-foot-nine frame, his speed and agility had always been as remarkable as his shooting ability. With the Redmen's fast-break offensive style, he was always with or ahead of the flying

Wiseman and McKenzie as they headed up court. Not any more. For the remainder of the season he would play in intense pain. His once balletic movements became a painful shuffle.

The Ashland game would go into the record books as a 121-61 win. But the toll it exacted on Francis, who scored 53 points, was devastating to the Rio Grande offense.

Oliver's well-calculated plan could withstand almost anything: a jealous faculty, a board of trustees that mistrusted and resented him, an Athletic Council that tied both his arms, a college president who turned his back on him in deference to threats from the Ohio College Conference and others, sniping from the press and the major college coaches, and the NCAA's blatant crusade to discredit him and his star. The one thing Oliver's strategy could not withstand was an injury to Francis. Without Bevo, the plan would fail. It was the worst thing that could have happened.

The Redmen had played twenty-three games and had three remaining regular season games scheduled when Bevo was hurt. Oliver, in a move that was and remains unheard of in college basketball, rescheduled the remaining contests to allow his star time to recover. That he was able to get away with this move speaks volumes about Bevo's unique and massive public appeal. All three remaining foes readily agreed to Oliver's demands. Without Francis, they knew, a game with tiny Rio Grande would be hard-pressed to attract flies.

"After that injury, the bubble just burst, and it all began to fall apart," Wiseman said. "Bevo couldn't practice at all, and the ankle was really bothering him. He and Newt were still butting heads, and without being able to practice Bevo got a little bit out of shape. We were all a little tired after all the travel and the tension around us all the time."

No one noticed that Newt took a day off to make a quick trip over to West Virginia. He never discussed it with the players, and no one knew where he went. He was back the same night.

It was late enough in the season that fans and sportswriters were speculating about postseason play. Once again, officials of the National Invitation Tournament failed to issue an invitation to the Redmen. The Adelphi loss hadn't helped their cause.

"I had seen a lot of pressure brought to bear on the selection committee to get some teams into the tourney," Milton Gross said. "But this was the first time I ever saw pressure exerted to keep one team out."

Instead, the Redmen accepted an invitation to participate in the

National Association of Intercollegiate Athletics (NAIA) Tournament. To earn the right to compete in the finals in Kansas City, the Redmen would first have to survive a qualifying round in Cleveland.

With little time to heal, Francis and the team left for Cleveland. En route they met up with one of the worst snowstorms to hit the area in years. Traffic slowed to a crawl, and visibility was down to a few feet. Drifts, whipped by the wind, reached as high as six feet across some stretches of road. With conditions deteriorating by the hour, the team managed to make it to a train station. There, in the face of howling winds and swirling snow, they hopped a train to Cleveland.

Once there they found that the horrid conditions had grounded the other three teams. Road conditions were so treacherous that the tournament officials, wisely realizing they would never recoup their $2,500 guarantee under the snow emergency conditions, canceled the event. The organizers chose the Redmen, by virtue of their overall record, to represent the district in the finals at Municipal Auditorium in Kansas City.

The NAIA Tournament was one of the most demanding in college athletics. To reach the finals the team would have to win five games in six days. One loss and it was all over.

Rio Grande was seeded first among the thirty-two teams in the field. Tournament officials could barely conceal their pleasure at having the top attraction in the nation in the field. If Rio Grande were to reach the finals (the bracket it was put in was decidedly weaker than the other side of the draw), the tournament would be a huge financial bonanza.

A sellout crowd of 10,500 greeted them as they took the floor for their opening round game against Arizona State University-Flagstaff, a satellite campus of the larger Tempe school. With Ripperger, Wiseman, and McKenzie enjoying success from the floor, the Redmen rolled over their foes in an easy 90-74 tourney debut. Francis, hobbled badly by the ankle injury and in obvious discomfort, accounted for 28 points. Nonetheless, the fans applauded his every move.

After a day off, the Redmen were in front of another capacity crowd. The night before, when they were not scheduled to play, attendance had shrunk to six thousand. Now, as they prepared to play Southeast Louisiana State, there wasn't a vacant seat in the house.

Southeast Louisiana had a big strong front line and used it to throw up a picket line in front of and behind Bevo. With his ankle reducing his mobility, he was unable to spin free the way he had throughout his career. That left him a stationary target, and Wiseman and McKenzie could not penetrate the defense surrounding him. Their passes were batted harmlessly away or intercepted when Bevo couldn't make the moves to catch them. "He was really roughed up by their big men. He was already hurting from the ankle injury and couldn't move well at all," McKenzie recalled.

The Redmen fought valiantly before being overwhelmed by their bigger foes, 78-65. They were eliminated, much to the shock and dismay of the promoters. A gimpy Francis could manage but 27 points in the losing effort. The absence of his average 47-plus points cost them the game.

They would have no national championship to cap off their season. Dejected, the Redmen boarded the train for the final three games of the season. The contests, against Shurtleff College, Rockhurst College, and Creighton, had all been pushed back after Bevo's injury.

The first stop was St. Louis for the game against Shurtleff, which was 19-4 that season.

Ever since the ten-day break that they had spent on campus amid the swirling currents of uncertainty and acrimony, the Redmen had felt a subtle shift in their energy. They found it increasingly difficult to get up for the games. Bevo's injury only exacerbated the situation. The bickering between Newt and Bevo was louder and more frequent than it had ever been. And the nagging injury was adding to Bevo's growing displeasure with his coach's persistent prodding to be more accessible to the press.

Bevo was tired, angry, and in constant pain—not a good combination for a winning performance. Yet the schedule and Newt dictated that he perform as planned, whether he liked it or not. "They were at each other all the time. It hurt the team," Wiseman said. Barr recalled, "It was obvious to all of us that it was coming to an end. Everyone pretty much knew by then that the team wasn't going to be back next year."

Wiseman recalled, "One particular incident that took place at that time was when Newt came home and found Bevo sitting in the living room having a beer. [Newt] climbed down [Bevo's] throat about training rules and conditioning, and Bevo went right back at him. It went on for quite a while with each one screaming at the other. Neither one would give in."

Of course, Francis was old enough to legally consume the beer, and when Newt barged in, Bevo was probably enjoying it in one of the precious few moments of privacy that he'd had in two years. The incident was typical of their relationship at that point, with Oliver constantly asserting his control over his player and Francis resisting it with growing ferocity. He could not free himself from Oliver's dominating persona and all the unpleasant activities that he was forced to endure at Oliver's behest, not even in the privacy of his own home. "I didn't have a private life," he would say of that time.

"I didn't feel he was training like he should be. I was hard on him and he resented it," Oliver recalled. "It just got to the point where I couldn't control Bevo any more."

"Newt could have been more diplomatic about the way he treated Bevo. But that wasn't his nature," Wiseman said. "I noticed Bevo's attitude wasn't the same as it was before. It just seemed that he really didn't want to be there. I really don't think Rip or I or any of us could have handled all the attention as well as Bevo did. The amount of attention he received everywhere we went was simply unbelievable. And it never let up."

The demoralized Redmen managed to pull themselves together in St. Louis. With a fourth-quarter rally they managed a 72-70 win over Shurtleff in front of three thousand fans. Francis, with his ankle hampering his every movement, still managed to contribute 37 points.

Oliver's two-week postponement of the Rockhurst College game turned into a great opportunity for the promoters of the East-West All-Star game in Kansas City. At the request of the Shriners, the charity game was shifted there and would be played as a preliminary to the featured game. The college All-Star classic was still in its infancy and the sponsors felt—and rightly so—that another Kansas City appearance by Francis would be an added boost to the box office. A full house responded for this second renewal of the classic, many undoubtedly drawn by Francis and Rio Grande's appearance in the preliminary game.

Rockhurst College proved to be anything but a roll-over-and-play-dead opponent for the showcase appearance of Bevo and the Redmen. Rio Grande managed a one-point lead at the half, but the Redmen were playing sluggish and uninspired ball.

The game, like so many others that season, was a rough-and-tumble contest, and the officials were displaying a marked lack of interest in the brutal tactics. The lead changed hands nine times in the final period, and there were eight ties. With less than three minutes remaining, Rio Grande trailed by a single basket. Ripperger was whistled for a foul as he and Wiseman applied pressure to the Rockhurst guards in the backcourt. In obvious disgust at the call against him and the frustration that he and the other Redmen were feeling because of the officiating, he slammed the ball to the floor. That action, by the usually reserved Ripperger, drew a technical foul call as well.

"It had been a really rough game, and Bevo was really getting worked over all night, and they weren't calling anything," Ripperger said. "I just lost my temper in the heat of the moment." Oliver was on the bench, waving and yelling wildly in protest of the call. "He was screaming at the referees and was halfway out on the floor when they called a technical on him too," Ripperger said.

Red-faced and animated, Oliver refused to obey the referees' order to sit down. When the foul shooting was over, Rockhurst held a 56-50 lead. Veins bulging from his neck and his face crimson with rage, Oliver tossed a large towel out on the floor with a vengeance. Stomping toward his players on the court, his arms swinging wildly, he announced, "That's it. Let's go. We're walking out of here."

"I was on the bench next to him when he went charging out there," Carl Benner said. "I couldn't believe what I was seeing." Bevo added, "I didn't know what the hell to think when he came out there."

"I asked him what he said," Wiseman said. "I couldn't believe it." Oliver repeated his orders to leave the floor. "He had told us at the last time-out, 'One more bad call and we're leaving,'" Barr remembered. "Of course, we didn't think he really meant it."

Whistles were blowing shrilly and the crowd was in an uproar as Oliver rounded up his stunned players and motioned them off the court to the dressing room. Slowly, they began to realize in the melee that swirled around them that Oliver really was leaving. He was stomping angrily toward the dressing room, where the College All-Stars had gathered at the entrance to watch Francis.

In confusion, disappointment, anger, and weary dismay, they silently began to troop off behind him. Shrine officials had scurried down from the stands in an attempt to intercept Newt and get him to finish the game. Oliver, jaw jutting and firmly set, brushed on by them without listening. As he reached the dressing room door, he was in full-tilt rage when he ran into Adolph Rupp.

Selected to coach the East All-Stars, the courtly baron grabbed Oliver by his elbow. "Now, Newt," Rupp said, his Kentucky drawl thick but insistent, "you know you ought to go on back out there and finish this game. It's just not right taking those boys off like that."

Oliver shook free from the court legend's grasp and stormed on toward the dressing room, head shaking and hands and arms thrown downward in rejection. It was obvious to everyone that Oliver wasn't coming back.

Out on the court, Benner had reached Francis. Bevo was still standing there, his ankle throbbing and instep bleeding where the tightly wound adhesive had cut through the skin. Amid the chaos and uncertainty swirling around them, the diminutive manager threw a comforting arm around Bevo's waist. "Come on, Beeve," he said softly. "We'd better go." Dragging the large canvas equipment bag with one arm and encircling Bevo's waist with the other, Benner urged the limping center gently from the court. As they made their way slowly through the milling crowd of players and officials, all of whom were confused about what had transpired, Benner shook his head sadly. "It shouldn't have ended like this," he said.

The crowd, now realizing what had happened, stirred as Benner and Bevo approached the edge of the court. They rose and cheered the departing duo but certainly not for Bevo's performance on the court that evening—he'd scored but 22 points. Instead it was a spontaneous outpouring of affection by fans who were expressing their gratitude and liking for an athlete who had thrilled and entertained them for two incredible seasons. The cheers followed them as they disappeared into the locker-room tunnel. The echoes of the ovation carried to them eerily in the darkness.

With the unorthodox, abortive ending to the Rockhurst game still a disquieting presence in their minds, the team flew to Omaha to meet Creighton University in the season's finale.

Although they had lost two of their last three games, the Redmen were still a hot ticket in frigid Omaha. The game had been shifted from the Creighton gymnasium to Boys' Town in order to accommodate the unprecedented demand for tickets.

When Rio Grande made its way onto the court, the doors to the gym had been closed for an hour. Three thousand people had been turned away. The crowd of sixty-five hundred had filled every available seat, until fans occupied even the seats on the Rio Grande bench. Room was cleared for Oliver and the reserves in front of the bench, where they sat cross-legged as the starters took the floor.

With Francis still hobbled by his badly injured ankle and the team dispirited from recent events, this game was nothing like the first time the Redmen had met Creighton that season. Throwing a defensive blanket over the limping Francis, Creighton jumped out to an early lead and was never headed. The listless play of the Redmen reflected their mental and physical anguish. "I think we just wanted it to be over," Wiseman said.

Creighton easily avenged its earlier loss at Troy and dominated the contest that the Blue Jays won, 93–75. Bevo scored 41 points.

The Redmen wound up the year at 21–7, including the Erie Tech game. Officially, their record would stand at 20–7, with three of those losses coming in the last four games while Bevo was injured. Even the staunchest of their critics had to agree that the Redmen from tiny Rio Grande had acquitted themselves well against major basketball power-houses.

For Francis the season had been one of personal trial and vindication. With the Erie Tech contest thrown out, he had scored 1,255 points in twenty-seven games, an average of 46.4 points per game. He had accounted for more than half of his team's total points.

His average, attained against major basketball powers, nearly equaled the pace of the previous year—the one that the critics had scoffed at and the NCAA had erased. Bevo had met the unspoken challenge to do it all over again, silencing the NCAA by reestablishing the single-game mark with his 113-point performance against Hillsdale, and he had helped establish the credibility of the fabulous exploits of the Redmen under the sternest of conditions.

The Redmen had established themselves as the equal of almost any team in the land. And they had done it without the advantage of a single home game.

15

Turning Pro

While the team made its way back to Rio Grande, The Associated Press released its All-America team selections. Francis had been named to the second team, even though he had received more first-place votes than Bob Pettit for first-team honors. By a strange quirk in the rules, Francis, with 119 first-team votes, was supplanted by Pettit, who had garnered but 102. Because more writers had named Pettit than Francis as their second team choice (131-26), the AP used the cumulative total, and Bevo was relegated instead to the second team.

On the AP's first team were Frank Selvy of Furman, Don Schlundt of Indiana, Tom Gola of LaSalle, Cliff Hagan of Kentucky, and Pettit of LSU. Francis headed the second team, which included Bob Leonard of Indiana, Frank Ramsey of Kentucky, Dick Ricketts of Duquesne, and Tom Marshall of Western Kentucky.

A sidebar story that most AP clients ran chronicled reaction to the results by some of those who had participated in the voting:

Paul Frink, *Lima (Ohio) News*: "Bevo Francis has definitely proven himself major league."

Dave Weiser, KEYY, Provo, Utah: "Francis and Selvy have sufficiently made critics eat the ball."

Jim MacDonald (Ansonia, Conn.) *Evening Sentinel*: "Gola and Green (Duquesne), best all-around. Francis, best shot."

Walt Hickey, (Burlington, Vt.) *Free Press*: "Bevo, best of them all."

Don Smith, *Long Island Star Journal*: "Viva Bevo."

Cliff Tauscher, WTSK-TV, Knoxville, Tennessee: "Bevo Francis has made a believer out of me."

Ray Fruger, (Elgin, Ill.) *Courier News*: "Francis has demonstrated his ability to mix in fast company."

Not surprisingly, there were dissenters. Among them was Bob Russell of the *Chicago Daily News*, who offered, "No Kentucky players should be considered. If we're picking an Alumni All-America, we should consider George Mikan, Goose Tatum and Hank Luisetti, along with Baron Rupp's overage boys. Francis doesn't belong either. He's a one-man sideshow, not a basketball player."

None of those familiar with the events of a year earlier were shocked when *Collier's* magazine announced its selections, chosen by a panel of major college coaches headed by Howard Hobson, and Francis was accorded no better than a regional honorable mention. That was a distinction he shared with another under-appreciated sophomore: Bill Russell of San Francisco.

�֎ ✖ ✖

Their season-long odyssey over, the Redmen returned to the campus and got less than the heroes' welcome they deserved.

Oliver, increasingly piqued at the administration, had been quoted on numerous occasions recently about his displeasure with the treatment that his team was receiving from the college. He had repeated his thinly veiled threats to leave, Bevo in tow, "for greener pastures." Rumors about a barnstorming trip with the team continued to surface.

The Rockhurst walkout had only added to the administration's unhappiness with Oliver. The move had drawn a stern reprimand from the NAIA, further upsetting President Davis and the trustees.

Even before the final road trip, the situation had deteriorated to a dangerously low level. Rumors abounded about the college's desire to rid itself of the abrasive coach who refused to adhere to the administration's advice and who openly defied and criticized college officials. By words and deeds, Oliver had done nothing but make matters worse.

Instead of a welcoming party of grateful faculty and students, what met the Redmen upon their return was a sternly worded note. Its message was clear. Oliver had pushed too hard, too often. And the school wasn't going to be pushed anymore.

"When we got back to our dorm, there was a note stuck under the door," McKenzie related. "It said if we played any postseason games, our scholarships would be revoked."

"Newt had talked to all the starters about going out on a tour together," Dick Barr said. "He wanted the whole team to leave school and go out on a tour with him. When Moses, McKenzie, and I turned him down, he dropped the idea."

For his part, Oliver said, "I had offers on my desk with guarantees of over $50,000 for us to play games the next season. But I could see by then it was never going to work there. They wouldn't work with me and what I was trying to do. They tried to drive me. You can't drive Newt Oliver. Nobody in the world can drive me. They told me it was going to be this way or else. Well, it was going to be 'or else.' I should have formed a pro team and taken them out on a tour. We would have made a million dollars. There was talk of getting a pro franchise in the Cleveland area, and then that fell through."

What Oliver did instead surprised even those closest to the team.

"When we got back and returned to class, Bevo wasn't there," Ripperger remembered. Added Wiseman, "Before I realized what had happened, he [Bevo] was gone."

Newt had left for more verdant pastures and had taken his star player with him.

"When we got back [to campus]," Bevo said, "he told me, 'I got you a contract.' I asked him what he was talking about. What kind of contract? That's when he told me he'd been to see Abe Saperstein in West Virginia and that he was offered a contract for me to sign with the Globetrotters' organization. I had been looking for[ward to] that last game ever since the injury. I really needed a break. But I knew from the last year that I wasn't really going to get any break from the press and publicity. I was tired of being cooped up with reporters hounding me all the time. The money wasn't that great at the time. But my daddy never earned more than five thousand dollars a year digging clay with a pick and shovel until his back was nearly broken. So being paid to play basketball sounded pretty good to me. Besides, I was tired of all the attention and publicity and saw it as my chance to get away from it all.

"Newt made it sound real good. Only then did he tell me that the contract was only good if I took him with me. He told me it was a combined deal. I thought it over some and decided to give it a try."

Without making up the midterm exams he'd missed while on the road, Bevo notified the school that he had signed a contract to play professionally and was going to withdraw and go home. He retreated to the Chrislips' home in Wellsville.

Saperstein was a shrewd businessman who had started the Globetrotters on a shoestring and turned them into a worldwide attraction that combined basketball skills with slapstick comedy routines, to the delight of millions. He was more than a little interested when Oliver turned up, asking to join the Globetrotters' organization and offering to bring along the nation's top scorer and gate attraction. The package that Saperstein offered was that Bevo would perform for a team that would provide "opposition" to the Globetrotters and would be coached by Oliver.

"I didn't know where else to go," Oliver explained. "The NBA had a rule that you couldn't play until your college class had graduated."

Despite the repeated threats that he'd made during the year about moving to another school, Oliver had never really had any plan to do so. Among other factors, he had not even considered the possibility that Davis and the trustees would reject the coach and players who had brought so much money to the cash-strapped campus.

Oliver felt both unappreciated and increasingly unwanted at his alma mater. Given his immense pride and ego, he felt he had little choice but to move on before the ax fell—and that it would fall was inevitable.

In an article that appeared in the *Gallia Times* shortly before the team returned to campus, Oliver was quoted saying, "We have received several offers. Neither of us has made up his mind definitely." In all likelihood, he regarded his spouting off to the reporter as a last-ditch effort to get the school to respond with an offer that would permit him to stay with dignity and complete the plan he'd started. If that was the strategy, it didn't work.

"Up until the time Newt told me we had a contract, I never thought about leaving or going to another school," Bevo remarked.

It is more likely that Oliver, with Saperstein's offer in his back pocket, had already determined that he was leaving. And Bevo would, by necessity, be going with him. According to Oliver, Saperstein had flattered him with praise for the public relations job he'd done at Rio Grande. The same action that had brought him nothing but enmity from Rio Grande had evoked admiration from a master promoter himself. This, Oliver felt, was the kind of appreciation that he had deserved but hadn't received from the school. The choice was easy: They were leaving.

On campus the other Redmen returned to class and began to take the exams they'd missed while traveling. "Bevo wasn't there," Ripperger remembered. "He had just gone on home to Wellsville," McKenzie said. "He'd done it before when we had returned on a weekend, and he'd always come back. This time he didn't."

Sportswriters speculated wildly about what was happening at Rio

Grande and what Newt and the absent Francis were really up to. On April 12, 1954, the Rio Grande College Committee on Instruction voted to expel Bevo Francis. "I think when he left, some of the professors saw it as an opportunity—'our chance to get him,'" Wiseman speculated. "They didn't like being left out of all the publicity and were anxious to get even with Oliver."

Citing "an excessive number of unexcused absences, failure to make up more than one of his missed midterm examinations, and failure to attend classes the past two weeks," they formally and publicly kicked out their most famous student. "It was a face-saving move on their part," Dave Diles said. "They knew Bevo had no intention of going back to school."

Wiseman said, "There is no question that it [the expulsion] was a reaction to Newt and his ideas. From the president on down they had become envious of Newt and the team."

The college's decision made national headlines. When reporters tried to reach Oliver at the Wicklines' apartment house, the person who answered said that Oliver had packed his bags and left the night before. Nor could the reporters find Bevo. He had gone fishing.

Later, when he learned of how the school had handled the affair, he was deeply embittered. "That was some of old Doctor Davis' doing," Bevo said. "I had told them I had signed a contract and was leaving school to go home. Two weeks later, I read in the paper that they kicked me out because of my grades. I thought, 'How the hell can they kick someone out who has already quit?' If I had not been going to class, I would have been ineligible to play. They'd probably have been the first to tell me that too."

Rio Grande's self-serving public renouncement of him was one of his greatest insults yet. The bitterness and humiliation that Bevo felt would remain for many years. It would be a decade before he could bring himself to return to the campus. The wounds inflicted by college officials festered, and he healed very, very slowly.

"It was wrong. It should never have ended that way," Wiseman declared. "You just don't treat someone that has helped you, as much as he had helped them, in that way. You don't kick them in the face. It was uncalled for."

"I hated to see it end that way," Ripperger said. "It was really hard for everyone to understand what had happened."

The reaction to the end of Oliver's reign at Rio Grande was immediate. Speaking at a banquet at East Liverpool High near Wellsville, the Geneva College coach Cliff Aultman declared, "Some boys are misguided. And I think you know what I mean."

Newspapers ran stories chronicling Bevo's colorful and stormy career at Rio Grande. Many Ohio papers ran two- and three-part series retelling the rapid rise from obscurity to national prominence of tiny Rio Grande. Opinion seemed equally divided about the school's expressed desire to return to normality.

While some debated the tawdry tactics of Oliver in their critique of the Rio Grande-Bevo Francis phenomenon, no one could deny that without Bevo Francis, Rio Grande College would not have survived into 1954.

❀ ❀ ❀

Within two weeks, Oliver and Francis were off to New York for the much-ballyhooed signing ceremony with the Globetrotters. With his usual flair, Saperstein arranged to have a pile of crisp new bills crammed into a peach basket to symbolize the abundant sum that he was bestowing on Francis and Oliver.

While they were in New York, Don Allen contacted Bevo Francis. "It was the first time I had ever spoken to him at length," Bevo recalled. "Newt had always kept him away from me. He tried to talk me into going back to school. But by then, it was too late. I told him about the way I felt about the manner in which they had treated me there as a reward for the thousands of dollars I'd helped earn for them. Now, at least, as a professional, the money I earned would go to me and Jean and the baby. And we could certainly use it."

Allen tried to persuade the player to return to school, but the millionaire auto dealer and Redmen benefactor could not refute what Bevo said about the college's profiteering from his heroics. Rio Grande had earned nearly $50,000 that season from basketball guarantees generated by the Redmen, or more than a quarter of the school's entire operating budget for a *year*.

In return, Bevo had received a scholarship of $600—provided by Allen—and $50 per month for groceries, again provided by Allen. In short, he had generated $50,000 for the school and had received in return a public expulsion. No wonder Allen's argument didn't work.

With the departure of Oliver and Francis, the trustees got what they wanted most: Rio Grande College returned to the normality—or, more accurately, obscurity—from whence it had come and with which it could cope. The glory days—and all that came with them—were over.

Part 4

Bevo the Whirlwind

Newt Oliver hands Bevo Francis his new
Boston Whirlwinds jacket.

16

An Unhappy Globetrotter

If you can meet with triumph and disaster
And treat those two impostors just the same . . .
Yours is the Earth and everything that's in it,
And—which is more—you'll be a Man, my son!

— *Rudyard Kipling*

Abe Saperstein had arranged for a lavish press conference on April 26 at the Empire State Building to announce the signing of basketball's all-time scoring champion with the Globetrotters' organization. Reporters crowded into the conference room to watch.

They missed altogether what took place in a small room adjacent to the conference room.

"The first time I ever saw the contract was just before the press conference," Francis recalled. "It was written so that Newt would get $12,000 and I would get $8,000. I said, 'No way am I signing that.' I told Saperstein that I was going to leave and started to walk out of the room. Then they said they would rewrite it so the contract was for $12,000 for me and $8,000 for Newt. And that is the one we signed."

Obviously, no lawyer had checked the contract on Bevo's behalf. "I never talked to anyone about it or consulted anyone," the player said. "The only information and advice I had gotten about it was from Newt. He always made it sound real good."

With their professional relationship off to a rocky start—right where their amateur one had ended—Francis and Oliver, along with Saperstein, faced the press.

"After you had been living on nothing for two years and then someone offers you $12,000, you don't do too much thinking about

215

it," he said. "My daddy would have to fill the car up with gas to get us back to school. We never had a penny in our pockets the whole time we were there. The money [the Globetrotters] offered looked real big to me then. It wasn't until much later that the salaries in pro ball took off. In those days it was a lot of money. My father had never earned more than $5,000 a year, and he was busting his ass digging clay with a pick and shovel all day. And they were willing to give me $12,000 to play ball! It looked like big money to me."

Saperstein held aloft a peach basket stuffed to overflowing with bills and poured the contents out on the table where Bevo and Newt sat as flashbulbs popped and newsreel cameras whirred. Ever the hyperbolic promoter, Saperstein claimed that he had signed the pair for $30,000 as a package to tour with the Globetrotters. The public accepted that not-insignificant sum as fact. Neither Bevo nor Newt disputed it publicly.

With the only coach he'd ever had at his side, Bevo Francis had affixed his name to a professional contract, trusting his coach's repre-sentations about the merits of doing so. In point of fact, the $12,000 that Francis received was a considerable sum for a professional basket-ball player in 1954. Most NBA players were earning less than $10,000. The game's biggest star, George Mikan, had earned only $25,000 at his best. For Bevo, $12,000 was an unimaginable amount of money.

Neither Bevo nor anyone else could have known or even guessed how minuscule that sum would look in comparison with the salaries offered to far lesser attractions by the NBA only a few years later. For now it looked like a small fortune, which, to the average wage earner of the time, it was.

Oliver submitted his formal resignation to the college, and the administration readily accepted it. In the opinion of the trustees, whom he'd driven to distraction, it hadn't come soon enough.

The week before the press conference in New York, Lowell Bridwell had written a two-part series for the *Columbus Citizen* that recapped the stormy two-year association of Rio Grande College, Newt Oliver, and Bevo Francis. Bridwell's analysis of the situation was insightful:

The spiraling, glistening bubble of national publicity and cold cash for tiny Rio Grande College has been shattered.
The bubble burst when Rio Grande's sensational basketball ace, Clarence "Bevo" Francis, was dismissed from school for non-attendance at classes. And in the wake of the falling pieces, there is dissension, recrimination and bitter disappointment.
The flare of the national sports spotlight, the ambitions of a few,

the desires of many and pressure from others combined to produce more stresses and strains than little Rio Grande could withstand.

The tiny 128-student college, its peppery basketball coach John "Newt" Oliver, and its amazing cage star emerged from the Ohio hills and splashed across the national sports scene in just two years. Now that the combination is breaking up, little Rio Grande is returning to obscurity. And the future for the lanky (6-foot-9) Bevo and his fiery coach is yet to be determined. But the immediate future doesn't include obscurity.

"It's a shame it happened this way," says Frank Allen, the pleasant, elderly fellow considered by many to be "Mr. Rio Grande." [Frank was Don Allen's father.]

[Frank] Allen has kept rooms for Rio Grande students for 53 years. He's seen the ups and downs of the little school. He was a trustee for 18 years.

He's seen times when there was doubt whether the school could open its doors another year. And he's seen times when it appeared the little non-denominational college was going to grow and receive the credit he believes is long overdue.

"This basketball team is the greatest thing that ever happened to Rio Grande," Allen said. "I feel sorry for everybody concerned. If it could have been handled right, all this wouldn't have happened." What did happen that wasn't handled right?

Oliver believes very strongly that the college administrators and trustees have yielded to pressure from the Ohio Association to put him and his program in shackles. He believes, and says vehemently, that he is being prevented from doing the very thing he was hired to do—namely, to build a winning basketball team, put Rio Grande "on the map," take the school's athletic program out of the red, and make money.

The college administrators and trustees, however, believe Oliver is drugged with ambition. And as a result, they say, he has refused to keep basketball within the overall school program, has operated the team as his own personal property, refused to follow school policy, and too frequently started talking before thinking. And sensational Bevo, who has scored more than 100 points in each of two games and gathered 11 all-time national scoring records, is standing right in the middle. He made it all possible, but now, he's a byproduct of the controversy.

To many of the students and interested outsiders, the whole fight is silly. They'd like to see Rio Grande, Bevo and Newt keep right on standing in the national spotlight.

But it's too late. There was a time when the controversy could have been settled quietly. But that time is gone. It's a toss up over whether Bevo quit school or was dismissed. Oliver is quitting, but the administrators and trustees are happy about that. It may be several days before it is officially announced, but there is no doubt that the stormy cage marriage of Newt and his cage court protégé to Rio Grande is ended.

Within a week of Bridwell's prescient analysis, Oliver and Francis were once again in the spotlight in New York, where their new affiliation was formally announced to the world.

Although Bevo had signed with Saperstein's organization, he would not be playing for the Globetrotters but on one of the teams, the Boston Whirlwinds, that Saperstein fielded to compete with the Globetrotters. The coaches of the teams that played the Trotters ran their teams on a franchise-like basis for Saperstein. He provided money for salaries, and the coaches would recruit and assemble the teams. Nothing was sacred about the names of the teams, and they would change from season to season and sometimes even several times within the same season. The players also changed, especially when the star players left the tour at the end of the summer to return to the NBA. Most of those remaining were journeymen and marginally talented players.

"I knew ten minutes after we'd signed those contracts it was a mistake," Oliver declared. "We got to travel and the Trotters got the money."

The Basketball Under the Stars tour that summer was an outdoor series that saw the Whirlwinds, led by Bevo and coached by Newt, meeting the Honolulu Surfriders, which featured the former Kentucky star Bill Spivey, a seven-footer. Also among the Surfriders was Frank Selvy, the major college scoring champ, who would join the NBA in the fall. The month-long series began in Miami and saw the two all-white teams play twenty-three games in thirty days throughout the south, where they could not compete with the Globetrotters.

Five thousand fans bought tickets to the professional baptism of basketball's all-time scoring king. The game was played on a portable court that was erected on the infield of the Miami Marlins' baseball diamond, then disassembled and repacked after the game before being put on a truck bound for the next venue.

His ankle healed after several months' rest, Bevo made his debut a successful one, scoring 27 points to lead the Whirlwinds to a 57-50 win.

Playing day after day against the likes of Spivey and Selvy was having a positive effect on Francis, and the challenge provided by the high level of opposition spurred him to standout performances in the crowded galaxy of stars. He responded by averaging 25 to 35 points a game, and a friendly but intense rivalry developed between the three scoring stars that helped alleviate the grinding monotony of the long tour.

After the southern trip the teams had a week off before beginning play in the Northeast. That swing began in the Catskills on July 27 and ended on August 30 in Springfield, Illinois. The schedule called for thirty-four games in a little more than thirty days. For this trip the Surfriders donned false beards to become the House of David, to conform to the image of the legendary five whose name Saperstein appropriated for Bevo's team. The trip took them up and down the coast and into Canada.

Wherever the teams appeared, Francis was the focal point of attention and grabbed the headlines from the more renowned members of the Globetrotters unit, which included the legends Goose Tatum and Leon Hilliard, as well as Walter Dukes, who had joined the tour a year earlier, and Nate "Sweetwater" Clifton. The eastern leg of the tour had the Globetrotters facing the George Mikan-coached U.S. All Stars, whose roster included Paul Arizin, Gene Shue, Red Holzman, Ray Felix, and Red Klotz, the former Baltimore Bullets star who long had played straight man for the Globetrotters. Despite this impressive array of talented players, many of whom were supplementing their NBA incomes with the tour money, sportswriters focused on Francis wherever the tour stopped.

"No matter where we went, it was always the same. They all wanted to talk to him," Klotz recalled. "They pretty much ignored the rest of us. That was the most unusual thing about it. It was always the Trotters' stars, Goose and Leon, especially, who were the attention grabbers before. But Francis was special."

After the summer tour the teams had about six weeks off before heading out on the road again. For Bevo the respite was a welcome one. For two hectic seasons at Rio Grande, he and his teammates had led a vagabond existence. The second year had been especially grueling, because they had only away games on their schedule and those were all over the map: the east, southeast, and midwest. When he left Rio Grande, he was off again with the Globetrotters tour. His professional obligations were even more demanding, thanks to Oliver. The one-night stands and the travel, usually 250 miles or more between sites, were physically debilitating.

So this reunion with Jean and their son was long overdue, and Bevo enjoyed every blissful moment of relaxation, savoring their together-ness as a family. The rest refreshed and rejuvenated him, but it was soon over and he was off yet again.

In early October the teams reassembled—minus the NBA-bound players—and prepared for the tour that would extend into April and take them throughout the western states and north into Canada.

Saperstein actually fielded three teams simultaneously, all called the Harlem Globetrotters. The tour that Bevo Francis made included one of those three teams, as well as the Whirlwinds, Washington Generals, and Philadelphia Sphas (which is how members of the South Philadelphia Hebrew Athletic Society were known).

Saperstein set up the schedule, which called for each of the opposing teams to play the Globetrotters every third night. On the other evenings they would play each other in a preliminary to the featured game. Those preliminary games treated the fans to truly competitive contests because those were the games that kept the players' competi-tive juices flowing. When they played the Globetrotters, they played to lose. It was simply not in Saperstein's game plan for any team to beat his Globetrotters—especially not teams that he had bankrolled himself.

Bevo had been familiar with the Globetrotters when he signed, but the extent of their on-court tomfoolery caught him by surprise. When he first became aware that he was supposed to be little more than an actor every third night, he was not pleased. "I wasn't happy about it," he said. "I'd played two seasons without hardly ever losing a game, and now I find out you aren't allowed to win one." In addition, the games were little more than comedy routines, with the Trotters using the opposi-tion teams as foils for their well-rehearsed and time-tested basketball shtick. The player who had been the biggest star in the sport only a season earlier now was reduced, thanks to Oliver, to a bit part in a farce promoted as a basketball game. "It went through my mind quite a bit about how demeaning it all was. It bothered me a lot," Bevo said.

Of all the promotional stunts, staged photo opportunities, outlandish claims, and fabricated stories that Oliver had foisted on the public, of the myriad courtside gyrations, grandiose claims, and head-line-grabbing scoring displays he had stage-managed, thereby cheap-ening the reputation of Bevo Francis as a basketball player, none would have as lasting an effect as the decision to sign with the Globetrotters.

The Globetrotters were (and are) a beloved organization that is credited with popularizing basketball around the world. They deserve the credit they have gotten. But what fans remember are the

Globetrotters themselves—not their token opposition. Thus Oliver's decision was nothing more than a shortsighted answer to his predicament at Rio Grande and an opportunity to cash in immediately. It would cost Francis dearly in terms of his reputation. Now college basketball fans were lapping up the story of Bill Russell and his San Francisco University Dons as they rolled to one victory after another. Bevo had been a member of the same incoming freshman class as Russell, who would join the NBA after graduation in 1956. Russell quickly emerged as *the* NBA star and soon was joined by Wilt Chamberlain; together they moved the NBA to a new level and in so doing launched an escalation in salaries that has never abated.

While the Dons were eclipsing the record winning streak set by Rio Grande, Bevo was playing out the contract that Newt had advised him to sign. None of the reporters who had followed Bevo's every move for two seasons bothered to report on his "games" now. After all, they were staged entertainment—not sport.

"For Bevo, playing on that team was truly a ticket to oblivion," Pete Bjarkman, a noted basketball historian, told ESPN. Actually, Bevo was in a worse place than oblivion. Now he was little more than an added attraction used by Saperstein to sell tickets and entertain the audiences. The Globetrotters were the stars of Saperstein's show. Bevo had no more status than the juggler and midgets in clown costumes who entertained the crowd at halftime.

"I always tried to do what I thought was best for Bevo," Oliver claimed. "But I wanted to improve my circumstances too. I didn't want to spend the rest of my life at Rio Grande." While Newt nearly tripled his income with the move to the Trotters, and Bevo was able to convert his name recognition into an annual salary of $12,000, the move did eternal damage to his long-term market value and how the always-skeptical reporters regarded him.

Then there was the travel.

"The travel just beat me to death," Bevo said.

After he badly damaged his lower back in a particularly nasty fall, Bevo was forced to travel from game to game in a jury-rigged traction device. The players tied some weights to straps and used the straps like a bandanna around Bevo's head, with the weights suspended over the seat back as they traveled. Each bump in the road brought another stabbing pain to his lower back. But Bevo played on.

While he endured the indignity of losing and the pain of the injuries, he wasn't about to endure much more of the stifling life with Oliver. "At first when we went out, he roomed with me," Francis said of Oliver. "That didn't last long, though. He treated me like some high school kid. He wanted to run my life like he had been doing all along. He was always telling me to save all my money and to eat only cheap hot dogs for dinner like he did. He was constantly harping on me about getting back to the room right after the game. I wanted to have a steak and a few beers with the guys. He wouldn't let me. We were battling all the time."

For his part, Oliver said, "I don't think Bevo ever trusted me. I never felt close to him, really. Later, when he started to listen to other people that were telling him I was living off of him, things started to go bad."

Francis remained with the Globetrotters for two and a half seasons after leaving Rio Grande. During that time he did enjoy a few light moments when some of his former Rio Grande teammates joined him on the Whirlwinds. As the fall tour started in 1954, Francis saw a familiar face in a Whirlwinds uniform: Wayne Wiseman had joined the team at Oliver's urging.

Wiseman, who had been a junior when Bevo arrived on campus, had graduated from Rio Grande, then taught in Anna, Ohio, and had accepted Oliver's invitation to rejoin his old teammate. Wiseman was closer to Francis than any of the other Redmen, and his presence made life on tour more bearable for Bevo.

"It really wasn't much different from what we had done the first year at Rio Grande," Wiseman remembered. "While the Globetrotters traveled in an air-conditioned bus, we traveled in station wagons. The hotels all were midpriced and looked the same from city to city. The dates and places and arenas all were just one big blur after a while. I got paid $600 a month, and the room was provided. I knew I'd be going into the service soon and was happy to get the money."

In fact, the biggest difference between college and the tour was that, when Bevo and Wiseman were in college, basketball had been a game. Now it was a business, and it wasn't at all the same.

Wiseman's education in basketball as a business began in St. Louis. The team had already left the hotel for the arena when Wayne arrived. He quickly made his way to the auditorium, where he was given a uniform. When he joined Oliver on the bench, the game was already underway. They exchanged greetings, and Oliver soon sent him in to play. No one had told Wiseman what the rules were when the Whirlwinds played the Globetrotters. Wiseman assumed that he was entering a real game.

"I was anxious to impress my coach and excited to be playing against the Globetrotters," he recalled. "I stole the ball from Leon

Hilliard, who had replaced the legendary Marcus Haines as the featured dribbling artist on the Trotters, and drove the length of the court for an easy lay-up basket."

Wiseman was smiling broadly as he drew cheers from the crowd and puzzled stares and glares from the Trotters. "I was all pumped up and went to work on Hilliard again," Wiseman recalled. "He was down on one knee doing his patented 'dribbling thing' when I stole the ball cleanly again."

Again he converted an easy bucket.

Hilliard, mouth agape, couldn't believe what was happening. It wasn't in the script for him to look foolish. The Whirlwinds were supposed to look bad, not him!

Quickly calling time-out, Oliver stood impatiently as the grinning Wiseman strutted proudly toward the bench, expecting to hear accolades from his coach. Instead, he heard: "Sit down. You're coming out." The wide smile faded as the ball-handling wonder from Waterloo learned the hard facts of life on the Globetrotters' tour. Wiseman listened sullenly as Oliver told him how he was to earn his money.

Wiseman had to endure life on the tour for only two months because his draft notice had arrived. His place was taken by another former Redman, Bill Ripperger. Ripperger had taken over Wiseman's teaching job in Anna, and when Newt called, Ripperger jumped at the chance to join his former coach while improving his finances.

"I was to begin receiving the same pay as Wayne, and I was making considerably more playing basketball than I had been teaching," Ripperger recalled. "But the staged games weren't really fun for me, and I hated playing the straight man. Thankfully, they would take Bevo out when they went into their routines. At least he was spared that indignity."

Not long after the tour began, Bevo left for an appearance in Chicago with the College All-Stars in the fifteenth renewal of their annual battle with the NBA champions. The game was played at Chicago Stadium for the benefit of Chicago American Charities. This year's match-up was between the Minneapolis Lakers and a galaxy of college stars.

Ray Meyer of DePaul University was the collegians' coach, and his squad included Cliff Hagan of Kentucky, Bob Pettit of Louisiana State, Gene Shue of Maryland, Frank Ramsey of the University of Kansas, Tom Marshall of Western Kentucky, Bobby Leonard of Indiana, Frank Selvy of Furman, Togo Palazzi of Holy Cross, Johnny Kerr of Illinois, Joe Bertrand and Dick Rosenthal of Notre Dame, and Chuck Bennett of Minnesota.

In an unusual turn of events Meyer led the college stars to victory over the pros. He remembered Bevo as a player who "fought for his position on offense. He had a super touch on the ball. He needed that type of competition in college to make him a pro player." Meyer, who had coached the game's first superstar, George Mikan, added, "Bevo had the tools, and if he had played in great competition, he would have survived as a pro."

But Bevo saw limited action in the game, accounting for only two points, and rejoined the Whirlwinds immediately after the classic concluded. The Globetrotters tour was a grinding endurance test. The Whirlwinds would play 180 games between October and April— roughly the equivalent of six college seasons.

The travel was continuous and invariably required all-night drives to the next city. The players would doze fitfully, catching furtive snatches of sleep in the station wagons, but it was difficult at best. After checking into their hotel, they would get perhaps five or six hours of sleep before they had to leave for the arena and another act in the never-ending show.

Once he had freed himself from Oliver's hectoring presence as his roommate, Bevo was able to enjoy some of the infrequent downtime that the tour afforded. He and Spivey would often enjoy a few beers and relax together before the wagons left for the next stop.

"I was sending home a considerable sum of money each month. I could not understand why [Oliver] kept hounding me about conditioning and money," Bevo said.

Oliver recalls it differently, of course: "I tried to counsel him as best I could about conditioning and such. But he just wouldn't listen anymore. I wasn't the most beloving of men. But I always wished him the best."

Bevo found Oliver's treatment of him an embarrassment, especially when one of Oliver's tirades took place in front of the other players. They battled constantly, neither willing to give an inch.

While the team was in Washington, D.C., Ripperger received his draft notice and had to leave the tour. "I had tried to serve as an intermediary between the two of them, but it was never easy," he said. With Ripperger's departure relations between the two grew even more strained. Finally, Francis had enough.

"None of the others would put up with it," said Francis, "and I finally got fed up with it too—and that's when I told Saperstein he'd have to make his choice. 'It's either him or me,' I told him. I had taken as much as I could take."

Saperstein reassigned Newt as an advance man. Oliver leaped at the change. After all, advance publicity was what he was all about. He excelled at it and relished his new assignment. Besides, he'd been coach to a team predestined to lose every game and was constantly bickering with his protégé.

Oliver shined in his new role. It allowed him to precede the Trotters into each city and trumpet their upcoming appearance. It gave him an opportunity to relive the glory days at Rio Grande with the press as captive audience. He loved every minute of it. And he was so effective that Saperstein asked him to reprise the role the following year as well. Oliver readily agreed and continued to traverse the country, beating the same drum he'd been pounding since he'd left Wellsville. "Bevo is coming—and this time he's bringing the Globetrotters with him." He was a natural.

For Jean the long months of separation from her husband were not easy. But, then, sharing her husband with the press and his fans never had been a picnic. While Bevo was at Rio Grande, and subject to Oliver's controlling and demanding manner, she had felt like she had no private life at all.

"It wasn't normal," she complained.

She sought only that—a normal family life with her husband and child. No third parties, thank you.

Now the Globetrotters tour was keeping Bevo away from home for months at a stretch, and her only consolation was a steady stream of postcards from places she had never heard of, pictures of places she'd never seen. "He'd write almost every day, and I would wait for [the postcards] to come in the mail and share the colorful pictures with our son," Jean related. Perhaps it would all be over soon, she thought. "We had never had a normal family life, and I was looking forward to the time when we could all enjoy life together. I had the support of my family close by, but it was a very lonely time for me."

For now, Jean had to be content with the few short months in the spring when Bevo was at home. That time gave her tantalizing glimpses of what "normal" must be like for other families. Somehow, some day, she was sure, it would be that way for them too. For now she would remain supportive of her husband and his choice of career and hide her aching loneliness from him.

In June 1955 Bevo packed his bags and was off again. This time he would be joined by still another former Rio Grande player, Al Schreiber. Al, the Long Islander who had joined the Redmen during the second half of the final season, had left the rustic campus after the 1954-55 school year ended.

"For a city kid that campus held little allure," said Schreiber, who had grown up in New York City. "I saw that Bevo and Newt were out on the tour and figured it was a good opportunity to earn a little money and see some of the country as well." He would stay on after they had departed, touring Europe with a Trotters unit before settling down back in Brooklyn.

The second year on tour was even worse for Francis than the first had been. In Spokane he again injured his back and neck, once again was fitted with a cervical collar, and again was told by the doctor to get complete bed rest. Instead, he rejoined the team and traveled in considerable pain, strapped to the crude traction system he'd used the previous season. His countenance bore the furrowed frown of a man in pain. Yet he continued to perform night after night.

As the second full season of the tour wound down, Francis decided he'd had enough. He had managed, despite Oliver's concern, to save enough money to build a modest home for Jean and his growing family. Jean had recently given birth to their daughter, Marjorie. In the tiny hamlet of Highlandtown, not far from Wellsville, Bevo Francis set down roots near the town he'd left as an unknown almost five years earlier. He was twenty-four years old and owned his own home—a considerable accomplishment for those times and one he was justifiably proud of. The road held no allure for him.

"When I had come home during that second year for a short break, my son fled at the sight of me to his grandfather's arms. He didn't even know me," Bevo recalled. "I decided then and there that I had had enough. It wasn't worth it to me to have my own kid see me as a stranger."

At about that time the NBA held its annual college draft. The Philadelphia Warriors chose Bevo. That was the same draft in which the Boston Celtics' boss Red Auerbach traded for the St. Louis Hawks' No. 2 overall pick and chose Bill Russell.

Eddie Gottlieb, general manager of the Warriors, drafted Bevo in the third round, 24th overall. "I had seen him play on the Trotters' All-America tour and had been impressed with what I had seen," Gottlieb said. "He showed his ability to hold his own in fast company, and I felt he had real pro potential."

Nor did it hurt to add the name of Bevo Francis to the roster, along with that of Tom Gola. That gave the Warriors two major drawing cards. The combination was, Gottlieb was certain, "a sure-fire box office attraction in Philadelphia, and our club could benefit by that."

Shortly after the Warriors drafted him, Bevo went to Philadelphia to meet with Gottlieb. As Bevo recalled that meeting, Gottlieb "explained that he felt that I would be an asset to the team, and he wanted to sign me to a contract for $10,000 a year. I had been making $12,000 with the Trotters and told him that. I figured with all the travel that I would have to do in the NBA and the added expense of a place I'd have to get to live in Philadelphia during the season, it wasn't worth it to take less than I had been making."

The two talked some more and finally agreed to disagree. "I told him if I accepted his offer, I'd have just as much travel and more expenses and be making less money. We just couldn't reach an agreement, and I told him, 'Thank you very much, but I'm going to go on back home,'" Bevo recalled.

Gottlieb tried to convince Bevo to reconsider. Success in the NBA, the general manager said, would mean that "you are as good as they say you are." But Bevo wasn't interested. He'd been proving himself ever since Wellsville High School. "By then, Bevo was in the early stages of basketball burnout," explained Earl Gutsky of the *Los Angeles Times*. Francis simply had no interest in proving himself yet again, not to Gottlieb, the critics, or the NBA. His mind was made up, and his decision was final. He was going home to Jean and the kids, where he belonged.

Jean's gain was basketball's loss.

"There is no doubt in my mind [that] under the right circumstances, he could have made it in the NBA," said Marty Blake, the NBA's former director of scouting.

It is hard to resist the temptation to consider what might have been. The Warriors would have boasted Gola, Paul Arizin, Neil Johnston, *and* Bevo Francis, and a few seasons later, they had Wilt Chamberlain too. One can only imagine what that lineup of talent would have meant.

Instead, Bevo returned to his family home in the hills above the Ohio River. He found employment in the anonymity of the shipping department of a pottery near his home. For the first time in their marriage, Jean and Bevo felt that they could truly enjoy life together.

Reporters continued to call. But their approaches soon became infrequent and more sporadic. The bedlam that had characterized the Francises' life since Bevo scored 116 points on one night was slowly replaced by the serene laughter of their children.

⊛ ⊛ ⊛

"It was as if this primitive came out of the woods and ran around naked for two years and suddenly said, 'I don't like this. It's not me.' So he goes back into the woods. And that's the last we ever saw of him," suggested William Nack, the long-time writer for *Sports Illustrated,* when he appeared on the *Sports Century* special. "He rose, but after he fell it wasn't as if there was a void people could visibly see or feel. It was like a comet. That name—Bevo—what happened to him? What happened to that comet?" mused Larry Donald of *Basketball Times.*

What happened was that Bevo retreated—if not to the woods, then to the blessed anonymity of the local pottery, where he joined hundreds of other anonymous, lunch-pail-toting factory workers. He was, at last, at home and at ease.

When basketball season rolled around, he was busy with the local barnstorming team he'd put together, mostly local players from his Tri-State Tournament days. They called themselves the Eastern Ohio All-Stars. Although Bevo's name still sold tickets, they struggled to make a profit.

Once they played the Cleveland Stars—a basketball squad comprised of Cleveland Browns football players who used basketball to supplement their meager professional football salaries in the off-season. Chuck Noll, later the Super Bowl-winning coach of the Pittsburgh Steelers, was a Cleveland Star, as were Babe Parilli, Don Colo, Maurice Bassett, Tom James, Fred Morrison, and Horace Gillom. Bevo and company taught the gridders some hoop lessons, vanquishing them in Massillon, Ohio.

The Eastern Ohio All-Stars continued their local touring the next season as well; the games allowed Bevo to play the game that he loved and broke the monotony of his day job.

In 1958 he accepted an offer to play for the Hawks of Hazleton, Pennsylvania, of the Eastern Basketball League. The minor league professional circuit featured a number of former NBA players as well as some older former college stars. It also included players who had been banned for life by the NBA because of their roles in the betting scandals. Richie Regan, who played in the EBL after he retired from the NBA, recalled that it did boast "a lot of talented players." All the teams were based in the Northeast and played their games on week-ends so the players could hold down regular jobs.

"It was a pretty rough-and-tumble affair," Regan said. "The referees had a very high tolerance level for fouls." The rough play and weekend trips away from home held little appeal for Francis, whose signing had created a stir in the eastern press. His association with the Hawks was short-lived; he returned to Ohio after one season.

The next year, 1959, a Detroit promoter approached him about joining a tour that featured the Harlem Satellites, led by Ed "Rookie" Brown, who had starred in the motion picture that chronicled the Harlem Globetrotters' success story. The slick, fast-talking promoter, Ted Raspberry, had a long association with prizefighters, the Negro Leagues of baseball, and barnstorming with black basketball teams.

"He told me stories that sounded too good to be true about what he was going to do with me," Bevo recalled.

His instincts were correct.

After several weeks of touring with the knock-off Trotters' team organized by Raspberry, Francis found his paychecks too few and even those were less than he'd been told he would get when Raspberry had regaled him with promises of riches. Soon after, the checks began bouncing higher than a basketball. Disillusioned and disgusted with the shifty promoter, Francis left the tour and went home. As it turned out, he was yet another victim in a long line of victims whom the unsavory promoter had left in his wake.

Francis subsequently sued Raspberry and testified against him about the predetermined outcomes of the "games" he was supposed to play against the Satellites. Although fans knew these were not real games, the testimony in open court caused a major media flap, and Bevo Francis was once again in the news, under very unwelcome circumstances.

Ultimately, the court awarded him the money that he was owed, as well as damages. When Bevo tried to collect, he found that the nimble Raspberry had filed for bankruptcy protection. There were no assets. Francis had won the case but was left holding the bag.

The poor clay miner's son, whose ticket out of poverty was the game of basketball, at which he excelled, had found that the game he loved was also the source of many difficult events in his life: the unjust suspensions he had suffered in high school, the hellish life he'd endured at Rio Grande, the shunning and humiliation by the faculty and staff at the school he'd helped to save, the dreadful career choices that Oliver made on his behalf, and now Raspberry's thievery.

Wiser but no richer for the experiences, Bevo Francis moved on with his life. He eventually found a good-paying job with one of the steel mills that dotted the Ohio River valley. Except for a few charity events and a local basketball tournament here and there, he concentrated on making progress at the plant and spending time with his family. He earned steady promotions, and he and Jean enjoyed a comfortable, if not ostentatious, life together. At long last, basketball was a secondary consideration in their lives.

On the rare weekends that saw him suit up for a local tournament, his fabulously soft touch showed few signs of rust even if his girth had expanded and his legs were slower. The low-pressure games offered him sheer enjoyment, nothing more. Here, at home in eastern Ohio, he didn't have to prove anything to anyone, and the game of basketball became fun again.

In 1961 Abe Saperstein formed a new professional basketball league. The American Basketball League, Saperstein boasted, would soon rival the NBA. With Abe at the helm, the new league began play in the 1962-63 season.

A young Cleveland industrialist bought one of the charter franchises. He had inherited a shipbuilding firm and had an insatiable appetite for sports. While many people had forgotten Bevo Francis by then, George Steinbrenner had not. He offered Bevo the chance to play for his Cleveland Pipers in the new league. Steinbrenner, who had witnessed Bevo's incredible crowd appeal as well as his prowess, hoped that Bevo still retained enough of both to help his franchise succeed.

Competition from the established NBA forced the new league to offer recent college stars no-cut contracts to induce them to sign. Rosters were crammed with these players, and when the final cuts were made early in the season, Bevo, out of playing condition and away from top-level competition for years, was among them. His professional career had lasted just two games, in which he played 21 minutes and sank two of five shots from the floor.

The league that Saperstein had promised would challenge the NBA folded midway through its second season. A long-delayed career in professional basketball was no longer an option for Bevo Francis. He would instead find fulfillment in his job and family.

As basketball season rolled around each year, the old urge to shoot a few returned too. He would participate in the occasional local tournament, but now he was an old man playing a young man's game. But that soft touch remained. Long after he lost his legs to too many miles of pounding too many courts from coast to coast, he retained the ability to shoot. Though the lean, lithe frame had grown considerably rounder with the years, it still responded when urged, almost unconsciously, as the adrenaline pumped through it for one more effortless basket.

By the mid-1960s Bevo's public appearances were sporadic. In 1968, when he was thirty-six, he hung up his sneakers for good.

17

A Shooting Star

I think if Bevo had played for anyone else but me, he would never have made it, as such. To become a legend.

—Newt Oliver, 1979

I really believe I had a lot to do with Bevo getting where he was.

—Newt Oliver, 1979

Perhaps one of the greatest joys in God's creation is the sight, on a crystal clear night, of a shooting star. Its sudden emergence, hurtling speed, and majestic splendor are ours to behold for only a moment. But in that twinkling of fleeting majesty and wonder, its momentum separates it from the billions of other stars in the galaxy. Its uniqueness dominates the heavens. Then, just as rapidly, it simply burns up and disappears forever.

The similarity of a shooting star and the career of Bevo Francis is inescapable. But it fails to differentiate between Bevo Francis, the nationally famous basketball star, and Clarence Franklin Francis, the man.

Those who played with Bevo Francis share an almost universal sadness about his abortive basketball career. But Bevo himself spends no time ruminating upon what might have been. "I really have few regrets," he said. "I established more of a home life together with my wife and kids. That's worth something more to me than fame."

And that's not just talk. According to his childhood friend Bob Grimm, "Bevo is the happiest guy walking around. He's got his low-key life and his family to share it with."

Francis worked for Crucible Steel for years, until imported steel took its toll on his employer in the mid-1980s. He was six months short of a pension when Crucible banked its furnaces for good.

Unlike the scores of other middle-aged men similarly affected, Bevo was not allowed to suffer the indignities of unemployment in private. "BAD TIMES FOR BEVO FRANCIS" blared the headline on a wire service story that appeared in papers across the country. Thirty years after his name had appeared in the sports pages, he was making news again. The story recapped his years at Rio Grande and detailed his current plight among the jobless. "I wish I had that diploma now," Bevo told the reporter. "It would come in real handy."

In his *Los Angeles Times* column, Rick Reilly related the plight of Francis and his family and looked back at his career and the controversy it spawned. In the last paragraph he concluded wistfully, "Maybe it is all for the better. Maybe the legend of Bevo Francis is best kept just slightly blurred, like a dream you are not sure you had—so bright and brilliant you are not sure it is real, so delicious you do not wish to know."

With a strong assist from Dick Barr, Bevo secured a job with a division of the Akron Goodyear Corporation and stayed until his retirement in 1994.

His bitterness toward the school that he helped save ebbed only slowly. "Nothing is ever going to take away the hurt he felt years ago, and that feeling that he was used," Dave Diles remarked.

Art Lanham arrived at Rio Grande College as basketball coach in 1960, and the icy relationship began to thaw. He persistently and patiently sought to bring the school and its most famous former student together. It took Lanham many years, but he was finally able to do so, and the relationship he fostered has remained strong ever since.

Lanham's efforts got a boost in the early 1980s from Juanita Dailey, who was doing her doctoral thesis on the era. She found that Bevo had in fact been a student in good standing when he left school. He could not have been expelled. The athletic director, Clyde Evans, made a public announcement of the findings, which, taken with Lanham's diplomatic overtures, were strong salve to deeply felt wounds.

Even after Lanham had effected the rapprochement between Rio Grande and Bevo Francis, Francis and Newt Oliver remained estranged for many years. Once, in 1973, Oliver appeared unannounced and uninvited on Francis' doorstep. They had not seen each other for twenty years. As Bevo recalled the encounter, Newt "showed up with a case full of the paperback book he had written and self-published. He wanted me to help sell them for him. I threw him out."

"I can see why he may have gotten mad at me," Oliver allowed. "I'm a kind of dominant person. I don't think I ever did anything to hurt Bevo, in any sense of the word. I tried to give him the best way out. I tried to protect Bevo the best way I could. But with all the publicity, it was hard."

Lanham again tried to bring the two together at the ceremony inducting them and other members of the team into the Rio Grande College Hall of Fame. "Bevo told me [that] if Newt was coming, he wouldn't be there," Lanham recalled.

The induction ceremony was lavish. Oliver was there. Bevo was not.

"There was a lot of resentment and hard feelings between the two for years. Bevo felt he had been exploited, and he probably had been," Wayne Wiseman said.

Time eventually softened the harsh edges of the enmity that Bevo felt, and the gentle, subtle prodding of Lanham and Bevo's teammates resulted in a semi-cordial reconciliation between the two—at least for the purpose of public appearances.

"As you get older, you mellow some," Jean offered by way of explanation.

In 1983 Rio Grande instituted the Bevo Francis Classic Tournament. Held annually at the beginning of the season, it brings together men's and women's teams in a weekend tournament format in the twenty-five-hundred-seat Newt Oliver Gymnasium, on Bevo Francis Drive on the campus of what is now Rio Grande University.

The campus that once consisted of four buildings set in a cow pasture now stands proudly atop a hill, a thriving university of sleek modern facilities. At its center rises a soaring bell tower whose chimes cascade down on a student body of nearly three thousand. Many of the buildings on campus harken back to the early difficult years. There is the Bob Evans School of Business, named after the son of the school's benefactor before Bevo's arrival, and there is the Esther Allen Greer Museum and Archives, endowed by the widow of Don Allen; she continued his philanthropic efforts after he died of a heart attack in 1959, days after the couple had dedicated Allen Hall, the administration building named in honor of his parents.

Community Hall has long since been razed. In its place a bronze plaque occupies the site, informing those passing by that this is where Bevo scored 116 points in 1953.

In 1986, at the urging of Rio Grande's president at the time,

Dr. Paul Hayes, the university that in large measure owed its very existence to Bevo Francis, awarded him an honorary master's degree.

In making the presentation, which both Bevo and Newt attended, Hayes cited the former student as "an unequaled success that will always be with us." The bitterness and humiliation that Bevo had harbored for nearly a half-century melted away in the warm smile that spread across his face as he accepted his degree. In the audience his wife and family beamed with pride.

In the fall of 2002 the university, then headed by Dr. Barry Dorsey, launched a two-year celebration of the fiftieth anniversary of the 1952-54 Redmen with a gala banquet that brought them and Newt Oliver together to relive the glory days once more.

The years since they last sped across the hardwood have flashed by. The Redmen of 1952-54 are now in their seventies. As their hair recedes and turns to silver, they are apt to reflect on their legacy.

There is no denying the role that they played in rescuing a college on the precipice of oblivion. Their precise contribution in saving the school, like so much else about their story, will be debated for years. But no one can deny that they played a pivotal role in rescuing the school that stands today as a shining monument to their success. That in and of itself would be a great legacy. But there is more.

The men who wore Rio Grande's red-and-white silks also resuscitated the sport of college basketball. In 1952 college basketball was reeling from the betting scandals that had left a noxious cloud over the sport and had emptied arenas across the land. University presidents rushed to assure alumni that they were de-emphasizing a sport that had despoiled their student athletes and betrayed the trust of their fans. Even mighty Kentucky and its legendary coach, Adolph Rupp, were forced to the sidelines by the scandal that began in New York and moved north, south, and west.

College basketball found its savior in Bevo Francis and his Rio Grande College teammates. During two glorious seasons they re-ignited fan interest, packed arenas, and dominated the sports pages nationally. Their unlikely success laid the foundation for the wildly successful Road to the Final Four and the $12 billion annual hysteria that is the modern NCAA championship tournament. It is a legacy that they can be proud to claim as their own.

Finally, they gave Americans something to cheer for in an age marked by the Korean War, the Army–McCarthy hearings, the nuclear arms race, and lynchings in the deep south whenever men and women of goodwill tried to change the culture that kept LeRoy Thompson off the beaches, out of the nightclubs, and consigned to the freight elevator.

From that shining moment in 1953 when Bevo Francis scored 116 points in a single game, all the little guys of the world had a champion. For those two record-smashing seasons, Americans could convince themselves that Peter Pan was right: "If you believe, if you truly believe—then anything is possible."

And that may be their greatest legacy of all.

Epilogue

I still get letters from kids all the time. I like that. If it keeps kids interested in the sport, well, then maybe it was worth it.

—Bevo Francis

The team scoring the most goals . . . wins the game.
—The only one of the thirteen original rules of basketball
that remains inviolate to this day

All the former Redmen translated their successes on the basketball court into successes in life.

Dick Barr, who constantly battled for rebounds against players six and seven inches taller than he, completed his education at Findlay College in Ohio after Bevo left Rio Grande. Barr enjoyed a long and successful career with the Akron Rubber Company, from which he retired some years ago.

Jim McKenzie, the confused youth who had his doubts about Oliver's plan, joined Barr at Findlay to complete his education. He coached and taught school for many years in the same district that produced the Waterloo Wonders.

Roy Moses, the bull-like forward who wore himself out charging through the opposition, taught at Oak Hill, near Rio Grande. He is active in the university's alumni program.

Wayne Wiseman, the talented ball-handling guard who triggered the nation's most potent offense, was a teacher and long-time coach of the basketball program at Springfield South High School, also in Ohio. He consistently produced winning teams there and sent several players

236

along to his alma mater.

Bill Ripperger, who survived Oliver's taunting to blossom into an accomplished player—perhaps the best rebounder for his size in the country—also taught and coached basketball in his hometown of Norwood, Ohio. He suffered a heart attack during a tennis match and died at forty-five, not long after recording his recollections of what he termed "the Fabulous Five" for this project.

Al Schreiber, who joined the squad midway through their final season, later joined Bevo with the Globetrotters organization. Following that, he founded a chain of convenience stores in his native Brooklyn and presided over their successful growth. He died in the 1990s.

LeRoy Thompson, who got to see all those cities Newt promised he would, went home and took his dad's advice. He got a job and settled down. He is retired from Timken Roller Bearing and remains in Canton, near where he grew up playing ball on the courts behind the coal yard. The negative aspects of his eye-opening experience with segregation on the swing through the south are something he doesn't dwell on. His thoughts are of a happier nature: "I still remember the feeling I got when the crowds cheered my name, I'll never forget it." He is a member of the Sandy Valley High School Hall of Fame (the consolidated district that absorbed Waynesburg), and the Greater Canton Negro Old Timers Athletic Association Hall of Fame. More than a half century since he left Waynesburg he remains the second all-time leading scorer in Stark County basketball history.

Reserve Don Vyhnalek left Rio Grande as well, and finished his education at Doane College in his home state of Nebraska. He achieved NAIA All-America honors as a senior and attributes his success there to the time he spent at Rio Grande. "I learned so much in that single, memorable season in the big time, that it carried over to help me at Doane." He is retired after a career with Ford Motor Company and resides in Indiana.

Carl Benner, the bespectacled student-manager whom Wiseman labeled "Stud," earned his degree at Rio Grande and added several advanced degrees. He held a doctoral degree in mathematics and was on the faculty at Wright State University near Dayton before his retirement in 1994. He died of cancer in 2003 after a long and courageous battle.

After leaving the Globetrotters organization in 1956, Newt Oliver entered teaching. "I tried to get a job coaching. But I couldn't," Oliver said. "I had an offer at the University of New Hampshire, but someone at Rio Grande squashed my chances. I made several other attempts and finally gave up. I decided to concentrate on wealth."

His promotional skills have served him well. He opened a drive-in root beer stand near his home in Springfield, Ohio. After working nearly around the clock, he finally gave up teaching to devote time to developing the business. Wiseman recalled that Oliver "had wooden nickels made up, and he'd stand in the school parking lot after class and handed them out to the kids. The nickels were used to buy discounted drinks at his restaurant." The business flourished, and Oliver invested the profits from it in land and securities.

"I'm a millionaire," he boasts within minutes of meeting a stranger. His holdings now encompass farms and acreage in southern Ohio, as well as blue-chip stocks and bonds. He has been a contributor to the Rio Grande University capital campaign for years. In what must appear to be the strangest of ironies, he eventually was elected to and served on the same board of trustees that he once drove to distraction as a coach—and had been fired by.

After selling his drive-in, he entered politics and eventually was elected to two terms as a commissioner of Clark County; he still lives in Springfield, the county seat.

"Newt lives in the past. He never really moved on," Wiseman said.

"I still wake up some nights and I can hear the crowd screaming," Oliver acknowledged.

He has self-published two books with two different co-authors about his years at Rio Grande, and he lectures before audiences that listen to him retell the story he calls "the miracle of Rio Grande."

As for Bevo Francis, he is quite content to "just forget about it all." The modest home he built in Highlandtown with the money that Abe Saperstein paid him holds no visible reminders that he ever played basketball. Instead, the living room is adorned with photographs of his children and grandchildren—they are what is most important to him. His basketball scrapbooks and trophies are buried away in an upstairs closet, out of sight. It is as if their presence is still too painful a reminder, even now. He opens them only with the greatest reluctance.

"Everything I've got, I got honestly," he said. "I get up in the morning and have breakfast with my wife. Then, weather permitting, I go hunting rabbits. About three or so I come back and spend time with Jean and the family. In the evening I get my coon dogs out, and we go hunting by moonlight in the hills and fields surrounding my home. That's how I enjoy my life."

One of his old basketball foes, Alex Severance of Villanova, said of Bevo, "I think he is a very fortunate man. There must be a lot of virtue in Bevo. Remember, he'd been taken up on the mountain and surveyed all the temples. Then he came down into the valley below, and he survived it all. Most men couldn't do it. I admire him for it. He was able to see through the glitter and tinsel and artificiality of it all and get back to the real world of living. He was able to endure it all without being disillusioned. Unlike most celebrated athletes, Bevo could let go and go on with living."

The man who first introduced the young Bevo to the world at large, Dave Diles, said, "Being content with himself is a tremendous blessing. For all the publicity and all the headlines and all that went with it, Bevo really didn't get anything material out of it. But he is rich in other ways."

It is certainly true that basketball never made Bevo Francis rich. But he and his teammates from tiny Rio Grande enriched basketball beyond measure.

"At that juncture in history, where he met that fork in the road, Bevo was the greatest shooter in the history of basketball," Bill Nack told ESPN Classic.

"There was no pretense about Bevo. He was the real deal," said George Steinbrenner. "He is an important part of college basketball history. Bevo's story is one of the greatest stories in sports. It's one that everyone should know about—and nobody should ever forget."

It is difficult to say how Bevo and his teammates will be treated by historians of the game. If the past fifty years are any indication, they will not be kind. In 1979 the name Bevo Francis was submitted to the Basketball Hall of Fame for consideration by its screening committee. It was rejected. Lee Williams, then the executive director, offered to paraphrase the comments of the Honors Committee: "The general feeling was [that] what he had accomplished was in terms of a 'freak' or 'contrived' situation."

Williams went on to point out that, "if, indeed Mister Francis' brief exploits in basketball can be determined as real and standard performances, and if his brief participation in the game can be equated to those who have played successfully for ten or more years, then, of course Mister Francis does have a good chance for election."

In the Modern Era section of the shrine dedicated to the sport of basketball in Springfield, Massachusetts, the ball and score sheet from the Hillsdale College game—the one in which Bevo tallied 113 points—remain on permanent display. There, they serve as a visual reminder to all who visit of a night in rural Ohio like none other in the history of the only truly American game.

❀ ❀ ❀

One would like to think that Bevo Francis would be remembered for what he was—a basketball player possessed of a jump shot so glorious that it separated him from all the rest. As each new generation of young players comes along and learns of his deeds, it would be nice if they could conjure up the real person, not the image surrounded by clouds.

They would see a willowy youth silhouetted against the fading twilight of an autumn evening. Alone on an empty asphalt court.

Just him and the ball.

With his back to the rusting rim and peeling backboard, he dribbles once or twice, and the sound echoes in the stillness.

Just him and the ball.

No screaming crowds. No hectoring, self-dealing coach. No carping critics and prying press.

Just Bevo and the ball.

His knees flex and his legs launch him effortlessly free of Earth's bonds. He turns gracefully in the air, his gaze fixed steadily on the rim. His wrist flicks almost imperceptibly as he lofts the shot skyward, imparting a gentle reverse spin. His long slender fingers follow its arc.

In the second or two that it takes the ball to traverse the space to the goal, the earth stops spinning and time stands still. Bevo is where he wants to be, doing what he wants to do—better than anyone else before or since.

Swish.

Acknowledgments

I n researching and writing this story I received the help and cooperation of many people without whom I could not have completed it.

First and foremost I must thank the two people who helped me to understand what their lives were like then and now and whose least favorite thing to do is to sit and talk to another writer about a very distant and difficult time in their lives. Yet Bevo and Jean Francis welcomed me into their home and shared their memories and feelings with me. For the intrusion I apologize, for their assistance and cooperation I will be forever grateful.

From the extended Francis family I had the cooperation of both half-brother Robert Francis and half-sister Norma Williams, who assisted in describing the early years in Francis' life.

The players who spent hours with me recording their thoughts, recollections and impressions on the two sensational seasons at Rio Grande were without exception cordial, open and candid about their days at Rio Grande and on the national stage. They also shared their scrapbook collections, which were a treasure trove of information to me and I am grateful to each and every one of them for their assistance and friendship. Bill Ripperger, the first player I met with and the one with whom I spent the most time, died suddenly within a week of taping his recollections of the days at Rio Grande. His taped interview, along with that of all the other players, are now available to future historians and researchers at the Rio Grande University Archives. Carl Benner, the student manager for the team, also passed away recently. He was very helpful in recent years in updating information for me and clarifying some points from conversations that were taped years before. He was very excited and eager to see the story he played a part in become available to the public. I regret I was unable to do that while he was still with us, but his role and remembrances are an integral part of the story.

Wayne Wiseman, Dick Barr, Roy Moses, Jim McKenzie, LeRoy Thompson, Don Vyhnalek and Coach Oliver were all cooperative and willing contributors and each spent a considerable amount of time with me taping the interviews needed to accurately reconstruct the events of those two years long ago. I am in their debt for their willingness to relive those days with a stranger for hours on end.

In Jean Lloyd Cooper, I found a resource more valuable than the archives she is custodian of at Rio Grande University. As a former secretary to the Board of Trustees during the Bevo years and as treasurer during that time, she was an invaluable source for verification and amplification on those days. She loves the university and wants nothing more than to see it treated with respect and dignity. It is people like her who have made the university a shining beacon of higher education in the hills of Ohio. They are as fortunate to have her in their midst as I was fortunate to have had her assistance. More recently Paul Harrison, Vice President for Administrative Affairs, proved to be a dedicated and caring individual who shared my enthusiasm for the project and was of invaluable assistance in securing photographs and other essential missing pieces to the story of the 1952-54 Redmen.

Dave Diles was an ABC-TV sports anchor when I first talked to him about the project years ago. Throughout, he has remained a staunch supporter and believer. The man who brought Bevo Francis to the attention of the world outside Ohio is a generous and charitable man and writer of great talent who never failed to encourage me in proceeding with the project. I am exceedingly grateful to him for his help and for his friendship through the years.

At Rio Grande, coach Art Lanham was a helpful guide to me in the early stages of this project and directed me in my efforts to track down firsthand sources in the area. His introductions and assistance were very helpful to me. In the Rio Grande-Gallipolis area, I spoke with J. Sherman Porter, John Halliday, Dr. Francis Shane, Dr. Raymond Allison and Bob Evans.

The many coaches with whom I spoke to in person, or communicated with by phone and mail, were all very giving of their time and offered their recollections and impressions of a team and player against whom they competed on the court many years ago. These coaches include George Faherty, Alex Severance, Vincent Cuddy, Ken Mast, Subby Salerno, Tony Hinkle, Ray Meyer, George Steinbrenner, Dave Wike, and Frank Solak.

I was also fortunate enough to have access to a number of writers and reporters from the era who were more than happy to assist me with the many questions I had about the period. This includes Bob Vetrone, Mel Allen, Marty Glickman, Dick Herbert, Bob Curry, John Condon, Milton Gross and Stanley Cohen. Bob Stewart of the Canton Repository worked diligently to help me in my effort to locate LeRoy Thompson, for which I am very grateful.

Ned Irish and Eddie Gottlieb, along with Red Klotz and the many players I reached out to in search of their firsthand appraisals of Francis and Rio Grande, were all helpful and I thank them for their special insights. Included among the latter were Bill Uhl, Robin Freeman, Tom Gola, Doug Howell, Richie Regan, Bill Spivey and a number of others who are named in the book. Norm Ellenberger provided interesting color on the scene at Butler University and Marty Milligan and Jack Devine added to the dramatic recreation of the stunning overtime win Villanova scored at the Arena as did referee Jocko Collins. Dickie Hemric and Ron Shavlik were both forthcoming with their remembrances of the doubleheader in Raleigh. For the Bluffton game, I had the assistance of Paul Jackson, who provided memories and clippings as well as a film clip of part of the game. For the Hillsdale game I was assisted by their former players, especially Jack Lowery, whose recollections were most helpful in understanding the other side of the 113-point performance. Smokey Blankenship assisted me with the Pikeville game information. The recreated game scenes in the book are all based on the recollections and conversations with the actual participants and coaches. Dialogue, except where attributed to another source, was constructed through interviews with the participants and others who were present when the conversations occurred.

Scores of people, players, athletic directors, sports information directors and alumni relations directors at the schools that played against Rio Grande during the two seasons Bevo was there were especially helpful to me. They went out of their way to help me track down the people who were participants and observers of the events described and I want to express my gratitude to them all for their help.

Those who helped me in my search to find participants and to understand the impact that their encounter with Bevo and the Redmen had on them and their team, as well as offer their assessments and appraisals from firsthand knowledge include the following: Alliance College: Athletic Director Thaddeus Holuck and Coach Stan Flowers. Adelphi College: John Condon and Coach George Faherty. Anderson College: Duke Ellis and Alumni Relations Director Donna Wheatley. Buffalo State: Coach Joe Adessa. Butler University: Dan Dullaghan, coach Tony Hinkle, Lodie

Labda, Jack Mackenzie, Col. Robert R. Reed, Col. Leon Redenbacher and Norman Ellenberger. Bluffton College: Coach Kenny Mast and Paul Jackson. Creighton University: Athletic Department Secretary Carol Ketcham and coach Subby Salerno. Denison University: Robert Laird, Dave Maurer, Theodore Bosler and the Alumni Office staff. Hillsdale College: Sports Information Director Mark Smith, Jack Lowry and referee Harold Rolph. Marietta College: Alumni Office Director Mrs. Vernon McGrew and Ronald Weekley. Miami University: Alumni Relations Officer Susan Cohen, Sports Information Director George Gallet, coach Dave Wike, Doug Howell and Sy Chadroff. Morris Harvey College: Mario Palumbo, David Rosen, Sports Information Director Greg McCollam and Secretary of Alumni Relations Louise Bentley. North Carolina State University: Ron Shavlik, Sports Information Director Ed Seaman, Joe Tiede (*Raleigh News and Observer*), Dick Herbert. Providence College: Coach Vinny Cuddy and spectator Bob Cousy. Villanova University: Coach Alex Severance, Marty Milligan, Jack Devine, Jim Smith, Referee Jocko Collins, Assistant Sports Information Director Tony DiFrancesco, Bob Vetrone, and spectator Tom Gola of LaSalle. Wake Forest: Dickie Hemric. Waynesburg: Edward Marotta, Director of College Relations.

I want to acknowledge the assistance of the many research librarians that helped me track down data and articles from many years ago. I especially want to thank Sue Chapman in the Indianapolis-Marion County Public Library, Debra Hines in the Chicago Public Library, the staff of the Flemington Public Library, the Research Desk at the New York Public Library, Robin Brown and the research staff at the Raritan Valley Community College, Brenda Galloway-Wright of the Urban Archives at Temple University's Paley Library and the research staff at Rutgers University Library. The local press coverage in Gallia County was researched in depth for me by Kathy Pertuset at Rio Grande. The librarians with whom I worked were all helpful and patient with me and never complained when I inevitably messed up their microfilm readers.

Dave Wohlfarth was a diligent researcher and fact checker for the elusive dates and places.

Both Henry Kearney and Dick Barr graciously read and reviewed the manuscript for accuracy.

Judith Wells in the Tampa headquarters of the New York Yankees never failed to provide cheerful cooperation and assistance.

I want to thank Steve Anderson of ESPN for making the Bevo Francis documentary available to me and for the permission to use it for this project. I encourage you to see it if you have the chance. It is a remarkably well done and balanced treatment of the story.

For Bill Faherty and the other members of his "team"—Bob Casciola and Bill Raftery—I am deeply appreciative of their support and friendship through the years. They never failed to be there for me whenever I needed a name, introduction, referral, or just a word of encouragement. I wish everyone could be as blessed as I am to have old friends like them.

From Barbara and Kyle Jr., I got the support everyone needs from the home team.

Kara Polhemus served as copy editor, research assistant and chief computer technician during the writing process—not an enviable task when working with a two-fingered technologically-challenged typist on a sensitive computer keyboard.

My agent Lawrence Jordan was with the project from start to finish and believed in it as much as I did, and always kept the faith for both of us that it would eventually be recognized by the right people at the right place at the right time. Thanks to SPORTClassic Books, Wayne Parrish and Jim O'Leary, who proved to be those people, and to Greg Oliver for his consummate production skills.

Finally, I want to thank my editor, Polly Kummel, for her competent and professional assistance. She is a writer's dream and the best in the business.

To all those who were contacted and responsive to my questions throughout the years, I am deeply appreciative. For all who posed the same inevitable question—"Whatever happened to Bevo Francis?"—I hope I have provided the answer herein.

Kyle R. Keiderling

Bibliography

Cohen, Stanley. *The Game they Played*. New York: Farrar, Strauss and Giroux, 1977.

Converse College Basketball Yearbook, 1953, 1954, 1955.

Hollander, Zander. *Modern Encyclopedia of Basketball*. New York: Four Winds Press, 1973.

Oliver, Newt. *One Basketball and Glory*, as told to Dan Hoyt. Springfield, Ohio: Author, 1969.

Oliver, Newt, and Danny Fulks. *Basketball and the Rio Grande Legend*. Springfield, Ohio: Author, 1995.

Porter, J. Sherman. *Lamp of the Hills*. 1976. Authorized history of Rio Grande College.

Appendix A:
The Rio Grande Redmen 1952–54

The Rio Grande College basketball team was, like the schedule they played, ever changing. During the two seasons detailed in this book, a number of players came and went. Some did not last much more than a day or two, leaving without playing a game, after surveying the schools' rustic setting and Spartan surroundings. Others stayed for a time and moved on. Some were discouraged by Coach Newt Oliver's strict training regimen, and others by the coach's strategy of only showcasing Bevo's talents and not their own. I have tried to include all those who lasted long enough to play on the court with Bevo. All of them contributed and, even if they are not profiled fully herein, were a part of the Bevo Francis story. They are:

Don Coyne, Delbert Davis, Bill Frasher, Jack Gossett, Bernie Lipkofer, Bob Miller, Bob Mundy, Dick Myers, Bob Renzi, John Viscioglosi, Don Vyhnalek, Lee Weiher, Bob Zurcher, Zeke Zempter, and student assistant coach **Caroll Kent**.

Nominate the Redmen to the Hall of Fame

In the spring of 2006 the Ohio Basketball Hall of Fame will enshrine its first class of honorees. Bevo Francis and his Rio Grande teammates will be among the inaugural inductees.

But if you believe the Redmen deserve recognition beyond Ohio, you can help secure their place in basketball's national history by filling out a form at www.bevofrancis.com and forwarding it to the Honors Committee at the Naismith Memorial Basketball Hall of Fame.

The Redmen of 1952–54 played a decisive role in rekindling interest in college basketball at a time when the sport was wracked by a betting scandal. Wearing the red-and-white silks of a school with barely 100 students, they faced a difficult schedule against major colleges and played before sellout crowds en route to being adopted as "America's team."

Their contribution to the sport was immense and their place in the Hall of Fame is long overdue.

Appendix B:
Bevo Francis' Statistics

1952-53 SEASON

	OPPONENT	SITE	RESULT	FG	FT	POINTS
				BEVO STATS		
				FG	FT	POINTS
NOVEMBER						
Sat. 8	Alumni	Community Hall	116-48	19	6	44
Sat. 15	Cumberland	Community Hall	84-75	17	11	45
Tues. 18	Sue Bennett	Community Hall	121-99	20	18	58
Thurs. 20	Waynesburg	Community Hall	108-70	13	20	46
Sat. 22	Dayton Freshmen	Community Hall	93-89	8	19	35
Mon. 24	Wilberforce	Community Hall	111-71	23	23	69
Tues. 25	Bluefield	Bluefield, W.Va.	93-63	8	5	21
DECEMBER						
Tues. 2	Denison	Granville, Ohio	88-78	10	6	26
Thurs. 4	Marietta	Marietta, Ohio	76-73	12	13	37
Sat. 6	Beckley	Beckley,W.Va.	90-71	14	18	46
Fri. 12	California State	Community Hall	105-73	27	18	72
Sat. 13	Sue Bennett	London, Ky.	114-68	19	21	59
Tues. 16	Stuebenville	Community Hall	107-58	18	14	50
Thurs. 18	Pikeville	Pikeville, Ky.	72-52	11	3	25
Fri. 19	Lees College	Jackson, Ky.	102-64	27	22	76
Sat. 20	Cumberland	Williamsburg, Ky.	78-49	8	18	34
JANUARY						
Wed. 7	Findlay	Findlay, Ohio	91-88	14	16	44
Fri. 9	**Ashland J.C.**	**Community Hall**	**150-85**	**47**	**22**	**116**
Sat. 10	Mayo State	Paintsville, Ky.	119-91	21	21	63
Mon. 12	Wright Patterson	Gallipolis, Ohio	113-85	18	19	55
Tues. 13	Bliss Bus.Coll.	Columbus, Ohio	101-53	19	13	51
Sat. 17	Lockbourne AFB	Groveport, Ohio	84-50	12	12	36
Tues. 20	Cedarville	Troy, Ohio	66-29	14	10	38
Thurs. 22	Cincinnati Bible Sem.	Dayton, Ohio	79-54	20	2	42
Sat. 24	Mountain State	Zanesville, Ohio	133-83	27	14	68
Fri. 30	Beckley	Huntington, W.Va.	102-69	15	16	46
Sat. 31	Stuebenville	Toronto, Ohio	78-65	15	11	41
FEBRUARY						
Mon. 2	Pikeville	Wellsville, Ohio	97-62	24	13	61
Sat. 7	Mayo State	Middleport, Ohio	126-98	24	12	60
Tues. 10	Cedarville	Springfield, Ohio	104-48	18	15	51
Fri. 13	Mountain St.	Parkersburg, W.Va.	116-65	16	5	37
Sat. 14	Bliss Bus. Coll.	Wellston, Ohio	105-69	16	17	49
Tues. 17	Lockbourne AFB	Portsmouth, Ohio	95-80	21	5	47
Thurs. 19	Lees	Chillicothe, Ohio	128-57	22	19	63
Fri. 20	Wilberforce	Cincinnati, Ohio	100-51	21	10	52
Mon. 23	Bluefield	Community Hall	128-73	20	13	53
Wed. 25	Ashland J.C.	Ashland, Ky.	70-63	6	13	25
Fri. 27	Cin. Bible Sem.	Gallipolis, Ohio	111-86	22	15	59
MARCH						
Tue. 3	Wilberforce	Cleveland, Ohio	109-55	22	10	54
Sat. 28	Shooting exhibition	Kansas City, Mo.				
1952-53 SEASON TOTAL			**39-0**	**708**	**538**	**1,954**
						(Avg. 50.1)

1953-54 SEASON

	OPPONENT	SITE	RESULT	BEVO POINTS	
		NOVEMBER			
Thurs. 26	Erie County Tech	Buffalo, N.Y.	120-59	64 *	
		DECEMBER			
Thurs. 3	Adelphi	New York, N.Y.	76-83	32	Loss
Fri. 4	Villanova	Philadelphia, Pa.	92-93 (OT)	39	Loss
Sat. 5	Providence	Boston, Mass.	89-87	41	
Fri. 11	Bluffton	Bluffton, Ohio	116-71	82	
Sat. 12	Hillsdale	Hillsdale, Mich.	82-45	43	
Sat. 19	Miami (Fla.)	Miami, Florida	98-88	48	
Tues. 22	North Carolina St.	Raleigh, N.C.	77-92	34	Loss
Wed. 23	Wake Forest	Raleigh, N.C.	67-65	32	
		JANUARY			
Mon. 4	Salem	Clarksburg, W.Va.	96-99	38	Loss
Wed. 6	Butler	Indianapolis, In.	81-68	48	
Sat. 9	Morris Harvey	Charleston,W.Va.	86-63	41	
Fri. 15	Alliance	Erie, Pa.	107-77	61	
Sat. 16	Alliance	Wellsville, Ohio	133-68	84	
Tues. 19	Ashland (Ohio)	Gallipolis, Ohio	117-74	55	
Thurs. 21	Findlay	Dayton, Ohio	74-71	32	
Sat. 23	Creighton	Troy, Ohio	96-90	49	
Tues. 26	Morris Harvey	Cincinnati, Ohio	74-62	26	
Sat. 30	Buffalo State	Buffalo, N.Y.	81-65	31	
		FEBRUARY			
Tues. 2	**Hillsdale**	**Jackson, Ohio**	**134-91**	**113**	
Tues. 9	Anderson	Anderson, In.	101-85	59	
Sat. 13	Salem	Huntington, W.Va.	115-76	58	
Tues. 23	Ashland (Ohio)	Ashland, Ohio	121-61	54	
		MARCH			
Mon. 8	Arizona State (Flagstaff)	Kansas City, Mo.	90-74	28	(NAIA Tourn.)
Wed. 10	S.E. Louisiana	Kansas City, Mo.	65-78	27	Loss (NAIA Tourn.)
Sat. 20	Shurtleff	St. Louis, Mo.	72-70	37	
Mon. 22	Rockhurst	Kansas City, Mo.	50-56	22	Loss
Tues. 23	Creighton	Omaha, Neb.	75-93	41	Loss
1953-54 SEASON TOTAL			**21-7**	**1,319**	**(Avg. 47.1)**
CAREER TOTAL			**50-7**	**3,273**	**(Avg. 48.9)**

Total estimated attendance—180,000

* Two year school—not included in official NCAA records.

1961-62 ABL (Cleveland Pipers)

GP	MIN	2PA	2PM	3PA	3PM	FTA	FTM	POINTS
2	21	5	2	0	0	0	0	4

Thank you to the Association for Professional Basketball Research for its help with these records.

Index